Writing your own scripts and speeches

Writing your own scripts and speeches

for corporate television, audio-visual and live presentations

Suzan St Maur

McGRAW-HILL BOOK COMPANY

London · New York · St Louis · San Francisco · Auckland
Bogotá · Caracas · Hamburg · Lisbon · Madrid · Mexico
Milan · Montreal · New Delhi · Panama · Paris · San Juan
São Paulo · Singapore · Sydney · Tokyo · Toronto

Published by
McGRAW-HILL Book Company (UK) Limited
Shoppenhangers Road, Maidenhead, Berkshire SL6 2QL, England
Telephone 0628 23432
Fax 0628 770224

British Library Cataloguing in Publication Data

St Maur, Suzan
Writing your own scripts and speeches for corporate television, audio-visual
and live presentations.
I. Title
808.066

ISBN 0 07 707349 5

Library of Congress Cataloging-in-Publication Data

St Maur, Suzan
Writing your own scripts and speeches for corporate television, audio-visual
and live presentations/Suzan St Maur.
    p.   cm.
Includes index.
ISBN 0-07-707349-5
1. Speechwriting. 2. Business presentations. 3. Video recordings—Production and
direction. 4. Business communication—Audio-visual aids. 5. Motion picture
authorship. I. Title.
PN4142.S67 1991
808.5–dc20   91-19194

1234   PB   9321

Typeset by Computape (Pickering) Ltd, North Yorkshire
and printed and bound in Great Britain by Page Bros, Norwich

To Paul, and the script that brought us together

Contents

Acknowledgements

My sincere thanks to the following people for their input, help, support (moral and otherwise) plus sheer patience while I was writing this book: Michael Barratt, Kevin Brewer, John Butman, Jenny Ertle, Charles Hodges, Jane Judd, Debbie Sinfield, plus of course Paul Webb and all at Bolney Motor Works (with special thanks to Chris Sutton, the finest coffee-maker in Sussex).

I would also like to thank the following production companies and in-house units who commissioned me to work on projects from which many of the script excerpts in this book are taken: AVI Communications Ltd, the Boots Video Unit, Charisma Communications Ltd, Christopher Swann Associates, Crow Lane Communications Ltd, Frontline Productions Ltd, Spectrum Communications Ltd, Videotel Ltd and John Woods.

Finally, I'd like to thank the numerous clients for whom the scripts discussed and shown in this book were written, but whose names have been deleted for reasons of confidentiality.

Suzan St Maur

About the author

Canadian-born **Suzan St Maur** is one of the UK's leading scriptwriters in business television, business theatre and AV. In her early career she worked as an advertising copywriter for agencies, consultancies and also direct clients.

Today Suzan is one of the most successful and creative innovators in corporate programmes and presentations. She is a regular contributor to many of the major business TV and business theatre production companies in Europe, and is recognized as one of the top UK scriptwriters in this field. She has become an experienced interviewer and presenter both off and on camera as a logical extension of her scriptwriting, and is now applying her scriptwriting skills to educational/documentary broadcast TV.

Suzan's previous books include *The A to Z of Video and Audio-Visual Jargon*, *Writing Words That Sell*, *The Home Safety Book*, and *The Jewellery Book*.

Introduction

There can be very few people in industrialized countries today who have failed to appreciate the growing value of audio-visual communications for corporate, marketing, promotional, motivational, educational and a host of other communications purposes. Synchronized sound and pictures operating together have been proved to work many times better than printed material generated to the same brief; the whole is greater than the sum of its parts.

There are a number of reasons for this—some statistical, some emotional. Research conducted in the UK and the US shows that a message communicated via the spoken word, with complementary pictures, is absorbed and retained two and a half times more effectively than if it is put over in print. In the past this difference was reflected in the cost gap between audio-visual (AV) and print media. However, technology and market pressures have reduced that gap quite considerably; today, the cost of producing a video is barely more than that of a glossy brochure saying the same things.

The growth of the AV media—particularly videotape—echoes the growth of television as the most important medium for public information and entertainment. Audiences of employees, students, customers and so on look upon TV as a powerful input of communication at home, and this has a useful spin-off effect when business or educational messages are put over to them in a similar style through video. Much 'business television' has capitalized on this effect quite unashamedly, particularly in its earlier days when it was considered something of a 'me-too' medium, aping TV, feature films and, in the case of business presentations, theatre and vaudeville.

Corporate TV and theatre have seen yet another 'me-too' effect, this time on the part of commissioning organizations. Just like a company's products, the quality of both its external and internal message communications is usually judged against that of its competitors. If the leaders within a market sector are using video and AV, those who wish to compete in that market sector must also use video and AV. Quite rightly, audio-visual communications are perceived as being a more effective and more sophisticated way of communicating than print. The company or organization that lags behind in this respect may well lose out to its more audio-visually minded competitors—in sales, in branding, in corporate image, in the quality of staff it attracts, in the effectiveness and motivation of existing staff, and even in its share prices. Audio-visual communications are used in all of these areas, and more besides; customers, suppliers, shareholders and staff now expect them.

Not surprisingly, therefore, the growth of the AV media has been meteoric. Since the 1960s, AV and videotape have metamorphosed from the magic lantern shows and the occasional flickering training film to a market worth around £500 million per annum in the UK alone. Apart from information technology and broadcast television, there are very few other industry market sectors that have grown so fast.

In parallel, there has been tremendous growth in the number and nature of production companies specializing in the creation of video, AV and live presentations on behalf of companies and other organizations. Apart from the occasional inadequate and amateurish production company which lingers on, the vast majority of those in business today have mastered the crafts of audio-visual communications and are providing their clients with a highly specialized and professional service.

In addition to this many companies, government bodies, institutions and other organizations have created their own in-house units to generate video, AV, and presentation software. Only a small proportion of programmes produced by in-house units (normally just those involving high budgets, for drama, comedy, or 'hard sell' promotion) are written by professional scriptwriters. The vast majority are documentary and/or didactic, and are written by personnel from the commissioning division or department of the company concerned.

Of all the processes needed in the creation of good audio-visual communications *the script* is universally seen as the most crucial. Far from merely being a written version of words to be spoken, the script is the blueprint for an entire production. Its purpose is twofold. One is to act as the final interpretation and distillation of the messages to be communicated; the end product of the client's detailed briefing and a considerable amount of background research. The other is to guide the whole production team in generating the finished on-screen product—a laborious and intricate process, all of which is driven by the script's indications. As such, writing the script is probably the most difficult and specialized activity of all.

Although there are a number of specialized scriptwriters working in the business today, there are very many more scripts written for video and AV than there are specialist writers to do them. This therefore involves a great many more individuals in the scriptwriting process, both within the commissioning organizations and within production companies. And even for those who do not necessarily need to put pen to paper, an understanding of the techniques required to create a good script assists people involved in two ways. Firstly, there is a need within the commissioning department or division of a company or other organization. Here, knowing something of scriptwriting techniques and audio-visual thinking can help managers and executives to define their objectives more clearly, and use a realistic interpretation of the media's restrictions and potential in doing so. This can save a great deal of expensive management time, and lead to a far more efficient and productive relationship with the internal department or external production company who will actually make the programme. Secondly, knowledge of scriptwriting techniques is extremely valuable at all levels of the production process. Because the partnership between words and pictures must be inextricably close if a programme is to work at all, every creative employee *must* understand how scripts are put together before they can interpret them. Even at administrative and secretarial levels, a knowledge of script structure, plus dialogue and narration techniques, help in costing, editing, typing and a number of other ancillary activities.

Most significantly, though, there are the people in a company or other organization who—though not specialist writers—*must* write scripts. Although specialist professional scriptwriters are available, the vast majority of scripts are not written by them, as suggested above. This may be for one of a number of reasons. Usually, there are not sufficient funds in the budget to cover the cost of hiring a specialist writer, or there may not be sufficient time for a specialist writer to be found and briefed. Sometimes, the script may be too sensitive, technically or politically, to be given to an outsider. Many executives and managers are unaware that specialist professional writers in the corporate field even exist; and if they are aware of that fact, they're often unaware of how to contact such a writer. And so on.

There are also people in business, government departments, educational and training establishments and other organizations who *want* to write scripts properly, not merely out of need, but out of a desire to expand their own range of communication skills. As the non-broadcast, non-theatrical audio-visual media grow in international importance for communications of all kinds, more and more people want to benefit from the opportunities these media offer. Training and education in scriptwriting techniques do exist, but in insufficiently available and thorough forms for today's growing needs.

This book can't set out to turn its readers into professional scriptwriters in the time it takes to read it from cover to cover. But with the expertise of Suzan St Maur behind every word—the result of a decade of experience in the UK, Europe and North America, writing scripts for many of the largest and best-known companies and organizations in the world—readers will emerge from this book with a great deal of knowledge. Armed with the information in *Writing Your Own Scripts and Speeches*, any reader will be equipped with the necessary theory, and will be ready to start the practice, of writing good, creative scripts to communicate the messages of the future.

Chapter 1

The media you use

There is one common denominator running through all forms of script and speech writing, and that is you are writing for the spoken word rather than for the printed word. (For more on this subject, see Chapter 6.) But within that, there are a certain number of variations dependent on the actual medium you're using and the restrictions it may or may not impose. To perform effectively, it helps to know a little about the various media, so here's a brief overview of each one.

Live presentations

Live corporate presentations today can be a far cry from the old days when the chairman would address the assembled multitudes in the staff canteen for an hour and a half, barking out the words while karate-chopping the lectern now and again to add emphasis. Even small business meetings today are 'produced' using sophisticated visual and audio-visual aids, interesting sets and a variety of speakers from the chairman to everyone's favourite soap actor to deliver the messages. Modern presentations like these obviously avoid the narcolepsy-inducing effect created by 90 minutes of a boring chairman, and also serve to add sparkle and emphasis to the messages concerned. Through the use of multi-media (AV, video and film), other live stage effects, the partitioning of information into digestible chunks, variety of presentation style that includes straight speeches, dramatized sections, and even song and dance acts, you cannot only keep your audience awake, but also get them to leave the presentation feeling well informed, motivated and uplifted.

The live presentation and, more to the point, the quality of its production also speak volumes for the quality of the organization giving it in the first place. If the audience consists of external groups—e.g. journalists, retailers, etc.—the quality of the presentation's production will position your company in their eyes just as much as the actual words will. And even to an internal audience, the overall themes and messages can and should be reflected in the way the presentation is produced, as well as in the speeches. To inform staff that you've just had a tremendous year and that profits have hit an all-time record, with a show given on a drab set with little or no dressing and a few tatty slides, will create a visual and environmental contradiction to the words. On the other side of the same coin, of course, a presentation to staff saying that last year wasn't too good and this year we really must get our acts together, given at an expensive venue with all the trimmings, will create a similar contradiction.

At the end of the day, though, from a writer's point of view, no matter what effects and audio-visual back-up you can use, you're still contending with human beings speaking live lines to a live audience. This can be seen as a limitation, but it needn't be—provided you understand the nature of the speakers you're writing for. These can range from a nervous company executive who is making his or her public speaking début, to an experienced and accomplished actor who is capable of having the entire audience crying, laughing or raging within minutes. So the key is to know who is to say the speech you write, and approach the writing of his or her section accordingly.

Overall, what makes live presentations different from the other media for which you can write is that, here, there is much more concentrated focus on the speaker than is the case with two-dimensional media. And although you can use slides and even video or film to highlight the speaker's words, the emphasis still rests far more on the speaker and the words than it would with pre-recorded material. Some writers see this as a drawback, and it's true to say that if you're saddled with writing a speech for a truly bad presenter, you'll often wish you could 'cut away' to some interesting illustrations or visual trickery to alleviate the monotony (as you could with video). However, even bad speakers can be made to present fairly well, provided they speak from a tailor-made script that avoids their own particular pitfalls and makes the best use of their personalities. And writing a good speech for a good speaker, whether it is your chairman or an actor, provides you with tremendous personal satisfaction—especially when you hear the audience applaud, which is something you normally don't get from video, AV and film.

Audio-visual presentations

This is something of a misnomer, because in theory any presentation or programme that consists of synchronized sound and pictures is 'audio-visual'. However, audio-visuals, or AVs, are now accepted as meaning a presentation consisting of a pre-recorded soundtrack illustrated by and synchronized with a number of still pictures in slide format (usually 35 mm). These are also called 'slide-tape' or, conversely, 'tape-slide' shows.

AV can be seen as something of a dying breed, because now that the cost of producing videotape programmes has come down proportionately many companies will choose this medium instead. At the time of writing, the cost per on-screen minute of good quality AV using up to nine projectors is about the same as that for reasonable quality video. Overall, video does seem to be replacing AV to a large extent, but I don't believe AV will die out altogether for some time yet; there are many influencing factors which still can swing the balance in either direction. Playback is more complicated with AV, but this can be avoided if you generate a programme on slides and transfer it to videotape for playback. AV has the advantage of being far simpler and cheaper than videotape or film to update after initial production; you simply swap slides in the magazine, provided that the soundtrack and original electronic cue remain the same. Video has the advantage of motion, rather than still images, but the quality of 35-mm stills when projected is superior to that of 35-mm motion picture, never mind that of projected video (although the boffins are working on that). The geographical situation of the material to be shot also comes into play, because it is considerably cheaper to send one stills photographer to shoot location material in Athens, Sydney, Hong Kong, Delhi, San Francisco, Toronto and London than it would be to send a full video crew. On the other hand, video gives viewers a much more realistic sensation of involvement in a programme than AV can provide, with the resulting increase in effectiveness and information retention. And so it goes on.

Most of us, at one time or another, have seen the typical example of a boring, flat, unexciting slide-tape show that consists of a monotonous narration behind a series of dull pictures, with perhaps a little music at the beginning and at the end. In fact, many people will think of this type of show when you mention AV. However, there is no reason at all why AV should be dull and boring. There is no reason why you should only use narration; you can include interviews, provided that the slides make it clear who is talking. You can make imaginative use of music to build up moods, or change the pace of the programme. You can also use sound effects to great advantage. In fact, as I say to participants in my scriptwriting workshops, writing for AV is rather like it would be if you could write for 'illustrated radio'—and, as you know, that medium manages to convey a wide range of moods and images through the use of different voices, music and sound effects.

If you're called upon to write for AV and you have little or no experience of it, you would do well to listen to a few radio plays and news magazine programmes (BBC Radio Four is very good) to get some ideas. People in my business will tell you that AV is very restrictive because you don't have the benefits of 'lip sync', i.e. both hearing and seeing people talk, and live action. However, these same people probably believe that an AV soundtrack never consists of more than narration and music only. I believe and, dare I say it, have actually proved that AV can be made extremely effective with imaginative use of the soundtrack. And there's a bonus here: sound recording, even when you use a lot of music and sound effects, location recording, etc., is very cheap when compared with the cost of videotape or film.

Apart from what I've described above, the same general rules apply to AV as to video and film. As with the others, with AV you should always try *not* to tell viewers what they can already see, but instead make the pictures and words complement each other. And never fall into the trap that is still sometimes set by the old-fashioned producer ... 'just write the words and I'll visualize them later'. If you want to create effective, powerful programmes whatever medium they use, you must think pictures and sound together right from the start—see Chapter 5.

Audiotape

Audiotapes are often used for training and other purposes, and can provide an effective and cheap way of communicating messages. If you are asked to write for an audiotape, you should bear in mind what I've described above, in the AV section, concerning radio. You have exactly the same scope as a radio programme, and that can be quite varied and interesting.

The other point that is very important—probably more so than is the case with a medium where you have visual input—is the circumstances in which the audience will be listening to the tape. Such tapes will probably be given to people to listen to in their own time, either at home or in their cars. As they are likely to be distracted visually while listening, it's important that you write the programme into short, crisp sections that don't require more than about four minutes' worth of solid concentration at one time. These programmes need to be very lively and interesting overall, because they tend to compete for attention with the traffic, the washing, the ironing, or whatever. And if the programme is to be listened to in-car, you should find out the average drive time from work to home of the audience, and ensure that the programme's running time is well below that. This way, the whole programme is likely to be listened to— many cars' radio-cassette systems are automatically stopped when the ignition is switched off!

Videotape

The 'corporate video' has become a leading piece of business jargon these days. As was mentioned in the Introduction to this book, many companies which even a few years ago would have used print for corporate, training, marketing or investment-raising purposes will now produce a video instead. At the risk of being cynical, there are probably only two basic reasons for this. One is that, today, producing a videotape programme is often not much more expensive than producing a glossy, multi-page, full-colour brochure. The other is the me-too syndrome. If your competitors are using video to communicate their sales or other messages, your company will look a bit cheap if all it can produce is a brochure, even if it did cost as much as a video would.

Naturally, there are a number of other reasons why video is so popular, all largely based on effectiveness of communication, efficiency of demonstration, etc. Some of these have been covered in the Introduction, and the others you probably know already.

In the final analysis most people in medium- to large-sized businesses will, at some time or other, be involved in the production of a video, and whether you're an in-company or external writer you're bound to be asked to write scripts for this medium.

Obviously, with video you do not suffer any of the restrictions mentioned above in connection with live presentations, AV, or audiotape. You have full live action, you have 'lip sync', you have the ability to portray the innermost intricacies of most methods and procedures, etc. What you may not always have is a large budget.

The purists of corporate television will tell you that because video offers you all this creative writing freedom, you can write scripts that will achieve all the objectives in the book using the scope of live action video combined with special effects and all the other tricks of the trade. That's fine, if you have an unlimited amount of money to spend. What the purists don't like to admit, however, is that companies producing corporate programmes must work to predetermined budgets, and that's where the writer's skill can be crucial.

Before you even begin to consider a video script, in realistic terms you must know how much you (or the producer) can spend on the project. To get into the nuts and bolts of budgeting here would be unwise, for two reasons: one, how far the budget goes depends to a great extent on the production itself and who is making the programme and, two, costings at the time this book was written will almost certainly be irrelevant by the time it is read. What you need to know, though, are two important things: how many days' shooting, and how many days' editing, are feasible within the budget?

Let's start with the shoot. On location, a good corporate video crew and director can cover, on average, about 20–25 'set-ups' in one location in a day. That means 20–25 different spots within a location where the camera is set up and lighting is arranged if necessary. The same number of set-ups are possible in a studio environment. Obviously, if you are shooting complicated sequences using complex methods and equipment, the number of set-ups comes down; and if all you need is simple 'camera-on-the-shoulder' set-ups with an ENG (small) crew using no extra lighting (e.g. outdoors), you can raise that number to about 25–30 per day.

Obviously, when you write your script you must consider the number of locations in which you recommend shooting, as well as the number of set-ups within each location. You must also remember to allow for crew travelling time from one location to another. If you find that you need to include, say, two locations in your programme plus a number of interviews, it may be possible to ask the interviewees to attend one of the locations where you will be shooting procedure sequences to save on another day's location shoot, which you would need if you were to do the interviews at the interviewees' offices.

The other point is editing time. If you know that a particular production can only afford two days' off-line editing and one day on-line, it's pointless to suggest that your programme includes many different selections from other taped material (e.g. previous programmes, library stock, etc.) if the likelihood is that your editor will be fully occupied cutting the original material shot for this particular programme. Similarly, if you only have one day to on-line edit, it would be foolish to suggest a number of complicated graphics sequences in addition to a full day's worth of edits with the live action material.

Now, all the above may seem comparatively far removed from the scriptwriting process, but when it comes to the production management of a video programme—especially when budget restraints are in force—it all becomes very relevant. If you're in any doubt, consult the producer of your video programme and ask just what is possible within the budget. This way, you won't waste your own time by writing scripts that are unproduceable within the financial limits concerned. And once you know what *is* possible, you can then use your creative ability to make the best use of the time available.

Interactive video

For readers who do not already know, interactive video is a useful medium for training, retail and other purposes. It consists of a linked system of videodisk playback and a computer terminal, usually a PC. The idea is that the viewer can interact with the programme, responding to questions by selecting one of a choice of options offered by the computer software. The selected option is then searched for and found on the videodisk, and played back to the viewer. In theory, it provides an excellent way to ensure that every viewer receives identical information (not always the case in live training or sales, as the information conveyed by humans is subject to variation).

When interactive video was first created, it was hailed in the trade press as the best thing since sliced bread, and was going to revolutionize audio-visual communications around the world. But, some years later, the revolution has yet to hit. The reason for this is that, although interactive video (often shortened to 'I/V') genuinely is a good idea, it is also a very expensive one. Improvements and refinements in technology may help in the future. But at the moment, the cost of the equipment required to play back I/V programmes, and particularly the equipment you need to record information on videodisk, is prohibitive to all but the largest and wealthiest companies.

If you, as an external scriptwriter, are asked to participate in generating an I/V programme, all that you are likely to be asked to do is to generate material for the 'options' described above. These can be dramatized or in documentary style, and are likely to be short cameos; but apart from this relatively unusual brevity, the writing techniques you will need are covered elsewhere in this book. The development of the programme and—if it is for training purposes—the didactic content and structure, are normally done by others. However, if you are an in-company person, your involvement may well extend to helping to develop the whole programme. In this case, you should enlist the guidance of one of the many dedicated I/V companies in the UK and other western countries, because creating I/V is a highly specialized activity—both in creating software and in driving the hardware.

Video wall

This is a medium utilized for exhibitions and other live shows (e.g. conferences) whereby, instead of using the conventional single screen area, the video image can be split up into a number of subsections—for example, 9 (3 × 3), 12 (4 × 3), 16 (4 × 4) or more. Each individual subsection can show something different, or all of them can be used together to display one large image covering the whole space. From the writer's point of view it's important to remember that this is an even more visual medium than ordinary video and, to justify the cost involved, programmes generated for video wall must make the best of the visual impact it offers. Creating programmes for this medium must be done by specialists, and if you're asked to write for it you would do well to seek their advice and work closely with them when writing your script.

Film

From the scriptwriter's point of view within the corporate/documentary area of production, there is no difference of any consequence between film and videotape. The only point which may influence the content of a script arises if you are making any changes to live action dialogue as you shoot the programme, or if you're shooting interviews.

Because videotape is an electronic process, it is possible to play back immediately anything that has just been recorded. This is a very valuable feature, because it allows you to check that the dialogue works, or that the interview content is satisfactory, while the camera and performers wait *in situ*. If the material concerned isn't right, you can then shoot the sequence again. With film, because it is a photographic process, it is not possible to watch your material back at the time of shooting; it may be a day or two before the 'rushes' come back from the processing laboratory.

The use of film in the corporate area waxes and wanes in popularity, but generally speaking the vast majority of corporate programmes are shot on videotape for this and other reasons. If you do use film, it is a good idea to hire a simple VHS camera and playback machine and run that at the same time as the film camera during the shoot. This way it's possible to watch each sequence back in the way that you would with a professional videotape system. The quality of image and angle of each shot will obviously be an inaccurate representation of what the film camera is capturing, but at least with the VHS playback you can check up on dialogue and interview content on the spot.

The emerging media

At the time of writing, new developments within the audio-visual business are largely variations—and improvements—on a theme. The area on which the boffins are concentrating is, not surprisingly, videotape/ television. Here, improved formats of tape are being announced almost every week, and improved standards of television systems are also being discussed at great length. Recent examples of this are, on the format side, S-VHS, Betacam SP, BVU SP, etc., and on the standards side, HDTV

(High Definition Television). However, in the main, these new developments only affect the quality of sound and picture, plus things like editing versatility and efficiency of camera use. They do not have any noticeable effect on the way in which scripts should be written.

DBS, or Direct Broadcast by Satellite, is becoming popular for conference work, as it can bring together members of a geographically dispersed organization without the need for travel and disruption to work schedules—albeit at a price. Video conferencing, as this is known, in theory should come under the heading of live presentations. And when writing scripts for these occasions, the only point to remember is to use your common sense. Keep scripts simple for foreign language nationals and/or simultaneous translation, and also bear the same point in mind in case the sound transmission is poor or begins to break up.

'Sponsored television' is also being talked about at the time of writing, and there have even been hints in the TV trade press that one day there will be a 'corporate channel', no doubt run by one of the UK's satellite TV stations. This would provide an outlet for corporations and companies to produce programmes to be shown to interested members of the public. If and when this becomes a reality, before writing scripts for such a medium we—as in-company and external scriptwriters—will have to make ourselves familiar with the guidelines set out by the broadcast organization concerned. Because, regardless of the current (1991) incentives to relax the sponsorship rules within TV, we're unlikely to see the day when we can make 24-minute commercials for a company and get them aired. Scripts for such a medium are likely to be put through a vetting procedure (rather as is currently the case with TV and radio commercials) to ensure that they contain the approved levels of documentary interest or entertainment and corporate flag-waving. And my guess is that the flag-waving will be severely restricted, 'corporate channel' or not.

Chapter 2

What is a script?

Many people, even within the audio-visual industry, believe that a script consists merely of a document showing the words to be spoken in a given production. However, the only instance in which this is true is in the case of a speech—and even then, the writer may well put in a few ideas for relevant speaker support slides. In the case of video, film and AV, the words to be spoken are only one part of the script.

In practice, the script is like a blueprint for a production. It sets out the logic and form, and describes the entire content from visual input to music and sound effects. It then acts as the working manual for the whole production team. A number of functions are essential to a production, and they can only be accomplished through consulting the script.

First of all, budgeting. Although many programmes are costed roughly on an approximation of how many days' shooting are required, how many days' editing, and so on, it is only when the producer or production manager sees a full script that he or she can break down the whole shoot and post-production process into an accurate assessment.

Then, location/studio management. The script will contain suggestions for establishing shots, location set-ups, studio or interior scenes, location interviews and so on, and all these have to be sourced, arranged and booked before shooting begins.

Casting is another activity dependent on the script. If actors are required for a production, the director or casting director will have to read the script carefully and understand the sort of characters the writer has created, and then cast the actors to suit.

The director can only begin to work on how the production will be shot once he or she has a script. If the writer has written a camera script, it will have been broken down into scenes and sequences. But then the director will need to break it down even further, deciding what length and style of shots to use for each sequence.

In post-production, the script is used as a working guide for editing, ensuring that the finished programme follows the writer's intentions as closely as possible.

And so it goes on. Without wishing to sound biased, I believe—and so do most people in this business—that the script is the single most important element of an entire production. Without a script it is virtually impossible to put any pre-planned production together. The only exception to this is the kind of TV documentary where a crew and director are sent out to shoot whatever material they can, and the final programme is in effect composed of edited sections of this material, some time later. In those instances the unit is more likely to be working to a treatment or outline of some kind. The narration will be written once the live action and other visual material have been off-line edited, and will be recorded during the sound dub.

However, the sort of documentary described above is very rare in corporate work as, understandably, clients prefer to see and approve the content of their programmes before committing themselves, and their money, to the project. Consequently, the script is usually the first major job to do in a production, and is undoubtedly the most important to get right.

This means that the writer—whether in-company or external—has a considerable responsibility in the context of the whole production. It is never a case of the writer being responsible for the dialogue and narration and someone else assuming responsibility for the pictures, although there is still the occasional old-fashioned audio-visual producer who will ask a writer to come up with the words for someone else to visualize later. This is bad practice, because if a writer is discouraged from thinking about the whole production, he or she runs the risk of writing words that can't be visualized for one reason or another. The most efficient and effective way of working is for the writer to assume total responsibility for the broad structure of the programme, and to write accordingly.

For this reason the writer must work very closely with the producer—if for no other reason than to ensure that the agreed number of locations/days' shoot, editing allowances, graphics and special effects, etc., are not exceeded and that the programme therefore does not go over budget.

Overall, writing the script in truth means designing the programme. And one of the main objectives of this book is to help you to do this, as well as to help you learn the crafts of writing the spoken lines that go into a script. Very often, it is not so much the ability to write that influences the success of creating a script, it is more the ability to *think* and to structure your thoughts into a logical, powerful and coherent production.

So read on!

Stages of a script

If we stay for a moment with the analogy of designing a production, you will recall that designing anything—whether it is a video programme or an article of clothing—requires preliminary work. In the case of designing fashion, for example, you would expect to do quite a few preliminary sketches and outlines before you arrive at the final drawing. With scriptwriting, there are also a number of preliminary stages which can help you and the rest of the production team order your thoughts and develop your ideas.

The synopsis or outline

This is usually a very short document—perhaps a page or two—which sets out the basic idea behind the programme you want to create. Outlines or synopses in the corporate context serve as a means of ordering the content of a programme, ensuring that the balance and flow of information is correct. If dramatization is to be included, it is briefly outlined and its purposes described in the context of the objectives of the programme.

Outlines are especially useful if you are putting together the content for a live presentation, where you're required to sort out the flow and content of information which will be divided into several subpresentations over, say, a 90-minute show. More often than not you will proceed directly from this to draft scripts and speeches, without going to the interim stage of full treatments first. And the great benefit of the outline is that everyone involved can agree the content and flow without your having gone to a great deal of trouble and time—e.g. had you prepared draft scripts. The following is an outline I wrote for the launch of a new corporate identity programme and new car, for a major motor manufacturer.

Teaser preview, opening AV

This should be an edited selection of material from the opening AV as described in 1., below, put together to form an intriguing collection of images designed to whet the audience's appetite without giving anything away. This section will be an AV (multi-image) multi-plexed to VTR and played back on loop tape VCR through monitors placed in the coffee/registration area. Content will consist of visuals accompanied by music and sound effects only; no live or recorded V/O narration is envisaged.

1. Style: evolving into the 1990s

This is a brief, fast-moving multi-image montage, giving a lively
conceptual overview of changes happening now in the style of many
aspects of our life. Subject areas include architecture, fashion,
technology, and corporate identities of a range of organizations. The idea
here is to impress visually on the audience the relevance of style and
image in every walk of life, and the evolutionary process through which
styles and images change to reflect the current and future climates in
which we live and work. Content will consist of visuals accompanied by
music and sound effects only; no live or recorded V/O narration is
envisaged.

2. Welcome and philosophy

Speaker X should speak on the following issues:

- the reality of Company X's current position
- its stance as the UK's number X, with good products
- its push towards greater, more upmarket 'desirability' in image,
  service and performance
- superiority in technology, ecological consciousness, and value for
  money
- the on-going intention to lead in everything Company X does
- current relationships and the desire to grow those into stronger
  customer loyalty
- the need for a new rationalization of all philosophies to clarify
  Company X's true image, both externally and internally
- Company X must change the way in which people perceive it.

3. Translating the philosophy into reality

This section is to be a documentary-style AV, narrated live by two actors.
The narration will focus on the following issues:

- the rationale behind the new initiatives
- leadership into the 1990s
- Company X pre-empting new consumer laws with better, greener
  products
- Company X's current investment in new plants and headquarters
- the continuation and consolidation of 'Think People First', the Quality
  Network, Company X College and other training initiatives, etc.
- the move to focus on Company X in UK, not Company Y and
  Company Z
- the vision for the future
- but, look how Company X projects itself now—uncoordinated and
  confusing image which does not convey to the public just what

Company X has to offer—and yet Company X is visible in such a wide range of ways. (Here we show current CI, and its visibility in such diverse locations as dealerships, stationery, motorsport, football matches, etc.)

- so now, the most important step forward into the 1990s and beyond, the new Company X corporate identity.

4. Corporate identity—the platform for leadership into the 1990s

The first part of this section is a brief, glamorous and exciting overview of the look, featuring the (symbol) and the Company X name. This acts as an *AV reveal*, using visuals, sound effects and music only.

The next part is a live presentation by *Speaker X, who covers the following issues:*

- what this corporate identity really means in global terms
- the relevance of the retained (symbol), and the focus on the Company X name
- a brief description of the look, colours and shapes, and the thinking behind them
- its far-reaching effect throughout the organization: a question of culture, not cosmetics
- how and where that image is visible
- the interpretation of the new image, and how it reflects Company X's innermost long-term policies
- the wide sense of integration with customers that the image provides
- what that interpretation means to dealers and their businesses.

The final part of this section is a *videotape presentation showing how the corporate identity works* within the dealerships, and how it will enhance sales, after-sales and customer loyalty. The video will consist of a number of detailed sequences illustrating the actual material dealers will be using, e.g. signage, furniture, flooring, lighting, etc. (to be shot on the prototype set), interspersed with more conceptual interior and exterior sequences to suggest mood and atmosphere (to be shot on location in Cumbria).

5. The retail concept

This section is to be a documentary-style AV, narrated live by two actors. The narration will focus on the following issues:

- continuing under the umbrella of leadership into the 1990s within the new corporate identity framework
- major initiatives following through, with development of franchises like (Franchise 1) and (Franchise 2)

- rationalization of LCVs into Company X vans
- the dealership benefits of providing such extended and rationalized services to customers
- why 'retail', not merely 'garage'.

6. Relationships

This is to be a live presentation given by an as-yet unnamed Company X speaker, who will discuss the following issues:

- leadership into the 1990s means fostering strong relationships
- the 'curves' of the new corporate identity symbolizing and embracing greater teamwork and partnership among Company X staffers, dealers, employees, suppliers and customers
- how existing initiatives like 'Think People First' and the Quality Network will enhance relationships even more in the 1990s
- the concept of those newly strengthened relationships resulting in better, more profitable business for both Company X and dealers alike.

7. Financial commitment: and CI implementation

This is to be a live presentation by an as-yet unnamed senior Company X speaker, who will discuss the following issues:

- Company X's commitment to the new image in financial terms: Company X's investment in the 1990s
- what that investment actually means, in terms of new buildings in (location), other new construction work, reorganization of systems, reliverying of vehicles, advertising/promotional material, stationery, etc.
- the benefits to dealers of financial commitment to the new corporate identity on their part, and the reasons why their investment in it will pay considerable dividends
- the new financial arrangements with dealers, i.e. lease deals rather than part-ownership purchase, and the benefits to them
- how much the new corporate image will cost dealers, using a few examples
- a timetable of activities in the near and mid-range future
- how dealers should implement the new corporate identity and other new initiatives
- what will happen next, when, and how.

8. (New car's name)—Introduction

This section is to be a documentary-style AV, narrated live by two actors. The narration will focus on the following issues:

- where Company X is today in terms of model range, styling, etc.
- technology update; clean engines, fuel efficiency, engine management, catalytic converters, etc.
- motorsports achievements
- how the motoring press perceives Company X today
- and now, a new car to symbolize the revitalized image of Company X and its relationships with customers
- a vehicular personification of Company X's new corporate identity, and its leadership into the 1990s
- the promising results of research.

9. (New car's name)—the car

This is to be a *videotape presentation of the new (new car's name) being put through its paces*, emphasizing its styling and shape, its performance, roadholding, etc.

10. (New car's name) implementation

This is to be a live presentation by an as-yet unnamed Company X speaker, who will discuss the following issues:

- the (new car's) market positioning
- the programme of the (new car's) implementation
- sales approach
- delivery
- what dealers should expect to happen next.

11. Finale

This is to be a very exciting, uplifting multi-image and/or multi-media celebration that visually summarizes the concept and feel of the new Company X for the 1990s, emphasizing the curve and flow of the corporate identity into better relationships and greater success, and symbolized in vehicular terms by the (new car). The audio track will consist of sound effects and music only, with no V/O narration envisaged. The objective is to leave the audience on a high, enthused and eager not only to implement the corporate identity and drive the (new car) but equally to participate wholeheartedly in Company X's leadership into the 1990s.

The above outline detailed the content, and to a limited extent the creative approach, of a complete 90-minute presentation in just a few pages. It provided enough information for the clients concerned to see how the presentation was mapped out, yet it only took a day or so to compile on the basis of preliminary research and the client's briefing.

The treatment

This is a longer version of a synopsis or outline, and in some ways you could look upon it as a prose version of the script; rather like a short story from which a screenplay is developed. Because a video or AV programme is intangible until it is completely finished, most people have a very difficult time visualizing and hearing what it might be like. But in corporate work—and, for that matter, in TV and the film world too—there are usually a number of people who have to know roughly what the programme will be like, because their approval/cooperation/money is required if the programme is to happen at all. That's why a treatment is often necessary—to provide these people with an understandable document that explains what the programme is all about without confusing columns of camera instructions and jargon everywhere to cloud the issue. Another important benefit of a treatment is that it helps you, as the writer, to crystallize your ideas and work them out without cluttering your own mind with all the shooting and editing paraphernalia that must be included in a script. Finally, the treatment helps a number of the other members of the production team to start planning for it, as mentioned above.

In corporate work, treatments are also useful in the same way that synopses/outlines are, from the point of view of providing all parties with a discussion document on content. By generating a detailed treatment, everyone can see not only what content you recommend, but also the amount of weight or importance you suggest giving to each topic. Because the treatment doesn't take as long to write as the final script (although the creative thinking involved takes time) and because the format is simple prose, it is much more satisfactory for content to be changed, moved around, expanded or contracted at this stage. This accomplished, you'll usually find that the script is quite easy to write from the final, agreed treatment, and that any alterations you're required to do will be comparatively small.

The following treatment was done for a corporate/educational programme for a UK water authority. It was broken down into two sections—first of all, a preamble to describe the style of the programme, followed by the actual treatment itself. The preamble on style helps readers to understand the general feel of the programme, so they can absorb the content that follows in the light of that.

The programme: approach and style

One of the most fascinating things about water is its visual mystique; it is the only element on earth which can combine total transparency with tremendous strength and movement. It is at the same time gentle, colourless, innocuous, yet powerful, awe-inspiring, and dangerous.

So for a theme to lead this programme, we need look no further than to water itself ... rushing, swirling, trickling, bringing the force of life literally from the heavens, through the water cycle, to us all. Helped by human-generated power and gravity, water is perpetually on the move; movement within a cycle that emulates the cycle of the life force which drives our world.

The programme will be based on a visual fluidity ... using existing footage, and new material, illustrating the constant movement of water both literally and metaphorically. Because ALL of the activity within the brief of this programme is intertwined with the driving force of water ... be it the activities of (name) Water, the technology designed to purify and regulate the water supply, the water cycle as perceived by the public, and even—to quote a simple, but topical example—the mysterious cycle of the salmon.

To relate the relevance of all aspects of (name) Water's work to the needs of the public, we will use two links throughout the programme.

One, will be the constant motion of water, picked up visually—and matched musically—at every major link point in the programme. Whether it is the movement of water down the River (name), the rushing of water through the mains, the whirling of water in and out of purification equipment, the dropping of water into test tubes, the running of water out of street standpipes or household taps, or even the trickling of water as it drops from a contented child's hands ... the movement, with its haunting, emotional, matching music, will constantly remind us of the life force water truly represents.

The other link, which will appear at brief intervals throughout the programme, is that of an ordinary family, living in an ordinary household, to be pictured in a 'fly-on-the-wall' drama-documentary style. We will begin the programme by looking at water from the user's point of view; underlining the way in which people take water for granted, in blissful ignorance of the essential role it plays in their lives. At key points within the programme, we relate the activity being portrayed to a simple, nonchalant domestic activity involving water. The sipping of water from a glass, in safe confidence ... the result of years of research and many thousands of pounds spent on purification; the fast running of a bath ... the result of the work of multiple pumping stations and an intricate new ring main around (city); the flushing of a lavatory, and the resultant, expert sewage treatment that permits the water cycle to continue; the joy in a child's face, as he watches a salmon leaping a weir in the River

(name) ... the result of years of arduous work on the part of (name)
Water to cleanse the waters for the salmon's return; these are just a few
examples. And in this way, we will connect the importance of ALL (name)
Water's activities to the individual, briefly, in an almost subliminal way,
without preaching or lecturing ... providing entertainment and relevance,
simultaneously.

In all, though, there is only one true link. And that is, water itself. This
wonderful element, never still, always moving, always allowing us to
thrive ... is a constant, faithful, forceful, flowing, source of life. And hence,
the title of our programme ...

THE FORCE, THE FLOW

The programme: content

The programme begins with a swirling, flowing montage of slow dissolve
live action images of moving water. This is edited and timed carefully to
coincide with the tempo of haunting, timeless music that will have been
carefully selected to mimic the visual images. After a few seconds, we
come to rest on the last shot in the montage; water dropping through a
young child's cupped hands, shot from an intriguing angle. The music
fades, and we hear happy, contented gurgling noises; the sound of a
small toddler gleefully enjoying bath-time. Slowly the camera tracks out to
show our young friend, cheerfully splashing about, flashing us a grin from
time to time. We watch carefully for a few seconds, as the child shows us
how his or her prize duck scoops up water and allows it to be poured
from its back.

A narrator briefly points out to us how we take water for granted ... and
yet, without it, we would die—even faster than we would for the lack of
food. He or she tells us that 71 per cent of our bodies, and 80 per cent of
our brains, are made up of water. We need water for health, for hygiene,
for a myriad of tasks and activities; each person uses up to 200 litres of
water every day. Then, we learn that in the (name) Water region, XX
million people depend solely on (name) Water, to bring them that force
... and that flow. But do we realize just what is involved, in providing
pure, clean water for our little friend to bathe in?

We now see something highly unorthodox, which jars us into realizing the
importance of our narrator's words. We watch the flow of water in our
'example' household ... but this time, it is going BACKWARDS. It
disappears from our toddler's bath, back into the taps ... it flows from a
glass, up into a cold water tap ... it runs at speed from its coverage of a
car being washed, back into a hosepipe ... from a kettle, into the tap ...

and so on. This sequence lasts only a few seconds, but leaves its mark. Now, we are ready to appreciate the enormity of the tasks (name) Water undertakes.

From the last swirling image of water running backwards, we dissolve to a swirling image of the (name) Water logo. We learn, by watching perpetually moving images of the (city) and (name) Valley area, combined with moving graphics and other live action, of the complex nature of (name) Water's area ... the dense population (over a quarter of all UK inhabitants) and high domestic and industrial demands over 5000 square miles ... and the fact that (name) Water is the largest water authority in the world.

After a brief, swirling, visual and musical link, we see our 'example' family out enjoying a walk by the banks of the River (name). A child's face glows, as he or she catches sight of a salmon or other fish. We move gently into a short clip or two from the 'Return of the (name) Salmon' VTR, and briefly learn of the painstaking efforts made by (name) Water's scientists in order to purify the river from pollution, and return it to its status as one of the major salmon rivers of the world. After seeing our family in a rowing boat, enjoying the tranquillity of water in a recreational context, we then cover the other major environmental points, and stress the efforts made by (name) Water to attack the effects of pollution from nitrates, industrial waste, etc. We now go back to our 'example' family, and watch for a couple of seconds, as one of them dabbles a hand in the gently flowing current.

Then, we relate this peaceful scene to the water cycle, and the sources of water available to (name) Water; the rivers, the wells, and the boreholes. We watch water flow through a weir, then dissolve to water gushing into a reservoir, and learn of the ways in which water is stored. After we see one member of our 'example' family take a refreshing drink from a water fountain, and we dissolve from the flow of this stream to the flow of water underground, we learn how the pumping stations, gravity, the mains network and the (city) ring main all function.

At the end of this sequence, we return home with our 'example' family. Here, we see someone fill a kettle from a cold water tap, and dissolve through this flow of water to flowing graphics of the movement of water at distribution points ... in other words, how water gets from the mains and/or the ring main, into our 'example' family's house.

Then, we move on through the sound of water rushing through the mains, accompanied by some music, to the sound of a lavatory being flushed. We see someone washing his or her hands at a bathroom sink, and glimpse the flow of the warm water there before looking at the water whisking around the lavatory bowl. We go on to see a swirling, graphic representation of sewage as it follows its course through the drainage system. As our graphic representation flows on, we dissolve to the rushing of water through sewage works, once again accompanied by music. Now, we learn about sewage treatment, and how waste water is prepared to serve us once again.

After another visual and musical link, we see a member of our 'example' family filling up a tumbler from the cold tap. The glass is nearly full, and the last few drops are just falling into the tumbler as we dissolve to drops of water falling into a test container in one of (name) Water's laboratories. Now, we learn about water purification and quality control, showing perhaps one or two very short interview clips (off-camera interviewer) with the scientists there. Lastly, we learn of the specialist water testers, who taste water for purity and palatability. We see one of these people tasting water from a cup, and then dissolve through to a member of our 'example' family, who is helping himself or herself to a drink of water from the hosepipe, while washing the car. Then, he or she resumes the hosing activity.

The narrator asks—rhetorically, we assume at first—if we, the public, appreciate water for the life-giving force it really is. A (name) Water van drives past in the street, slowly. The narrator points out that (name) Water, as the experts, are achieving great things. But are we doing our bit? As the narrator says this, the person washing the car looks up, quizzically, at the camera. The nozzle of the hose, still in the car washer's hand and pumping out water at full force, strays wildly in the direction of the (name) Water van, spraying the driver's face. He grimaces, grins, drives on a little further, and parks. We focus on the hose spray, still, and then dissolve through to a leaking pipe, with jets of water surging from various fissures in its surface.

Now, still using our 'example' family members, their day-to-day use of water, and fast-moving images of water as links, we look at the various aspects of what individuals should know about their own water supply. We look at each aspect in turn, using a combination of live action and graphics to describe what we should know, the importance of having a header tank, how to guard against problems, how (name) Water will warn and advise people when serious problems are likely to occur, how to solve local problems when they do arise, and when it's time to call in an expert plumber. We cover any environmental and conservation issues that pertain to individuals.

If relevant, we can also mention any other advisory service (name) Water may offer, and we reiterate the point that (name) Water is the expert body where ANY water matter is concerned. The last shot should be of a plumber successfully running a previously broken tap, smiling at our 'example' family; the camera zooms in on the flow of water from the tap, and we then dissolve back to the wildly straying hosepipe, zooming out to reveal the idle car washer once again.

The previous sequence may have been a 'dream'; but it was one which has had an effect on the car washer. In a pensive mood, he or she picks up the hose and resumes work, efficiently now. The driver of the (name) Water van gets out, and waves in a friendly fashion to the car washer, who smiles apologetically. We return our concentration to the forceful flow of the hosepipe once more.

Now, we close the programme on a montage of the force, and the flow of water, leading from the simple hosepipe back through a recap—in visual terms—of all the aspects of water, and of (name) Water, that we touched upon earlier. The haunting music accompanies our final sequence.

The narrator sums up in a couple of well-chosen lines, and mentions the fact that (name) Water is working hard to anticipate the growing needs of the future. We end by learning that it is only the expertise, technology and dedication of (name) Water, that can bring the force—and the flow—of life-giving water, to XX million people within the largest water authority area in the world ... for a very long time to come.

The skeleton script
This is largely self-explanatory, as it consists of a script written fully where the information exists, and holes where the information is yet to come. Sometimes skeleton scripts have to be produced if some final information is not available until the last minute. Also, if the people who will be approving the script understand script format well, the skeleton can be a viable alternative to a treatment. Skeletons can be useful, too, if you're writing a script that contains a mixture of documentary and dramatized material; it is often possible to generate the dramatized sections right away, before the documentary research has been carried out. By producing a skeleton script containing the dramatized sections in full, leaving gaps for the other sections, it will be easier for you to match in the documentary material when it eventually does arrive.

The full script
This is also self-explanatory, and consists of all the necessary material, sometimes including interview transcripts if they're relevant. There are three basic methods of laying out a full script.

Side-by-side   First there is 'side-by-side', which is always used for AV scripts and is often used for film and video as well. The layout consists of two vertical columns; on the right, you include all audio material like the voice-over narration, dialogue, interview suggestions/transcripts, music, and sound effects. On the left, you include all visual material. This can either be a general description of what should be seen on screen at the time, or a precise list of shots. How technical and detailed this column should be depends on (a) the level of technical literacy of the people reading/approving it and (b) how much visual input the director/producer requires from you.

Vision	Sound
We open on a series of still dissolves of the doctor sitting at his consulting desk. Then through a full screen wipe, we see that a patient has entered and sat down opposite him.	Music over.
We now see a series of tight shots of the two faces as they engage in deep conversation.	*NARRATOR:* A common problem faced by GPs today occurs when patients return for repeat prescriptions of one of the minor tranquillizers. Dependence, though common, must be reduced with care.
We see a reaction shot of the patient, looking upset.	And helping patients to come to terms with their dependence on benzo-diazepines takes a great deal of tact and understanding.
We snap change to graphics illustrating the recommended reduction dosages of Valium.	Reducing dependence must be carried out very gradually, to minimize withdrawal symptoms and anxiety.

Screenplay   The next layout is known as screenplay format. This comes from the feature film business, and contains voice-over narration and dialogue in indented sections, with descriptions of visuals set out between dialogue chunks at full page width. Margins should be fairly generous to enable the other members of the production team to scribble notes and comments next to the relevant lines.

We open on a long shot of the doctor sitting at his consulting desk. The patient is sitting opposite him, talking in undertones. The patient listens intently, then speaks.

> *DOCTOR:* Well frankly, Mrs Murphy, although I understand your concern I really think it's time we thought about reducing your intake of tranquillizers.

We cut to a close reaction shot of Mrs Murphy, who looks horrified.

> *MRS MURPHY:* Oh, no, Doctor! How can I possibly manage without them?

We return to the original two-shot. Their conversation continues in undertones as the narrator speaks over.

> *NARRATOR:* Helping patients to come to terms with their dependence on benzo-diazepines takes a great deal of tact and understanding . . .

TV drama   Finally there is TV format, or TV drama. This in effect is the reverse of screenplay, with the visual instructions indented and the dialogue spread across the page to the full margins.

Which layout of script you use is largely a matter of preference. AV producers and some video producers/directors prefer you to use side-by-side, as it leaves you in no doubt as to what visual action takes place at which point in the soundtrack—each visual activity is described directly opposite the relevant sound section. However, screenplay and TV drama flow better if you're reading them. And from a purely secretarial point of view, these two are far easier to generate. If you use a word processor, you'll find it can be quite difficult to lay the pages out—and even more difficult to edit later on, although that depends to an extent on the WP software you use. Although you should really pick the format which seems easiest for your needs, it is a helpful courtesy to speak with the producer and/or director of your programme and ask which layout suits them best.

The camera script

In the main, the only difference between a full script and a camera script is that the full script runs on continuously from start to finish, but the camera script starts each new scene on a fresh page, with each scene numbered and described as follows:

1 INTERIOR: DOCTOR'S OFFICE   **DAY**

We open on a long shot of the doctor sitting at his consulting desk. The patient is sitting opposite him, talking in undertones. The patient listens intently, as the doctor speaks.

> *DOCTOR:* Well frankly, Mrs Murphy, although I understand your concern I really think it's time we thought about reducing your intake of tranquillizers.

We cut to a close reaction shot of Mrs Murphy, who looks horrified.

> *MRS MURPHY:* Oh, no, Doctor! How can I possibly manage without them?

The reason for starting each scene on a fresh page, and numbering each one, is because when a programme is being shot it is not necessarily done in 'linear' fashion—i.e. shooting following the exact order of the finished programme. With each scene separated off, the director can then shuffle the paperwork so that the scenes can be shot in the most practical and cost-effective order. In addition, splitting the scenes up this way can allow more space on the paperwork for the director's notes, etc. Once again, whether or not you develop a full camera (or shooting) script depends on the requirements of the producer and/or director. If they want you to do it and you're able to use a word processor, it is really quite simple to do a reassembly job.

The director may also want you to put more technical information into the script, but if you're an inexperienced scriptwriter, you will need to learn directing and editing jargon. The more commonly used terms are described in Chapter 5. Here's how the previous example would be worked out in more technical/shooting detail:

1 INTERIOR: DOCTOR'S OFFICE   **DAY**

Long 2-shot doctor and patient sitting either side of consulting desk.

> SFX talking in undertones

Cut to new angle CU listening shot, patient.

> *DOCTOR:* (OOV) Well frankly, Mrs Murphy, although I understand your concern …

Cut to MCU reverse angle doctor.

DOCTOR: ... I really think it's time we thought about reducing your intake of tranquillizers.

Cut to BCU reverse angle reaction shot Mrs Murphy, horrified.

MRS MURPHY: Oh, no, Doctor! How can I possibly manage without them?

Chapter 3

What is a brief?

There is a popular misconception, floating around corporate programme commissioning circles, that a brief is a document stating what the programme commissioners want the programme to consist of.

What a brief *should* be, is a document that defines what a programme should achieve in terms of the message it communicates to its viewers/audience. What the programme commissioners want to see included in the programme really is very secondary in importance; the only important consideration is to include whatever will communicate their message in the most effective way.

For the in-house person with the job of writing a script, however, flaunting this point under the noses of his or her superiors will not always create an atmosphere of cooperation and enthusiasm. The instigation of a 'corporate video' often seems to become the personal baby of senior company personnel, and as you well know, when egos get involved priorities sometimes get stood on their heads. Frequently, then, if a good brief is to be generated, the scriptwriter—in-company or external—has to play the role of diplomat as well as interrogator.

Ostensibly, the brief for a programme should have been established before a scriptwriter is called in. This is usually the case when you use an external scriptwriter. But there are two problems here. One, as an in-company scriptwriter you are far more likely to be involved in the development of a brief for understandable reasons—you're there, on the spot, and you're probably part of the communications team who regard the programme as part of a broader project anyway. Two, even if you are an external writer of sorts—perhaps a member of an in-house video production team—you'll probably need to work with the programme commissioners to redefine or redevelop the original brief you were given.

Even if you, as the writer, do not have to deal with egos, politics, personal bugbears, etc. (and I must point out that, in any case, these problems do not always arise), there is still a very strong tendency for people to forget what the programme has to *do*, in favour of who appears in it, how much it will impress the Board, what to include so that it might win an IVCA or AV award, and so on. Even those of us who work in the production industry occasionally are guilty of forgetting what we get paid to do—when there is the lure of some highly creative computer graphics, the chance to write poetic narration, the possibility of a helicopter shoot, and more. So in this criticism of the way in which briefs are sometimes put together, no one is being left out.

What, then, is the answer? It's a preaching job, I'm afraid. You, as the writer, have the initial (and probably foremost long-term) responsibility to represent the viewers throughout the writing process and, yes, that also includes the development of the brief. Clients and colleagues alike can get very bored with the sound of the scriptwriter's voice, nagging perpetually about what we want the viewers to think, feel and do, but if you're to do your job well then you have to put up with the flying rotten tomatoes and well-aimed water cannon. You have to preach your point, and practise it.

If you're very fortunate, of course, you may not be dealing with a committee of brief-makers, but will have sole responsibility for the project from initiation stage onwards. Why do you need a brief if there is no one else to agree it with? You need a brief, because it will provide you with not only the guidelines but also the focus you need before you begin to think about concepts and scripts. You need a brief to establish beyond a shadow of doubt just what it is *you* are trying to achieve with the programme, never mind what others might want. You need the freedom associated with this totally non-creative, non-visual document to draw up your programme's objectives, without the clutter of communications media. And finally, you need a brief because a brief—no matter how long it takes you to compile—will save you a lot of potentially expensive time in the long run.

What a brief needs to establish, and why

A good brief must examine and discuss a number of factors, and include the necessary conclusions. These are:

1 *What sort of programme is it—corporate, marketing, sales, promotional, internal communications, external communications, recruitment, training, etc.?* This is an obvious question which should receive a straightforward answer. But sometimes programmes are made with the intention of covering more than one of these areas, which is to be avoided if possible. Hybrids—e.g. corporate programmes doubling up as recruitment programmes, which are typical—never really achieve either job properly, because the different messages necessarily become diluted if they are to run together.

2 *The* raison d'être—*why is a video/AV necessary in the first place?* Is the need management-perceived (pro-active) or is it reactive (e.g. to address a particular problem or set of circumstances)? This will influence your approach. If the programme comes as news to the viewers, they are more likely to sustain interest and a positive attitude to the programme. If the programme is being made to address an existing issue, the viewers are more likely to have preconceived ideas about that issue which you will then have to address—particularly if the programme is intended to change attitudes and perceptions.

3 *Who are the viewers (customers, dealers, retailers, wholesalers, the public, all staff, certain staff members, etc.)?* You must define the target audience very thoroughly; and if there is more than one group, you must know what percentage of the total each group represents. This will then help you to put yourself in the shoes of the target audience, and will direct you in your research.

4 *In what circumstances will the viewers be seeing the programme?* If viewers will see the programme as part of a live presentation or trainer-led training exercise, the programme you write can be set in context by a speaker before people watch it. If the programme is to be watched in people's own time at the workplace, without any preamble or led discussion afterwards, it will have to be rather more attention-grabbing. And if viewers are likely to chat informally afterwards about it among themselves, you will have to ensure that you don't write anything into the script that could trigger some people's cynicism and scepticism, as in a discussion not led by an expert these attitudes have a way of spreading. Finally, if viewers are to take the programme home and watch it, you should consider making the programme entertaining as well as informative. After a day's work, people are more attuned to the idea of watching a comedy show, a good documentary, or a soap, than they are a serious business programme. If your programme is as entertaining to the viewer as his or her favourite TV programme, yours will be retained much better.

5 *What is the principal message to be conveyed to the viewers?* Normally, whoever is commissioning the programme will be keen to get as many messages into the programme as possible. Obviously this is understandable, but there should always be one message which emerges as number one. This ensures that the programme has direction and overall cohesiveness. A plethora of messages given equal importance will result in a diluted programme that leaves the viewer feeling confused and oversaturated with information.

6 *What—if any—secondary messages are to be conveyed?* There are the other messages that don't make it to number one. They should be reduced in number to the basic minimum, and then placed in order of importance. You won't necessarily approach them in this order when you come to write the script, but you will know how much time and 'weight' to allocate to each when you're putting the programme together.

7 *What are the background politics behind the messages?* Is there a 'hidden agenda'? Very often video and AV programmes are made to overcome political problems and sticky issues within the viewing audience. This is fine, but it has to be done in a way that doesn't leave viewers feeling that their intelligence has been insulted or that management is trying to con them. When you write the script, it will be your job to address the sticky issue and then generate the changes of attitude, behaviour, etc., that are required—sometimes a tough job, but made easier if you know the facts and have researched the whole problem (viewers' side included). Consequently you need to find out the full story—not just the official version in management-speak. External scriptwriters often find it difficult to extract this information from programme commissioners, but in-house writers will usually be aware of the whole story to start with. In a way, your role in these circumstances will be like that of an investigative journalist. If you should encounter any resistance from the programme commissioners when you try to extract the 'dirty linen', it's worth pointing out to them why you need to know—it's because you're trying to do the best possible job, not to be nosy. And it's also worth pointing out that, although you need to know everything, you're not necessarily going to use all of that information in the script. It's merely a case that the more you know, the more likely it will be that your script is on target.

8 *What is the primary audience's level of technical literacy and general understanding of a business message?* Once again, this may seem obvious. In many ways, the most important point here is that the programme commissioners should know and understand just how much the viewers can absorb and at what level, so they don't expect you to include more information or more complex information than is reasonable in the circumstances. It's also important that everyone understands what and how much information the viewers will find of interest to them. Many programme commissioners succumb to the temptation to add in a great deal of issues of interest to management, but which viewers—especially if they are shopfloor staff or external groups like retailers—will find boring and irrelevant.

9 *On what medium, and at what level of quality, will the programme be played back?* This is more of a production point, and affects the choice of medium on which to initiate the programme. However, obviously you must know whether you're to write for video or AV. In the case of video, you need to know if the programme's visual content is to be updated at any time, as you could make things easier for the producer and editor when the time to update it comes, by writing the programme as narration only with no 'lip sync' dialogue.

10 *In which languages is the programme to be produced?* You must know if the programme is to be translated into different languages. If it is, you should avoid dramatization altogether for two reasons; one, overdubbing costs are likely to be high and, two, drama—especially humour—in the culture of one language does not always translate well into the culture of another. You should also avoid lengthy interviews, although short ones can be overdubbed or subtitled into the language concerned. Finally, allow plenty of time in your English language narration for music gaps, etc. This is because many foreign languages require three words to say what can be said in English in one. For example, a French translation of an English narration will be about 20 per cent longer, and a German translation will be up to 35 per cent longer. For programmes falling into this category, you should ask the producer to ascertain the languages that are to be used, and how much extra time you will need for the longest overall.

11 *If you could choose one thought to be in the viewers' minds after they've seen the programme or presentation, what would that be?* This is the final question to ask of the programme commissioners, and it ties back into one of the earlier criteria of what is the main message to convey. The response to the question may be predictable, but on the other hand it may also be revealing and help you to crystallize the tone of the programme in your own mind.

Live presentations

To a large extent your job in obtaining a good brief is a little easier here, because the audience concerned is (a) captive and (b) much easier, in many circumstances, to define. However, most of the points raised in **1–11** above are relevant to live presentations and speeches, and it is a case of adapting these points to the needs of a live presentation.

Chapter 4

Getting the approach right

Once your brief has been established, you then normally need to enter into research phase. The amount of research required will obviously depend on the subject matter in hand, and also on the nature of the messages to be communicated; sometimes your research will consist of a few phone calls, and at other times it will involve several days of 'field work'.

The most important thing to remember about researching a script is that collecting the factual information is normally the easiest part of the job. And no matter how technical a programme is to be there is always some suitable expert available to tell you how to approach the complicated parts and even read them afterwards to make sure they're technically accurate. That is the least of your problems.

The most difficult part of researching a script is finding out the cultural/emotional background, and angling your approach to ensure that the correct *feelings* are generated through the programme you write for. This information is not always established through the briefing process, and even if it is it's likely to have been management-generated, which may mean it is a little one-sided. If your programme is to get results, it must be written in a way that grabs the audience in their own language, and that demonstrates a realistic understanding of their needs and problems. No matter how well-meaning management are, they do not normally operate at the sharp end and cannot possibly understand how it feels there. You, on the other hand, must find out.

It is extremely important for you to spend some time—even if it is just on the telephone—talking to typical representatives of the audience in question. If they are trainees, go and spend an afternoon with them and really find out what it feels like to learn their job. If they are retailers, go into their stores and get the feel of the atmosphere, their customers, their displays, etc. I have spent hundreds of hours in retail stores, factories, workshops, offices, hotels, fast food outlets, power stations, foundries, even down a coal mine, talking to representatives of video or AV programme audiences. Apart from the new information I learn, I also enjoy the experience of meeting new people often in intriguing circumstances. So far, I think the coal mine was the most interesting, with the turbine room of a fossil-fuel-fired power station running a close second!

If the programme commissioners ask why you need to do this when they've already told you what they feel you need to know, you should always reassure them that you don't think they're lying—because they're not. It's just that you must have the total picture, including the views of the audience, if you are to communicate the programme commissioners' message properly. I've never encountered a serious problem in this respect; most management are usually glad that you care enough about the job to go to that sort of trouble. Sometimes, when there are potential political minefields, you will only be warned about them when you ask if you may talk to the audience, and this in itself can give you a better insight into the project.

If you are to write about a process which is not particularly technical, it's a good idea to try it out for yourself. For example, if the programme is to be part of an existing training exercise, you should attend part of the course as a participant. This helps you to understand the subject matter, and also gives you the chance to talk to other course members, who are likely to be your audience.

If you're writing about a particular product, go and see how it's made. If you're writing about a service—let's say a car-valeting service—get your car valeted by the people concerned, or watch how they valet someone else's car.

Above all, remember to put yourself in the audience's shoes. Try to understand how it feels to be in their position—understand their motives, their problems, their needs. Once you've achieved this, you can then put the feelings and attitudes you've gathered together with the feelings and information the programme commissioners want you to communicate, in a balanced and realistic way. That's what leads to a truly effective script that will achieve its objectives and give the programme commissioners value for their money.

Determining your approach

Many people still feel that the only way to make a corporate programme is to use a documentary or 'news item' approach. This couldn't be further from the truth. Television and, to a lesser but still significant extent, AV are emotional pot-pourri and for the purposes of your writing you can virtually take your pick from the wide range of styles you see on broadcast TV. Humour, drama, pathos, shock, threat, sympathy, empathy, stimulation, aggression, etc., are all there for the taking, provided that you remember not to let the tail wag the dog. In corporate work, these entertaining and stimulating types of television are fine, providing they are used as vehicles for the message to be conveyed and not purely on their own merits. We can all learn a lesson from the TV commercial world, whereby you can remember every last detail of a wonderfully creative and exciting commercial you saw last night— everything, that is, except the name of the product. Often these commercials, especially for beer or cars, are stunning examples of cinematography, but they're a total waste of the client's £300 000 or so if all they're doing is to sell the competitors' products or the director's talent.

During your briefing and research phases you will have got a good grip on the message, the nature of the audience, and the circumstances in which the programme will be seen, which are the three key triggers in how to decide on your approach. There is no such thing as the right way or the wrong way, and each case has to be judged individually. Let's take a look at some general points to consider first.

AV: more than meets the eye

Many people feel that AV is restricted when compared with videotape, because all you have to play with are mute pictures with a soundtrack. But having said that, with a little imagination there's plenty you can do with these tools at your disposal. As mentioned earlier, AV is like illustrated radio, if that were possible, and can use any of its techniques to good effect.

On the picture side, the most important consideration is to think in terms of sequences of images—not one-off photographs. There is nothing more irritating than a slide-tape programme that jumps about from subject to subject. When you're writing for AV (and therefore recommending the visual content as well) you need to think in a progression, almost as you would with film or videotape; pictures should follow each other in a logical sequence. Just as you would with videotape, think of establishing shots, followed by more detailed pictures unfolding the story. If you're describing, for example, a new computer building, show the outside first, then go indoors and show the details.

Stills film is cheap, so you don't need to recommend that the photographer is mean with it. You should never keep one image up for too long; even if you're describing one object, show several different angles of it rather than use one static shot. Staying with the computer example, try to get some human interest into your visuals and words by showing shots of hands using the keyboard and highlighting the benefits of the new product as well as the features ... show people's faces, studying, smiling, talking to colleagues, etc., to bring the benefits of the machine alive. Suggest that the photographer should use his or her creative flair freely on any project; even the most boring metal box can look interesting through a filtered lens, using artistic lighting.

Graphics (charts, diagrams and so on) are useful if you have a particularly complicated process or topic to describe. However, too many charts and diagrams illustrating long sections of statistical information are boring. Remember that AV, like TV, is largely an emotional medium rather than a suitable place to give lots of information—you should use the audio-visual media to highlight the main points and create the right attitudes, and put the details in accompanying printed material. To attempt to do this in an AV will mean that viewers lose the main messages in among all the clutter.

With AV, if you don't have sufficient pictures and, for one reason or another, it would be impractical to shoot new material, you can always recommend the use of a library. There are good picture libraries in most major cities and, although library shots aren't cheap, the odd one or two can be cost-effective and brighten a programme up considerably.

Then, there's the soundtrack. Sound recording is cheap, and so are sound effects. Library music is relatively cheap, too, and most recording studios have a wide selection on hand for you (or the producer) to choose from. Never fall into the trap of thinking that an AV soundtrack should always consist of a voice-over narration with a little music behind it. This definitely isn't true.

Video: the documentary approach

Let's take an example, where there is a limited budget, and your purpose is to communicate a new product or process to employees. You need to include some sort of address to staff from the chairman, and show how the new product has been developed as well as what it does.

Many such programmes that you'll see show a 'talking head' of the chairman, straining to read a teleprompter, followed by a voice-over reading out brochure copy while a fixed camera is pointed at a metal box. The occasional graphic arrow appears on the screen to point out a particularly interesting widget. After four minutes, the audience is asleep.

There is a tendency among inexperienced or overly enthusiastic corporate people to think that the natural way to shoot a programme is to go and shoot what's there. 'We'll start at reception because we have a lovely new switchboard, and Bridget is quite attractive, then I think we should proceed through the corridor because we spent a fortune on the new downlighting, then directly into the corporate fitness centre because that demonstrates how committed we are to our people, and from there right on to the machine shop where we really should get the milling and drilling operations of the three types of computer controlled machines . . .'

Wrong. The brutal fact of life is that, apart from a few people from the company, no one in the audience will care deeply about such things as new switchboards or expanded offices or corporate fitness centres, even if they are an internal audience. They want to get an image or impression of your message—not the office furniture or even the lovely Bridget. Whoever your viewers are, never write programmes based solely on *things*—you should write programmes about what things do for *people*.

Next, let's look at the chairman. Many chairmen, being chairmen, have developed a bit of an ego over the years and may fancy themselves as performers. Others may be shy and have no interest in being on screen, but their subordinates think it would be a good idea. Performing on camera is in fact a very difficult thing to do. The natural reaction for an amateur is to go completely blank . . . to repeat . . . to look sideways . . . to stutter and say 'er'. So, sticking the chairman in front of a camera can be courting disaster, and you should think carefully before recommending it—or succumbing to pressure to include such a recommendation in your script. No matter how revered the chairman is to his or her staff, to the viewer the chairman is simply a sweaty, stammering non-actor with a high, squeaky voice. But what do you do if you *need* to include that chairman in your programme, whether it is for practical or political reasons?

First, get the chairman out of the office and on to the factory floor. Or outside the building by a big sign that reinforces the company's image. Or if, say, the programme is about a new car component, sit the chairman in a car, on a car, in the back seat of a car, driving along. If he or she can't remember the words, don't allow them to be read out—that sounds stilted and very unbelievable. Instead, interview the chairman off-camera (see Chapter 12) and use your questions as prompts, dropping your bits later in the edit. If the chairman can remember what to say, get him or her to walk around; the camera can follow. If you take them from the formal environment of the TV studio or the boardroom, many chairmen turn into real, interesting human beings. Not only is that very important for your purposes—it's also very important to the audience.

Next, we move on to objects. Never simply plonk a machine or other product in front of a camera, and never use brochure copy as the narration script. Instead, get someone in a white coat to describe lovingly the baby he or she has just given birth to (see Chapter 12 on interviewing experts). Real words from a real enthusiast are much more illuminating than any narration script you or I could write. If a product does something, show it doing it. If it has an interesting internal activity that can't be seen from outside, don't stick a graphic arrow over the place in question, but dissolve through to some well-designed, lively graphics that show how it works.

Don't just say 'it cuts fuel consumption by twenty per cent'. Show someone driving into a petrol station, filling up, paying, and smiling. (A two-hour shoot, and there's got to be a tame petrol station nearby.) Push the camera into the back seat of your car and shoot a close-up of the petrol gauge.

Above all, let people and places talk; that's what television is all about. People don't go about their working lives without saying a word—factories and machines are noisy. Let your viewers see things and hear things as they really are. Never shoot mute tape and stick a voice plus a little music over the top; this results in no more than a moving AV show, and with a boring soundtrack at that (you can still have sound effects in AV—see above). The whole point of documentary video is to make the audience feel, as far as possible, that they're participating in the action on screen. Unless you're writing for an audience of deaf people, silent movies are a waste of money. Even if your programme is to be translated into a number of languages—which will restrict the amount of 'lip sync' sequences you can use—the sounds of industry are pretty much the same in any language, and you must use them freely.

Where possible, use interview clips for descriptive sections, and keep them as short as possible. Interview people at their place of work rather than in an unfamiliar environment; don't let yourself get talked into moving interviewees into strange places for production reasons, because although the sound quality might be better the interview's content won't be as good if your interviewee is nervous. (See Chapter 12 for details on how to conduct corporate interviews.)

That's real life, which is what documentary TV is meant to convey. Now, what about using fiction?

Video: dramatization

The first thing to remember is: don't be frightened by drama. You're not about to compete with Harold Pinter or Tennessee Williams.

Dramatization in this context is simply the re-creation of 'a slice of life' and dialogue is simply the way ordinary people say ordinary things.

So how can dramatization be used in the corporate context?

The most obvious place is in training programmes. There is no better way to illustrate the wrong ways and the right ways of doing things than by a dramatized example. This is particularly true where you're training people to deal with other people—'interpersonal skills'.

But there are other ways in which dramatization can be useful. A very relevant, and often missed opportunity for drama is in the demonstration of a product or process. Instead of describing what something does in two-dimensional terms, you can make a demonstration much more meaningful by showing a dramatized example of the product or process being used in a realistic context.

In corporate work—particularly in training—there is usually a need for some kind of documentary/didactic explanation to accompany dramatizations. This is fine, but don't clutter one up with the other. Let your actors do their job without the narrator breathing down their necks every thirty seconds. Use narration to link, then let the characters do the demonstrating or teaching. In some contexts, you don't need narration at all; remember, viewers are not idiots who need to be led by the nose. It's very important to remember that video is usually much more self-explanatory than people think—yet many corporate programmes you see over-explain, with pictures, actors and narrators all saying the same things, to the point of insulting the audience's intelligence.

Combining drama and documentary styles is a useful ploy, and can be approached in one of several ways. You can blend the two smoothly so that the joins are not very visible—this helps to reinforce the overall message, without jogging the viewer's attention every time you change from one style to the next. Remember, it's the message that counts, not whether the person talking is an actor or a director of the company. You can also make a feature of the relationship between the narrator and the dramatized characters, using the camera itself as the 'eye' of the narrator and, by implication, of the viewer as well. This creates an interesting, slightly surreal effect.

A word of warning: never use amateur actors, unless you and the director are *convinced* they can do the job well. In the main, though, if the budget won't stretch to hiring professional actors, avoid dramatization altogether. It doesn't matter how many times the financial director has starred in 'A Streetcar Named Desire' with his local amateur dramatic society—he is unlikely to impress your viewers by trying to play an agitated customer in a corporate training programme. Amateur acting looks like what it is—dramatization made on the cheap. And the last thing you want to do is reflect *that* image on the company or organization concerned.

Video: comedy

Be careful of comedy; don't let the tail wag the dog.

In the late 1970s and early 1980s when Video Arts—that well-known production company specializing in humorous corporate training programmes—was in its heyday in Britain, everyone in the UK wanted training and other corporate programmes to be shot at Fawlty Towers or the Ministry of Funny Walks ... both classic examples of a special type of humour attributed to John Cleese, who was one of the original Monty Python characters.

The Cleese-esque brand of humour is still brilliant, of course, but it was done to death, and badly at that, by 'me-too' production companies and in-house units everywhere. People were so entranced by the genre that they would even try to force it into business messages that were totally unsuitable for humorous portrayal.

The result was that not only did the genre become very tired, but it made a lot of companies look very silly. Other types of humour were exploited to death as well—especially sitcoms. Many professional writers were called upon to rip off a number of popular UK sitcoms for corporate purposes, with very mixed results. We could produce the words, of course, but trying to match a well-known style of comedy plot to a corporate message doesn't always work, no matter how experienced and talented the writer.

Writing for this type of script is a specialized job best left to professionals. Comedy writing courses are available in some major cities and there are a number of good books on the subject, if you're interested in this type of scriptwriting. But whatever you do, don't try to tackle humour unless you're certain you can do it well. Comedy writing runs a close second to children's stories in the league table of the most difficult writing styles (surprising, as it appears easy, but true) and no one should take it lightly. A corporate programme that contains bad comedy is the most efficient way I know to make the image of the company concerned look very funny indeed.

If you do use humour, it only works if you tailor the content to the message—not adjust the message to fit around a funny plot. In-jokes for an internal audience work well and will usually bring the house down, as well as make a point. Bending a well-known entertainer's style of humour around a specific brief and set of objectives takes practice, but it works, too.

Often comedy is not a case of writing lots of funny one-liners, but of placing ordinary actions into extraordinary circumstances. A man sneezing in the bathroom isn't funny; but the same man sneezing into a bowl of freshly sifted flour on the kitchen table, can be. If you want to tackle humour, good luck—just remember not to labour it. Use it sparingly to emphasize your message, and never let it dictate the programme's content.

Some examples

As I said earlier, there is no such thing as the right way or the wrong way to approach a corporate script. The styles I have outlined above are generalizations, of course, and you can create a number of variants on each. But to set your own thought process in motion, here are a few examples of how I've tackled some typical corporate programme requirements.

1. Retail staff training VTR programme

Message: To create staff awareness of new additive-free range of own brand foods, which has been introduced rather as a concession to current fashions than as a major marketing exercise.

Audience: Store staff, who feel that the whole additive issue is a bit of a storm in a teacup and aren't really that interested in it.

Viewing circumstances: As part of regular staff-training session, conducted one Monday morning each month, trainer-led.

Requirements: To tackle staff cynicism head-on, and say, in effect—OK, we all know that the additive issue is a bit overrated, but there are customers who take it seriously and we must care about their needs. Programme should entertain and generate questions afterwards.

Approach: Open with a spoof 'horror' sequence which is funny, but sets up the problem by showing the lurking dangers of additives creeping round a comedy 'customer' character who is obsessed with food. She then goes to a branch of the store in question, paranoid and convinced that all food will now poison her, only to find out through the helpful assistant she meets that she may now buy additive-free food there.

Comedy sequence demonstrating how product knowledge and good customer-care techniques on the part of the assistant bring the customer down from near-hysteria to confidence and satisfaction. Occasional voice-over narration here and there to point out factual information, but the main bulk of the information coming through the dialogue. Also includes an interview with an in-house expert who discusses the relevance and true importance of additives in food.

2. Graduate recruitment VTR programme

Message: To attract graduates with a wide range of degrees to work for a relatively autonomous government department which has something of a boring, stuffy image.

Audience: Final year students at universities, who will almost certainly think that this organization is stuffy, boring and impersonal, but who are not necessarily high-fliers themselves. They want interesting careers in a secure environment.

Viewing circumstances: The university 'milk round', which means that this programme will be shown at presentations, etc., along with dozens of others. Consequently it has to stand out from the crowd, and also set up what it's offering very quickly and effectively before it gets into any detail. Might be taken away by graduates and watched at home.

Requirements: To show that working for this organization is not stuffy and boring, and that the work it does is highly relevant to the lives of everyday people.

Approach: To use four case studies typical of the work this organization does as a 'core'. Each case study is described in 'off-camera' interview clips by one of the team involved in it. The interviewees must all be young people and, preferably, recent graduate recruits themselves. Then, we develop a dramatized sequence at either end of the programme, based on four university students sharing a house. Each student tells his or her own little cameo story, which unbeknown to him or her is directly linked to one of the case studies. At the beginning, their stories unfold to set each one up, and they query how activities relevant to their stories are dealt with by the government. There is then a short V/O section which introduces the organization. We return to the four students, who recap on their stories after which they all go off for the weekend. We then go into the documentary case study section of the programme, and finally return to the four students returning from their weekend. In the meantime one has been given some information about the organization, which they discuss briefly. The final tie-up between drama and documentary is in the last few shots of the programme, where we see one of the students attending the organization's HQ for an interview. (Excerpts from the script for this programme appear in Chapter 10.)

3. Educational/PR VTR programme for a UK Water Authority

Message: To explain what the authority does, and how the water process and 'cycle' works in that region.

Audience: General PR purposes, schools, etc., plus information for potential shareholders. Viewers tend to take their water supply for granted, and haven't the faintest idea how the water is supplied or what happens to the waste. Water is not seen as a glamorous or interesting topic—just a utility.

Viewing circumstances: As part of a live presentation, then as give-away for people to watch at home.

Requirements: To make people realize that they get good value for their water rates, and that without water they couldn't live. Also to establish the complicated and extensive amount of equipment and activities needed in order to maintain a healthy water supply, particularly in this region which contains one of the UK's largest conurbations. Programme has to be really interesting and attention grabbing, as when people take it home it will be competing for attention with the usual broadcast TV programmes.

Approach: A very beautiful, poetic, almost romantic documentary approach. Highly emotional, uncluttered voice-over narration with stunning photography of water, and the minimum of nuts and bolts. Concentrating on beautiful images even when discussing sewage treatment, etc. Central pivot around a typical family home. Surprising sequence early on which discusses what life would be like without water, showing many examples of water flowing *backwards* up pipes, wash handbasins, sinks, etc., plus resultant drought and even loss of life. Also concentration on ecological issues, restocking of rivers, etc., to emphasize that a Water Authority's work is not just about sewers and drains. Shot on 16-mm film for more subtle and artistic lighting and effects—'oil painting' style, transferred to VTR for playback. (The treatment I developed for this programme is shown in full in Chapter 2.)

4. Sales/marketing AV

Message: To attract new business for a major UK construction company, in the area of building for the retail industry. This particular division of the company is already very successful and experienced in the retail field, but wishes to expand its customer base even further.

Audience: Two levels; major decision makers (e.g. Chairman/MD) and also middle management (development managers, etc.) in large retail organizations. Secondary use as high-level mailshot to potentially interested parties, usually the result of an enquiry, accompanied by brochures and covering letter.

Viewing circumstances: As opening part of a live presentation to a small audience. AV chosen as initiation medium in preference to VTR as it is easier and cheaper to update. Programme will be shown as an AV in live presentations where possible, but will be transferred to VTR for mailing out and for showing when an AV rig is not available. Programme therefore must be made to single-screen format, 'TV safe'.

Requirements: The company would use this programme when asking a potential customer if they can be considered to tender for a particular project, whether it forms part of a live presentation or in response to an enquiry. We can assume therefore that the audience will already be interested in seeing what they can do. Much of the expertise in building for retail is involved in the construction company knowing the nature of the retail business, and organizing the building work so that trade can continue in the store as smoothly as possible while the work's being done. The attitude of the construction company's management is crucial, too, as if they're enthusiastic about retail the job will be done better and more quickly. This company's management were all brimming over with enthusiasm, and they were all good, fluent talkers during the briefing and research activities.

Approach: To capture the hustle and bustle of retail in series of fast-moving AV sequences, interspersed with slower sequences that showed the rich texture and high visual appeal of the materials used in various projects. To show examples of the excellent refurbishment work they had already done for a number of top High Street retail names, as well as new build projects within edge of town and greenfield site developments. And rather than use voice-over narration throughout, use the voices of the construction company's management in short, atmospheric clips in a vox pop style, to illustrate the depth of their knowledge and high degree of lively enthusiasm. Narration just used as a link between sections. Some short sections just using sound effects and music, capturing the spirit of retail and the ingenious way in which the construction company could manage to refurbish an entire store while still keeping the customers flowing through the check-outs. (An excerpt from the final script for this programme appears in Chapter 9.)

As to whether or not all the above examples work, all I can say is that the four programmes concerned were very successful and did a good job for the companies who commissioned them!

At the end of the day, logic and reasoning are never enough to produce a good corporate programme or presentation—creativity, indefinable though that is, has a large part to play in determining whether or not the programme works. In corporate writing you should never be afraid to be a bit daring, because however outrageous an idea might appear on paper it will never normally translate into something quite as outrageous on screen.

However, there is one overriding factor you need to consider at all times: money. If you don't have a great deal of money in the budget, then you should forget trying to be too creative and daring and stick with a good, simple approach that will convey the message properly with few frills. But don't let a low budget depress you. There's a lot you can do with one camera and a simple two-day shoot, and (in the case of AV) with a couple of days' worth of stills photography.

Chapter 5

Visual thinking

Before you put any words down on paper, please take careful heed of this one piece of advice. In writing for any of the audio-visual media, *you're not just writing words*. Just as television or feature films must have a successful marriage of words and pictures, so must the corporate versions. Always, always visualize what you're writing. Even the most straightforward corporate documentary, with a narration and general views and not much else, must still have a strong partnership between what the narrator says and what the viewers see. It certainly is not a case of one duplicating the other, as I've already said; you should never tell viewers what they already can see, or show them exactly the same things that a voice is describing. The key is to use words and pictures as extra dimensions of each other.

When you're writing a script you *must* think of the pictures at the same time. You don't necessarily have to work out every shot length and every camera angle—that's usually the director's job, although your suggestions are helpful when you write the camera script. (The main terms for shot lengths and camera angles are given below for reference.) All you need to start is a clear idea of what should be happening on screen.

In many ways it is unproductive to go into a lot of visual detail until the broad content and creative approach of the script are agreed. But if you can't work out what viewers should be seeing on screen most of the time, you can be certain that no one else will, either. Writers who focus only on the verbal content are usually cursed by producers and directors who struggle to make some visual sense out of very pretty but often totally unpictorial words. These writers are living in the past, in the days when the audio side of a slide-tape script consisted of excerpts from the brochure copy which the producer then tried desperately to match to still photographs. That's no better than a 'magic lantern' show, or somebody talking a bored audience through their holiday snaps, and none of us—professional scriptwriters or beginners—should be writing awful programmes like that.

Visual thinking isn't difficult. It's just a case of colourful story-telling. If you're writing narration, try to complement words with visuals so that the words and pictures work together to encompass an idea. And narration doesn't have to tally exactly with what's happening on screen. Narration can also act as a commentary, pointing out issues which are allied to the action on screen but not necessarily identical to them. Remember that viewers are not idiots; their ears are perfectly capable of functioning independently of their eyes, providing there is a logical link between the two senses. If you're writing dialogue, you need to become the character—see the person you've created and feel what he or she is feeling; but more of that in Chapter 6.

A useful exercise in visual thinking is to tell a story to a child. The quickest way I know of putting a child to sleep (useful on occasions, but not the point here!) is to describe the big, bad wolf as a cruel, unfeeling individual with deep-seated psychological problems and an innate hatred of people wearing crimson-coloured headgear suited to equestrianism. Talk in terms of the big, bad wolf's huge ears that flop over his forehead, his nasty, gleaming eyes, his ugly black teeth and smelly breath, his slimy, growling voice and his horrible smile—his sudden change from being sweet and charming to being evil and terrifying as Little Red Riding Hood runs away, screaming with fear, and then hides behind a chair, crying and trembling—and the child will be awake until midnight. What you're doing is stimulating the child's imagination and, through your use of visual words, making the child see the entire story in his or her mind's eye. I don't suppose the big bad wolf will ever star in a corporate programme, but the principle of visual thinking for these media is much the same.

Visual thinking in AV

Although much of what I've written above pertains to VTR, most of it is equally relevant to AV. I've already laboured the point elsewhere that AV is *not* as visually restrictive as most video producers will tell you, and it's worth repeating here. In fact the visual effects you can achieve with multi-image, multi-screen AV shown live to an audience are in many ways more interesting and impactful than those of film or video. Large format AV has a number of practical drawbacks when you compare it with the portability and idiot-proof playback qualities of video, but as a creative visual medium there's nothing like it. The thing to remember about the visual side of AV is that even with just two projectors you can create the sensation of movement, through gentle dissolves and sequences of slides shot in registration. And, as I've mentioned, the intelligent and imaginative use of the soundtrack—with atmospheric music and a good choice of sound effects—can add a great deal to the perceived quality and meaning of the pictures.

Once you get to AV programmes made with a number of projectors, especially if you can use more than a single screen, you can create stunning effects of movement with a slightly surreal, abstract quality. You can capture human expression and emotion through the high quality of 35-mm still photographs much better than you can with the electronic harshness of video. One of the most emotive and heart-rending programmes I have ever seen, on any corporate medium, was an award-winning single screen three-projector AV programme about the work of a charity in the Middle East. The images the photographer had captured of poverty, desolation, hunger and apathy literally brought tears to my eyes, especially coupled as they were with narration words that stung me with the vivid pictures they conjured up in themselves, and the strong yet subtle music and sound effects that subliminally underlined the plight of these people. All that, with no 'lip sync' and no live action, and a low budget as well.

How to describe your visual thoughts

As mentioned in Chapter 2, when you begin the script process with a treatment and draft script it is not a good idea to clutter things up with a host of camera and editing terms. There are two reasons for this: (a) it may disrupt your own flow of creative thought, especially if you're not too familiar with the jargon and (b) if the script has to be approved by people who are not technically literate it will confuse them and obstruct their own thought processes.

However, the time comes in any scriptwriter's working life when use of the jargon is called for. As with most industries, VTR and AV production have their own languages which, contrary to popular belief, are not designed to blind clients with science, but are used to guide the director and editor as to what you want the programme to look like. The place for this jargon is in the camera or shooting script, and here is a selection of the most commonly used terms to help you describe your visual thoughts.

AV terms

Animation   Any effect of motion, created by showing a series of slides shot in registration with minor differences in each one, progressing through to a new image.

Bar chart   A chart using horizontal 'bars' of varying lengths to illustrate quantity.

Bracketing   A means of shooting the same thing using different light exposures. This way you can show something going from dark to light and back again, or create a 'dawn coming up' reveal sequence.

Build-up   A series of graphics slides, usually with the same heading. With each new slide another line or two is added, building up to the total list which is contained on the final slide of the sequence.

Column chart   A chart using vertical 'bars' of varying lengths to illustrate quantity.

Dissolve   A means of changing from one image to the next whereby the first slide slowly fades out as the new one slowly fades in. A soft, gentle change.

Graphics   Slide content which consists of words and figures, or drawn symbols—in other words virtually anything which is not a 'photograph'.

Lock down sequence   A series of images where the camera is 'locked' into position, but each shot is slightly different—usually of a different length, using a zoom lens. This can simulate a 'zoom in' effect as you would see on film or VTR.

Pie chart   A chart showing a circular symbol divided into segments, to illustrate quantity.

Snap change   A simple change of slide from one to the next, without dissolving.

Videotape terms (shooting)

The following are in order of length, starting with the subject (in this case a person) furthest away from the camera. Distances are approximate only.

ELS   Extremely long shot—subject in far distance.

VLS   Very long shot—subject in middle distance.

LS   Long shot—subject in good view, but with background around him or her.

MLS   Medium long shot—subject almost filling frame (from top to bottom, at least)

MS   Medium shot—subject in view down to around the knees.

MCU   Medium close up—subject down to the waist.

CU   Close up—head and shoulders.

BCU   Big close up—head and neck.

ECU   Extremely close up—face only.

Wide shot   A shot taken with the camera on wide angle.

2 shot   Any shot with two figures (people) in it. Hence 3 shot, 4 shot, etc.

OTS shot   Over the shoulder shot—usually used in interviews with the camera pointing at the interviewee over the interviewer's shoulder, or sometimes in dramatized sequences.

On the shoulder   Where the camera is not on a tripod but on the camera operator's shoulder. Useful to get at tricky spots where there isn't any room for a tripod. Creates a 'newsy', urgent look, in the style of TV news items.

Crab   A camera movement where it emulates a crab—camera, tripod and dolly moving sideways. Hence crab left and crab right.

Pan   Where the camera swivels on the tripod from one side to another, hence pan left and pan right. This word is often used by the non-technically literate to describe virtually any camera movement at all, but its true meaning is as I've just described.

Tilt   Where the camera tilts vertically on the tripod, hence tilt up, down.

Track   The camera and tripod are placed on what looks like a portable railway track, which allows steady movement. Hence track in or out, moving towards or away from the subject. You can also use a 'tracking shot' so the camera can accompany a presenter who is walking along. Provided you're shooting on a very smooth surface and the camera is on a good quality wheeled dolly, you can simulate a tracking shot without the railway by pulling the whole assembly along on the wheels.

Zoom   Where the camera appears to move towards or away from the subject, without moving—done through the use of a zoom lens with the camera static on the tripod.

Videotape terms (editing)

Animation   Any sequence where a normally inanimate object or symbol is made to 'move' on screen, through the use of special effects.

Caption   Words and/or figures put on to the programme during the edit.

Cut   A short, sharp change from one sequence to the next.

Dissolve   A slow change from one sequence to the next—see AV section above.

Graphics   Usually done by computer; anything which appears drawn, and also any graphic treatment of live action material.

Superimpose   To add one image on to another electronically.

Rather than duplicate with examples of how to use these terms here, it would be better for you to look through some of the script examples later in this book where you'll find most of the above terms in context.

Chapter 6

Writing for spoken speech

(This chapter contains contributions from John Butman, one of the most successful corporate scriptwriters in Eastern USA.)

At the risk of over-simplifying things, my view is that there are only two worthwhile points to remember about writing style for any kind of modern business communications, whether it is for the audio-visual media or for print.

1 Write as people speak; not as you were taught at school.
2 Keep it simple ... no unnecessary long words, no long sentences, no meaningless clichés and incomprehensible jargon.

Easy, isn't it? Wrong. These two points, together, are difficult to learn and even more difficult to put into practice. When professional writers look back at scripts they wrote even five years previously, it usually makes them cringe. Those are not as good as the scripts they're producing now. And in five years' time, their output will be better still. It takes experience and practice, and no matter how much you have of both you can always get better. One of the aims of this book is to give you a starting point, to help you begin your voyage towards good scriptwriting. The following two paragraphs illustrate this point:

NARRATOR: The object in question is made of light wood, containing a cylindrical core of carbon. At end of this instrument it is necessary to sharpen the surrounding wood in order to achieve a conical point. In this respect it is possible to hold the object in the hand, and through the application of the correct degree of pressure, the carbon point will convey an image upon piece of paper placed directly beneath it. At this moment in time, it is not possible to demonstrate the action of this object as it would appear to have been temporarily located in a non-regulation situation.

NARRATOR: I'm talking about my pencil. It's made of wood, with some carbon in it. If you sharpen one end, you can write with it. I can't show you how it works now, because I've lost it.

The most direct form of communication, and interestingly the earliest form of communication we know, is spoken speech. Prehistoric society was selling ideas and products through speech long before anything was carved in tablets of stone.

Many find the conversion from written to spoken speech quite a difficult task. Ironically enough it is a lot harder to write simply, in the way that spoken speech is simple, than it is to lean on the support of carefully constructed phrases and sentences that come straight from the grammar books we all used to pore over in the classroom. Like any new concept, learning to write in simple, spoken speech means a shift in your attitude—in the way that you think, as well as in the way that you set out one word after another.

Understanding the logic behind the need to write in simple, spoken speech can be made easier if you look at the ways in which sales people deliver a pitch to a prospective customer. Here, a straight, uncluttered, simply worded sales pitch is probably the most believable one of all. Simplicity implies honesty, conviction and enthusiasm. On the other hand, a wordy, over-long, cliché-ridden sales spiel will often have the prospect wondering what all that verbiage is trying to hide, or if it's actually a replacement for a good, believable sales story.

Communicating through the audio-visual media involves exactly the same principle. A strong, simple message that says what it means in unfussy language will come over as a lot more believable than large amounts of flowery prose that do not fool anybody.

Talking to 'you'

Naturally, there is a dividing line between the 'spoken' speech you should write for printed material, and the 'spoken' speech you write for an audio track. This second category has further subdivisions when you consider the spoken style for writing narration, character dialogue and live speeches. However, there is one very strong common denominator which runs through most of them, and this is what the advertising world calls the 'you' angle.

And before you raise your voice to say that corporate programmes are not usually 'advertising', remember that regardless of the purpose of virtually any corporate programme, it is still selling something. A recruitment programme is selling a career in your organization to potential employees . . . a training programme is selling a new method of doing things to staff . . . a charity fund-raising programme is selling the idea of giving money to a good cause . . . and so on.

There are exceptions to this, like very technical scripts describing the workings of an industrial process. To an extent these need to be led by 'it' rather than 'you'. But that doesn't mean that 'you' can be forgotten, even when the narration is describing how many times the ionized widget revolves in the galvanized cylinder per millisecond. In these cases, perhaps it's better to say that you should remember who it is you're writing for. And even with your ionized widgets, you're writing about 'it' for 'you'; not for 'us' or for 'it'.

The cruel truth about selling anything by any means is that 'you' is the only important part of the deal. 'You' will only act on the words a person hears if there's something in it for that person, and if he or she is involved. For example:

> *NARRATOR:* We recommend that the choke be pulled out to the fully extended position, as this facilitates the starting of the engine from cold . . .

. . . won't motivate anyone. By phrasing the line in this way you're not involving the viewer in the process—yet (if this is a training programme) it is 'you' who is supposed to be operating the machine—not 'us'. By rephrasing the line to include the viewer as part of the action, he or she is likely to find the process much more interesting, and therefore absorb the information more thoroughly:

> *NARRATOR:* When the engine is cold, you'll find it much easier to start if you pull the choke out to the fully extended position . . .

'Situations at this moment in time'

Many satirical publications in English-speaking countries run columns about clichés. Business-speak grew out of lawyer-speak and more recently, computer-speak, elevated to world class status by the more pompously spoken business schools of the western hemisphere. Business-speak has its own fashions and trends, just like the clothing industry; remember 'parameters', for example? That was a great favourite of the 1970s and still hangs around today, with many people talking about parameters when they really mean perimeters, but never mind. Situations is another great all-time favourite; a useful alternative to far more explicit words like circumstances, conditions, problems, etc. Examples include 'a no-win situation' (deadlock), 'an on-going situation' (permanent arrangement), 'a management-led situation' (bosses rule), and so on.

Business-speak clichés can be strung together to make further gobbledegook that could be translated into something far simpler and easier to understand. Here are some more examples: 'at this moment in time' (now); 'within the parameters of our situation at this moment in time' (here and now); 'outside the parameters of my corporate responsibility' (not my job); etc. In some business circles it's considered a good thing never to use a short word or phrase when a long one will do. Business clichés that develop out of this ridiculous principle are supposed to lengthen simple thoughts and make them sound more business-like, more assertive, more corporate, etc. Nonsense. Business-speak clichés are just a prop for people—or companies—to lean on while they figure out what it is they really want to say, and then how to say it.

The value of pop conversation

It has already been stressed earlier in this book that you—as the scriptwriter—must know, understand, and to a large extent represent the audience right from the start of any project. When you put pen to paper (or fingers to keyboard) you must take this one step further and get yourself inside the viewer's mind. This does not mean you have to become a mental contortionist; it means that you should use the information you have already gathered about viewers' needs and circumstances to work out how they think. Many companies pay research organizations huge fees to find out this information, and if it is your company's policy not to let one corporate sneeze out of the building before researching the market for it, then that's fine. But common sense has a great deal to do with it, too. Many organizations find they spend a lot of money on research that tells them what they already knew, which was based on common sense. Although good old-fashioned horse sense is hardly the scientific way to assess your audience's needs, it can be a cheap and effective alternative, especially for the small business.

Once you understand how your viewers think, you can begin to speak their language, which involves the grammatical rule-breaking mentioned earlier. That's because people don't speak to the rules; even reasonably 'educated' conversation tends not to follow rules very closely. If you recall, the other main points about writing how people speak is to keep statements and thoughts as simple as you can; and that works in tandem with the grammatical rule-breaking.

A thought which is expressed correctly in grammatical terms, like this . . .

NARRATOR: Currently, increasing numbers of construction foremen are finding that the new Brill contract management system is the only satisfactory system to which they can turn.

... is lumpy and awkward. The grammatically incorrect, but far more human way of saying it, is...

> *NARRATOR:* Now, more and more construction foremen are finding the new Brill contract management system is the best one to turn to.

Picking up on popular conversation means *listening* to what people say—in particular, listening to what typical representatives of your audience say—and then writing in that language yourself. To suggest that a 40-year-old business executive should learn how to speak like a 16-year-old school leaver might sound like a tall order, but if you keep your eyes, ears and mind open it is possible. And you may find it hard to believe if you haven't tried it yet, but this process can actually be very enjoyable, too!

Jargon

The dividing line between specialist language and jargon is dangerously thin. Words that might be considered by one person as an indispensable part of the vocabulary might be considered by another as deliberately abstruse. Business language today seems to be growing ever more specialized, to the point where a visitor from a former decade would be totally in the dark when reading an ordinary business document.

It's difficult, if not impossible, to write effectively for many industries without being tempted to use specialized language that sounds like jargon. However, the questions of whether it really sounds like jargon or not is something for you to decide. Webster's *Third New International Dictionary* describes jargon as 'technical terminology or characteristic idiom of specialists in a particular activity or area of knowledge'. There is nothing wrong in that, except that jargon is also 'often: a pretentious or unnecessarily obscure and esoteric terminology'. Pretention and obscurity in scripts are very counter-productive indeed.

The technology business, particularly the electronics technology business—and especially computing—have the most complicated specialist vocabularies and the greatest number of newly coined phrases or new meanings for existing words. This makes sense. The computer industry is new, in comparison with banking or insurance or fashion or retail, and its vocabulary is still developing. If you complain that computing has altered the meaning of the word architecture forever, think how banking must have changed the meaning of the word draft, for example. There is no doubt that computing language will gradually work itself into general usage. Much of it already has—think of such words as software and information systems and programmer. Many computing terms (borrowed from other usages originally) have also been returned to the language in non-computing expressions. To 'crash', for example, is often applied to a general, catastrophic, complicated and serious malfunction of any kind of system. A 'bug' is any kind of small, annoying and recurring malfunction in any type of procedure.

The right words for the audience

When you're writing scripts and speeches of any kind you should always be searching for words that are the most accurate, least open to misinterpretation, and best suited to the tone of the project. People with excellent vocabularies often find themselves wanting to use a word in general conversation that they believe to be the best word for the job—let's say the word is inchoate—but hesitate to use it because some people will not understand it, and it will have the effect of confusing (or, even worse, irritating) rather than enlightening the audience.

The most important and really the only determining factor in your decision about where specialist language leaves off and jargon begins, is the audience. You must decide, with every word, whether or not your audience will understand the word, or can grasp its meaning from the context. If you decide that most of them won't understand it, you have two choices. You can use the word anyway, but explain or define it. This requires more words and takes precious on-screen or speech time—and may put a lump in the flow of the argument. Or, you can choose another word or phrase. You can also take the risk and use the word without explaining it—and hope that some people will look it up, hear it again, or learn what it means somehow or other. This is a rather high-handed approach and should only be used if the central meaning of the script does not depend on that word.

Overall, you can assume that external audiences will have less understanding of and tolerance for specialist language than internal audiences. However, when it comes to language—as opposed to messages—you may be able to broaden your definition of 'internal'. For example, if you're writing a speech for a conference of plastics engineers from a variety of companies, they might be considered an internal audience, because they're likely to have a common vocabulary.

Let's consider some computing terms, and try to determine where specialism in the name of accuracy ends and where pretention and deliberate obscurity sneak in. Take the terms end-user, host, system, network, desktop, mini, third party, application, protocol, connection, remote, multi-vendor, integration, transparency and architecture. Today, most people in the computer industry, whether technical people or not, would understand these terms. They would certainly not consider them to be pretentious or obscure. Most business people using computer systems, but not in the industry itself, would probably agree.

When you're writing for either of these groups, using such specialist language without explanation and without apology makes sense. In fact, to try to avoid it would probably lead to awkwardness and an amateurish tone. For example, the word 'host' has come to mean the main computer in a system, the one that essentially runs everything else, whether it is a huge IBM mainframe or simply the largest PC. To use the word host is, in computer circles, accurate and clear and much more elegant than 'the main computer in the system that runs everything'.

To replace the term transparency, you might need to write, 'state of accessing and interacting with many different machines, networks, users, services and databases in ways that are determined without the involvement of the person using the computer'. Brevity is beautiful, isn't it?

In the travel business, you have 'destination' referring not so much to the country you're visiting but to the place you are ultimately going to whether it is a resort, city, bungalow, hotel, mud hut or campsite. In manufacturing, you have the terms discrete and process; discrete meaning 'the manufacture of separate parts which are then assembled into a whole', and process, which means 'the manufacture of a single end product by working, modifying or adding ingredients'. The financial services industry is notorious for its terminology, including terms such as 'instrument', meaning a financial phenomenon that helps you do something with money.

Words like this have to be considered as acceptable usage because, even if some in the audience would consider them pretentious, they are generally accepted by those who must use them most. And they help to simplify your script, which can often compensate for the use of jargon and create a better overall effect.

Unfortunately in some business communications jargon is used as a weapon. The reason is obvious; if you use language that others don't understand, you can create an advantage for yourself. Your listeners will have to pretend they understand what you mean, which means they won't really understand what you mean—which means that you can alter your meaning later if it suits your purpose. Or they can choose to ask what you mean, which puts them at risk. Perhaps they really should know this term?

It's not surprising that, as specialist language has grown more complex and as the sheer number of specific, identifiable things there are in the world has multiplied, there has also evolved a new kind of generic language to help define categories of new things, and make life a little simpler. So now, instead of screws and nails, we have fasteners. Instead of glue or tape we have adhesives. Rather than parts or bits we have components and units. Rather than typists or computer operators, we have end-users. We have elements and platforms and systems and modules. Although it is easy to use these terms—because they are so broad and inoffensive—they're not very exciting. Use of too many generic terms leads to a kind of generic writing indistinguishable from any other.

Acronyms

The great bane of the business writer's existence is the acronym and the abbreviation. The number of these used in every type of discipline has grown beyond control. Why it is that people have the urge to create one for any and every phenomenon is a mystery. For example, in FMCG, or Fast Moving Consumer Goods, you have SKUs or Shelf Keeping Units. This means, essentially, anything you put on a shelf in a package whether the package is a bag, a tin, a carton, a bottle or anything else. SKU is therefore a more inclusive term than item, or product, or thing. But, to any but internal or trade audience its use would be out of the question.

From MRP (manufacturing resource planning) to RDB (relational database) to AGV (automated guide vehicle)—treat acronyms and abbreviations as severe forms of jargon. Avoid them, or at least explain them up front. For example:

> NARRATOR: By adjusting the anti-glare screen on the visual display unit, or VDU, you'll find you can block out all unnecessary light. This way, when you're using the VDU your eyes will suffer far less strain.

Writing styles

Having established that all styles of scriptwriting must be in spoken rather than written speech, we now need to look at the subdivisions within that. On the assumption that you will never script an interview (see Chapter 12) we should look at the three main areas for which you will write scripted words: narration, on-camera presentation and dialogue.

Narration
Narration is almost a writing style on its own. Yes, it must be spoken speech, as with dialogue. But because it is not to be spoken in a 'real-life'

context, and because most professional voice artistes are very good at their jobs, you can enjoy more freedom with narration than you can with dialogue. Many of us in professional writing believe that narration is similar to poetry, where the cadence of the words has a very important role to play in supporting the message the words convey. It is important to write simply, in spoken speech, but also to balance the words and the sentences, so that there is a certain music to it all. Single words and very short sentences can be loaded with emotion by the voice artiste, and convey a great deal. These are especially useful to break up longer sections of detail or technical matter.

Very often, you'll find that you develop your writing style for a particular programme from the visual thinking that goes into the treatment and, later, into the script. Try to balance facts with feelings, keep it uncluttered, and don't write 'wall-to-wall' words. Short silences, or short passages with music and sound effects only, can say more than words.

Here's the first couple of minutes of narration for a multi-image corporate programme, for a well-known computer company. As it was a slide-tape programme with no other voices, the narration had to convey all the messages, including the mood and philosophy of the company. Visually, the programme began with an exciting montage of images; the narration did not run wall-to-wall, but was punctuated with music:

NARRATOR: Welcome … to the information technology partnership of the future.

Welcome … to (Company X).

Pioneers … in partnership with a new era of progress.

The principle of partnership is not new. But the (Company X) style of partnership within information technology, is blowing a welcome breath of invigorating air back into the industry.

Up until now, most large computer systems have been researched, developed, manufactured, marketed and supported by one organization alone … straining, under the weight. And many companies have found the strain of such vertical integration too heavy. A rapidly changing market, rising costs, and avid competition, have forced a number of vertically integrated organizations to lose market share, or even go out of business.

Successful business, in this evolutionary time, is created by adaptable animals … not, by lumbering dinosaurs.

Now, the new way of doing business … the (Company X) way … is to form a network of strategic partnerships, in which a company concentrates on doing what it's really good at. These companies, and their partners, are very light on their feet. They respond fast and well ... to market trends, technological advances, and customer needs. (etc.)

You'll find a number of other examples of narration contained in scripts throughout this book. When you read them, try reading them aloud, and you'll get a better idea not only of their content but also of their cadence and rhythm. When you write narration of your own, always remember to read it back to yourself aloud—preferably into a tape recorder, so you can study it further on playback. Even scriptwriters as experienced (and old!) as I am should do this, as you'll often find that a line which reads perfectly well on paper just doesn't sound right when you hear it. By hearing it, you can make the necessary readjustments before the script is submitted for approval and recording.

Another useful tip, which applies to all scripted speech, is to make it very clear to whoever is likely to make alterations to your script that you will go over it afterwards and 'smooth it over'. (You should reassure them that any 'smoothing' will be a matter of style and will not alter the content or meaning.) No matter how well-intentioned other people are they are not likely to understand your script as well as you do, and even a small alteration or addition can disrupt its flow. By reserving the right to adjust other people's alterations if necessary, you can ensure that the final agreed script is readable and effective.

On-camera presentation
Writing for in-vision (on-camera) presenters is very similar to that for narration. On the assumption that you use a professional presenter (and unless they're very good, in-company people cannot do the job as convincingly) he or she will be able to put just the right lift, emphasis and drama into your words, as would be done for a narration. However, with narration the fact that the voice is heard but not seen allows, ironically, *more* room for verbal imagery and poetic licence than if you can see the person who is saying the words. With an on-camera presenter, you can get away with a little poetry, but too much might detract from his or her authoritative stance. To illustrate my point, here is the example of narration I gave above, adjusted for an on-camera presenter.

> We see the presenter in front of Company X's corporate HQ. The camera zooms in slowly to MCU.

PRESENTER: Welcome to Company X ... the information technology partnership of the future ... pioneers, in partnership with a new era of progress.

> We cut to a new angle of the presenter.

PRESENTER: Of course, the principle of partnership is not new. But the Company X style of partnership within information technology, is blowing a welcome breath of fresh air back into the industry. (TURNS AS IF TO WALK OFF)

> We cut away to a shot of the interior of the building, showing an open plan office with a number of people working busily. Cut to a CU of a computer newspaper on one of the desks, showing headlines announcing various bankruptcies, companies in financial trouble, etc.

PRESENTER: (OOV) Up until now, most large computer systems have been researched, developed, manufactured, marketed and supported by one organization alone ... straining, under the weight. And many of these companies have found the strain of such vertical integration too heavy, forcing them to lose market share, or even go out of business.

> We zoom out to a wide shot of the office again, and the presenter walks into shot. He picks up the newspaper.

PRESENTER: Successful business, today is created by adaptable animals ...

> The presenter points to an article in the paper. We then cut to a CU of his finger pointing at a headline which says something like 'Computer giant in trouble'.

PRESENTER: ... not by lumbering dinosaurs.

> We cut back to MCU of presenter sitting on desk, casually, talking to camera.

PRESENTER: Now, the new way of doing business ... the Company X way ... is to form a network of strategic partnerships, in which a company concentrates on doing what it's really good at. That means they can respond fast and well to market trends, technological advances, and customer needs. (etc.)

The differences are subtle and hard to define, but generally I would say that presenter scripts should be less emotional than narration. A useful exercise is to watch broadcast television and compare the style of narration for, say, a documentary programme about wildlife (usually quite emotional in style) with the style of on-camera presentation done on a consumer or similar programme. This will provide a useful illustration of the difference.

Dialogue

Here, more than in any other area of scriptwriting, you need to practise all the principles I've described above about writing as people think. There is a difference, though, because with dialogue you have to get inside the mind not so much of the audience (although this still applies in overall terms) but inside the mind of the *character*.

When I'm writing dialogue, I find it helps to imagine every possible detail about characters—what they look like, their names, where they live, what their hobbies are, etc. In exactly the same way as with the programme's audience, the better you get to know your characters the better you will write for them. Many novelists will tell you that they develop their characters so thoroughly they eventually take on a life of their own, almost dictating to the novelist what they should say and do. This is fine for fiction, but in the corporate field we have to retain a certain control over characters as we must use them to convey specific messages. However, if you will forgive the pun, we can all take a leaf out of the novelist's book.

It's important to make your characters real. Even in the thick of business life, business people are thinking and reacting to other issues. Sports, current events, food, each other. Bring some personality to them; nobody is just a truck driver or just a middle manager. Have their motives in mind. People tend to say things because they want something or need something, or have some hidden agenda that lies behind their spoken words. Always be reasonably sure what the subtext is, underlying the spoken words. And don't be linear. Conversation tends to be circular. One person has a pet topic, another has a different concern altogether. One person says something and the next person says something that sounds unrelated, but has a perfectly clear relation *for that person*. And whatever you do, *never* use a character as a vehicle for putting over corporate policy, mission statements, or other inappropriate information. No matter how important it is to the content of the programme, making a character say anything that he or she wouldn't say in real life will subject your programme to ridicule from the audience. Use voice-over narration, captions, or anything else, but don't turn a dramatization into an acted-out version of the company brochure or policy document—it will alienate your viewers and make them cynical about the whole programme.

When you're writing dialogue, don't write it directly on to paper; talk it through to yourself . . . try to project yourself into the character you're scripting. Imagine you are that person; imagine not only what he or she would say, but how he or she is feeling at the time. Even at the risk of making your colleagues think you've gone mad, get up from your desk and walk through the moves of a particular scene. Use not only the right words but the right body language for what the character should be doing. In drama, you have to work yourself up to feel all the emotion of any particular plot: sense what the murderer was feeling as he stuck the electric carving knife into his mother-in-law's jugular vein; sense how the love-struck girl felt when her boyfriend told her he was leaving her; sense how the mother felt when her baby died. In corporate work, we may not need these strong emotions quite so often. However, in the case of a dramatization of an industrial accident, there should be strong emotions. You would have to feel the pain of someone who has just tripped over a fire extinguisher and broken a leg, or feel the terrible guilt of the office manager who has forgotten to unlock the door to the fire escape. Practise good old-fashioned human empathy, and you're on the way to writing good dialogue.

Once again, you'll find a number of examples of dialogue in the corporate context in script samples throughout this book. And watch good TV drama when you can—I still marvel at the superb characterization by writers like Jack Rosenthal and Alan Bennett, and humbly hope that one day I can create characters even half as good as theirs.

Chapter 7

The corporate programme

In theory, any videotape or AV programme made for and about any aspect of a business or industrial concern, is a 'corporate' programme. 'Corporate video', as it is known within broadcast TV production circles, has largely replaced 'training films' as the most recent and somewhat patronizing cliché used to describe what keeps many individuals and companies in rent money when broadcast times are hard. However, the whole rather unfortunate story of the 'corporate video' image as the poor relation within the television/film world is not one to be discussed in any detail here. Suffice it to say that 'corporate television', as those of us who work in it refer to it, now represents more in terms of money spent per annum in the UK, than does the entire output of independent productions made for the BBC and ITV. In addition, several of the ITV franchise holders now have divisions or departments producing corporate programmes, which provides them with a very useful boost to their revenue.

Although many people in the industry would agree that the dividing line between corporate and broadcast programming is becoming harder to perceive (see Introduction), it is important to remember that there is one very significant difference between the two types of activity. Whereas broadcast television is about communicating entertainment and information to a large and usually general audience, corporate television is *always* about communicating defined messages to a much smaller, carefully targeted and highly specific audience.

Nowadays, with sophisticated televisual technology becoming more financially attainable, the techniques and approaches of broadcast TV can be used increasingly for corporate purposes. This means that the tools available to be used for a corporate programme are often of as high a quality as would be the case for a broadcast programme; even low-budget corporate programmes can now be shot to 'broadcast quality' and look and sound as good as everyone's favourite TV programme. But that is where the similarity ends, and where it will always end. Corporate television is *not* a branch of broadcast television or films; it is a separate activity with a completely different culture, and must be seen as such by everyone concerned—particularly by the scriptwriter.

As for AV, the techniques used to *make* corporate programmes are obviously quite different again, as has been pointed out earlier in this book. But although the way it is made is different, the concept of the corporate AV programme is much the same as it is for its videotaped cousin.

Having looked at the overall positioning of corporate programming, let us now look at its different varieties. Within the 'corporate' arena there are training programmes, recruitment programmes, marketing/sales programmes, and promotional programmes, all of which have their own chapters below. Then, there is also the true 'corporate' programme in itself . . . the programme which demonstrates a company or organization's image and capabilities, giving an interesting overview of the whole or at least of a substantial part or division.

The purposes for which such programmes are used are wide and varied, ranging from external sales to dealer motivation to staff induction (and recruitment, though that is not to be recommended—see Chapter 10). Corporate programmes can be used as scene-setters for conferences and presentations, and even as direct mail pieces to potential or existing investors and customers. For these reasons it is harder to define the audience for a corporate programme, and because of its multi-purpose role you need to write for a wider range of audience types than you do in the case of, say, training or recruitment programmes. However, this does not mean that such a programme needs to be bland or dull just because it must appeal to a more diverse group of people.

Many corporate programmes consist of a shopping list of the company's history, its present assets and staff, a summary of its products and demonstrations of its achievements. When portrayed in a dry and colourless way, this tends to be very boring. A good corporate programme is one that conveys all that information (without too much detail), and at the same time encapsulates the personality of the company—giving viewers not only the facts, but a strong feel for the company or organization's corporate culture. Quite apart from any other reason, this sets the company concerned in context with its competitors by conveying its character.

If you're called upon to write a corporate programme about an organization, it is essential that you spend some time researching and absorbing its culture. Obviously, if it is the company for whom you work, this shouldn't be too difficult. Getting it across can be done in many ways—through careful selection of interviewees, through showing some of the company's social activities, through emphasizing its contributions to local charities, etc. It can even be done through the odd chance remark made by a staff member in a vox pop, by showing a few seconds of the company's football team in action, or through the use of lively and uplifting music.

When writing for this type of programme, you should never allow yourself to forget that any company's greatest asset is its people, no matter what else it has. Where possible, you should use the company's people to convey its culture by imparting relevant information (through interviews—see Chapter 12) in their own words, unprompted by policy watchdogs. Obviously with AV it is sometimes unsuitable to use interviews for more than the odd few minutes, but it is still possible to convey a 'human' feeling through narration, even if it is comparatively low key.

Many people regard corporate programmes as audio-visual company brochures, and to an extent this is reasonable. However, do remember that the big advantage of the audio-visual media is that they harness two senses instead of one: sight and sound, rather than sight alone. With this added grip on the audience, an audio-visual 'brochure' can create a far deeper and more lasting impression on them than if they were merely to read printed words and look at still pictures. The key is to use the additional dimension to convey the emotional and cultural aspects of the organization, because it is often these aspects, rather than the hard facts and figures, which will give the organization the edge over its competitors.

In the following example—a corporate-style multi-image programme for a well-known telecommunications company about their presence in a huge development area of the UK—I focused very sharply on the 'people' aspect. The company concerned suffered from something of a 'faceless' image, which was a problem I wanted to address through the programme. Although this was about one part of the company rather than about the whole, and therefore not a traditional 'corporate' programme, the principles used were much the same. This is shown here in 'skeleton script' format.

> We begin with a lively visual montage of action shots of the (area) area, showing various stages of development. Interspersed throughout are shots of (Company X) installations, and (Company X) people at work both in the context of operational tasks, and also in working closely with customers. We see people using telephones in their homes, and we see people at work using all forms of telecommunications hardware.

> The soundtrack consists of lively background music, and a distinguishable cacophony of voices speaking on a variety

of telephones. We hear one-line comments from (Company X) Business Centre staff (e.g. '(Company X) Business Centre, how can I help you?') and other (Company X) staff (e.g. '(Company X) Engineers, good morning', '(Company X) (area) depot, how can I help you?') plus a selection of customer lines (e.g. 'I'd like to enquire about . . .', 'Can you tell me if . . .', 'I want to order ten more lines for my office . . .', 'I'm interested in (satellite link) . . .') and so on, relating to the range of (Company X) products on offer. These voices are mixed up, but when heard in sequence suggest the variety of services (Company X) offers, and the friendly, helpful way in which (Company X) staff respond to their customers over the telephone.

Towards the end of this, the music and sound effects fade, and the narrator formally introduces us to the programme . . .

NARRATOR: The (area) today, holds one of the world's finest—and largest—business and residential developments.

Here, is a major city, within a major city . . . living, breathing, thriving, twenty-four hours a day.

Here, is the site of some of the world's most sophisticated telecommunications.

And here, from the earliest of beginnings, setting the standards as always, is *(Company X)*.

Now, after a short musical interlude, we hear a selection of 'vox pop' clips taken from interviews with a number of (Company X) personnel.

These interviews should not be restricted to senior management alone, but also include a few sentences from operational staff, design staff, engineering staff, etc., who were involved in the early establishment of the (area) telecommunications work.

Edited together, the 'vox pops' briefly tell the story of the enormous challenge (area) presented, and how it was only (Company X)—with the necessary investment, technology, expertise, experience and resources, who could possibly realize the potential of the site, and create telecommunications to take customers efficiently into the twenty-first century.

The section also explains how the (area) development allowed telecommunications installations to be designed in from scratch, thereby avoiding the problems of older areas, but at the same time creating other challenges in terms of developing new systems and state-of-the-art technology, to meet a whole new generation of demands.

As these 'vox pops' are in progress, we see occasional shots of the speaker concerned, and material which illustrates the points each speaker makes. Finally, the words of the last 'vox pop' interviewee fade, we hear a short musical interlude, and the narrator links to the next section ...

NARRATOR: Working ... caring ... helping ... pioneering ... totally committed, to this exciting new environment. And, totally committed to needs, plans and future of every customer, from individual, to corporate.

The next 'vox pop' section consists of initial reaction comments from a selection of customers.

The first of these interviewees should be a domestic user, who is perhaps someone who has never had a telephone before, or who in any case was previously not accustomed to using the most modern telephone equipment. An elderly person in a sheltered home (if such property exists within (area)?) would be ideal. He or she says how it could only be (Company X) who would provide such an installation, and how nice it is to have such efficient communication with the outside world ... including the occasional conversation with relatives living abroad.

Subsequent clips should include a number of businesses, from small to very large. They should comment in general terms on how (Company X) was their natural choice, and also on the good personal relationship they had and still have with the (Company X) staff who worked for them. Appropriate illustrative material is shown on screen during this section. Then, after a short musical interlude and visual link, we see some exterior shots of the (Company X) Business Centre. The narrator links once again ...

NARRATOR: This, is (Company X) at its best ... caring for customers not only on *their* premises, but from a central focal point within (area) itself. Here, there's the opportunity for customers and staff to meet informally and discuss their needs, their business problems, and (Company X)'s solutions.

>Now, we go visually and verbally inside the business centre, and hear a few short 'vox pop' clips about its activities. For the time being, it may be necessary to restrict the interviewees to (Company X) staff only, but at a later stage, if and when a re-edited version of the programme is made, 'vox pop' clips of customer reaction to the Business Centre can be added. Then, we fade out of this section, and the narrator links to more specific aspects of the Business Centre.

NARRATOR: Within the (Company X) Business Centre is a massive, living display of the telecommunications products of today and tomorrow ...

>As we look at a few examples of the demonstrations, we hear two or three very short 'vox pop' clips from (Company X) staff (later customers as well) describing the demonstrations and their relevance to customer needs. Then, back to the narrator ...

NARRATOR: For customers who have yet to install their own equipment, there's a range of essential services.

>Brief 'vox pops' as above, describing services and also training facilities. Then, these voices fade, and the narrator links us out of the section (accompanied by further exterior shots of the Business Centre) and on to the next ...

NARRATOR: The (Company X) Business Centre at (area) ... a permanent, telecommunications forum where customers can see the latest technology for themselves ... and meet the (Company X) people who will help them benefit from it.

Expertise and flexibility, with a friendly face ... that's what (Company X) offers throughout (area). Whether it's for a small, growing business with simple requirements, or for organizations with some of the most complex telecommunications needs in the world ...

>Now, we examine three or four case histories in a bit more detail. Using a combination of short interview clips (as opposed to the even shorter 'vox pops') with both customer representatives and (Company X) staff involved with those customers, plus narration links where appropriate, we learn of the stories of (various companies named here).

>Suitable illustrative material accompanies this.

Although some technical detail is included to show the complexity of the installation concerned, considerable emphasis is also placed on the personal service that each customer received, and on the productive and friendly relationship that exists between customers and (Company X) staff.

Should a specialized module be required for certain viewing purposes, this could be incorporated after the case history section. It should be treated in a similar style: i.e., supposing it were a large office development, it would include 'vox pop' clips taken from interviews with the property developer, and with one or two existing or prospective tenants, as well as one or two senior (Company X) staff who would be responsible for the management of that particular development. The narrator would link appropriately.

Now we show the final, summarizing visual sequence, and the narrator takes us almost to the end of the programme . . .

NARRATOR: (Company X), is the world's third-largest telecommunications company . . . leading the international field in many technological areas . . . investing heavily in ever-improving the quality of performance, and service.

But communications, as we've heard, involve *two-way* conversations. (Company X) staff in (area) are people who *care* about their customers, *listen* to their needs, and work *hard* to make their contribution even more valuable, every day.

Together, (Company X) and its (area) customers *communicate*, for the good of national and international *tele*communic-*i*-*n*- . . . talking, working, and successfully striving . . . towards better business, in a challenging and exciting world.

The programme ends on a few very short, one-line 'vox pop' clips from a selection of both customers and staff. These would probably be in response to the question, 'in one sentence, how would you sum up your view of (Company X) here in (area)?' Any humorous comments, provided they were of a suitable nature, could be incorporated to end the programme on a friendly, human, up-beat note.

The next example is the narration script from an AV programme about a company which makes smoke and gas detection equipment. The subject matter is a little dry, so I tried to inject a 'human' feeling into areas of the script by bringing in some of the interesting aspects about how the company was founded, and some of the key people who made it what it is today. The programme's main objective was to describe the company's activities to internal industrial audiences, as well as customers, so it had to be written in the first person plural rather than in the more hard-sell 'you' tone of voice. To save space I have not included the visualization of the programme, but let me say the original photography was shot by excellent photographers in both the UK and in the USA. With good lighting, good imagination and plenty of talent, photography of equipment, even as apparently lifeless as this, can be interesting—and this certainly was the case here. At the beginning and at the end of the programme there were sequences of graphics and photographs depicting space and the universe; not a new concept, but one which worked well, especially treated as it was with a surreal overtone, underscored by appropriate music.

NARRATOR: Throughout the world, we work to improve our lives. Each year, we move further and wider to harness resources and develop our potential. And as each advance places greater demands on our ingenuity and technology, we meet new challenges ... and face new risks, often in hazardous environments.

Without risk, there would be no progress. But when the risk of hazardous gases or fire turns into harsh reality, consequences can be cruel. And such risk is an enemy of many faces ... often subtle, and even invisible.

Protection in our advanced industries, must come from a source that matches the technological complexity from which those risks arise. A source which regards protection not just as a business, but as a philosophy.

(Company X) ...

We, are a company totally committed to a mission. A mission to protect people ... to protect property ... to save lives.

(Company X): our promise is protection for today, and tomorrow ... protection, for life.

At (Company X) we are world leaders in the development and manufacture of gas monitoring and flame detection equipment ... with over 25 years' experience behind us.

Coal mines, petrochemical plants, pipelines, and offshore drilling platforms are the more immediately recognized areas where our products are needed. But they are also extensively used in the pharmaceutical industry, in food processing, pulp and paper production, coatings, semi-conductors, and many other varied manufacturing facilities. These are just some examples of where our equipment protects people, plant and property.

We invest heavily in research ... commit wholeheartedly to engineering excellence ... and ensure personal devotion to quality control at every level of operation, by every employee.

These are the values which have earned us our reputation for reliability, integrity and technological leadership in the gas and flame detection field ...

... with catalytic bead and semi-conductor sensors for gas detection ... with ultra-violet and infra-red technology for flame detection ... plus a wide range of complementary equipment, systems and services.

Protection by our equipment can mean greater worker confidence ... in their workplace, in their employers, in enhanced productivity. And in a world where environmental consciousness is growing, this protection can help promote good relations within a company's community.

Our story starts in 1961, when America's space programme was really taking off.

Four aerospace engineers led by (name), had developed a unique method of sensing hydrogen in the presence of other gases.

Having started work from (name)'s home in California, our four talented people were soon in business ... providing outstanding equipment to a number of US Government agencies.

One of their early orders was to supply a proprietary hydrogen-specific sensor to NASA for their manned space programme at Cape Canaveral.

In 1966 we were acquired by entrepreneurs, (name) and (name) ... but success didn't come easily. Their philosophy and dedication to the highest ethics, blended well with the technological progress made during their early years with us. This was when the focus shifted primarily to combustible gas detection in the oil and gas industries ... which were forging ahead to meet the growing worldwide demand for energy.

Soon, our products were selling all over the world from our base in (USA). And by the early seventies, our first (Company X) location in Europe was established with a manufacturing plant in (city). A few years later we set up a sales support office in (city).

In the early eighties, we opened a direct sales office in (city). And in 1988, we created a further sales office in (city).

Also in 1988, (name) took over as president. (Name) has been with us since January 1974, and in that time has worked his way up through most of our departments.

Today, under (name)'s strong and dedicated leadership, we are strategically placed to offer our philosophy, care, and fine products to customers, wherever their people and places must be protected ... anywhere in the world.

Even though our products are used far and wide, every one originates from the same technological excellence that has been our inspiration, from the start.

Technological excellence of this kind, can only come from a tremendous dedication to, and investment in, research and development. Some of the world's finest engineers and scientists work within our (Company X) team, using advanced equipment and modern facilities.

Whatever refinements the future may bring, the key to any gas or flame detection system will always be the sensor. It is on the sensor and detector, that the reliability and performance of the whole system depend.

Our sensor technology leads the field in gas detection. The combustible gas sensor uses catalytic beads to detect the presence of flammable gas. It achieves its inherent stability and functioning through the use of a proprietary design, for both the active and reference beads.

For the detection of hydrogen sulphide, we use our semi-conductor sensor. This sensor is in service world wide, and has been used more than any other device for the detection of hydrogen sulphide.

Both types of sensor can be configured as 'smart' devices, for easy maintenance and one-person calibration.

Our flame detectors identify ultra-violet or infra-red wavelengths ... or, a combination of both from a flame. The result is a very high degree of selectivity, which allows fast detection—and eliminates many sources of false alarms.

And total protection means knowing that EVERY product is completely inspected and tested under the most rigorous conditions. Quality assurance and total quality control, are our way of life—where life is at stake, there can be no OTHER way.

Our products are designed to fit together flexibly, to satisfy a wide range of requirements. Customers have multiple choices in how our products are configured and interfaced with others. And the products available range from single-channel instruments, to flexible, multi-channel systems.

We also work on behalf of our customers to design and build complete fire and gas systems. This includes support equipment like control panels, audible alarms, fire alarm systems, PLC systems, and a number of other field devices.

Sales support is also a major part of protection. From our sales offices in (locations named here,) a fast and responsive service operates using the latest telecommunications equipment and computer links. From these locations, our experts give customers advice on system selection and design, and complete after-sales support.

Another key element is our distributor and representative network, with facilities in every major market in the world. These organizations are hand-picked for their responsiveness and expertise. Their knowledge and experience, is shared throughout the worldwide network to the benefit of our customers.

No matter how important a role technology plays in our success, it is only PEOPLE who can harness that technology ... turn it into protection that performs for every customer.

Not surprisingly, our team of people is an international family. Many (Company X) people have been with the company for the majority of their working lives ... devotion to excellence, is a strong and lasting bond, around the world.

The world's countries ... their leaders and politicians ... their people ... more and more, they are concerned about their environment. More and more, they are demanding that greater care be taken of the world in which they live and work.

At (Company X), we are meeting that demand. And, in dedication to our philosophy to protect people and property, we're entering into the environmental monitoring field ... with a range of analysers and accessories for ambient and source measurements, in environmental and process applications.

Because as new technology develops, so does the pressure on people to use new and different techniques, to do new and different jobs. Jobs which demand new skills ... using new tools ... in new environments ... facing new hazards.

As we extend to the limits of Planet Earth and beyond, we can be certain of the exhilaration of discovery. But we can also be certain that risk will always be present.

So, our customers can be safe in the knowledge that we will also be there ... protecting people, protecting property, protecting the future ... for life.

The final example of a corporate programme approach was for one division of one of the largest computer companies in the world. Once again, strictly speaking this is not a 'corporate' programme in the traditional manner of setting out the entire organization's wares, but as this company is so huge even this one division is as large as many other whole companies. Here, the programme was to be used at the end of a live presentation. The presentation itself consisted of about one hour's worth of speeches and a couple of videotape inserts about a computer system designed for local government. About twenty guests at a time were seated around a huge table, with the speakers sitting there as well. Video monitors were lodged in the table at intervals, sunk into the woodwork, to run the videos and show speaker support material. In the centre of the table was a large 'model city', used during the presentations to show how the computer system could help local authorities control their various property and plant. This programme was shot using the model city and a 'motion control' camera, which gives the effect of travelling in, through and around small spaces, so that viewers felt as though they were compressing themselves into tiny elves and travelling around the model city. Background music was slightly surreal and mysterious, and the voice-over artiste had just the right edge of suspense to convey the point that the future for local government was going to be very different from what it was at the time, and that enlisting the help of the computer company concerned would be a very wise precaution. The programme was made in the mid-1980s and, in fact, many of the predictions discussed in it have begun to materialize. Although it is difficult to get a feel for the way the programme looked just by reading the bald script, the way it turned out on screen made it one of the best programmes I have ever been involved with—an instance where pictures and sound worked together in harmony to convey information and subliminal, emotional messages in perfect balance. The programme was shot for a very low budget; yet another illustration of the point that you do not need huge sums of money to create corporate programmes that work well. There is a lot to be said, too, for the fact that the programme's director and I were a good team (and still are!). Because he and I had a good understanding of each other's working practices, he was able to interpret not only the words I wrote, but the atmosphere I was trying to create, and the results were excellent. Here is the script.

> (This section will give a very strong, futuristic impression. The voice-over sections will be short and to the point, with much of the detail being conveyed visually.)

> The programme opens with a totally black screen. Suitably rhythmic, futuristic music begins, and after a few seconds a caption appears on screen, in stark white, pulsating in time with the music. It says:

> Caption: 'The information contained in this section of the programme has been taken from a recent INLOGOV research paper'.

> The pulsating message fades, and the music becomes a bit louder and livelier. The model city gives us an impression of dawn breaking over the horizon.

NARRATOR: In this, our generation of rapid change, there is amongst us an increasing urge to know what lies over the horizon.

> The model city now lights up, and illustrations of the narrator's words can be seen.

NARRATOR: Recent research shows three broad strategies on that horizon, which may well shape the local governments of the future.

One, is that there will be LESS government.

Two, is that the public will play a more prominent role; both under central control, and under local control.

Three, is that in many areas, government will be much more open.

This, will breed many new strains of organization.

> Visuals show 'Core Authorities', 'Two-tier Authorities', 'Location Dependent Organizations', e.g. Two-tiered Urban and Single-tiered Rural, etc.

NARRATOR: And the current fashion for breaking off discrete chunks of local government, may well continue.

> Visuals show hiving off of such elements as M.S.C., Water Authorities, etc.

NARRATOR: So, where will local government go?

The answer, is not so much where it will GO. On that, we can only speculate—even with detailed research.

However, one thing we do know, is what will NOT go.

Whatever the future holds in store, certain key services will always be needed by the community.

> Visuals show 'Housing', 'Education', 'Social Welfare', 'Planning', etc.

NARRATOR: Key people will always be needed, too.

> Visuals show 'Members', 'Chief Officers', 'Professionals', 'Clerks', 'Public'.

NARRATOR: And the key functional tasks will stay, as they always have.

> Visuals show 'Strategic planning for the organization', 'Operational tasks like rents, rates, etc.', 'Support functions like typing, communicating, etc.', 'Providing an interface to the public'.

NARRATOR: So, what will be new?

> Visuals show representation of chart as depicted in (name)'s document:
>
> This is to continue throughout relevant narration section below.

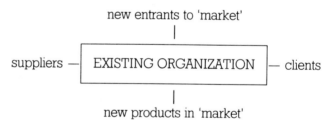

NARRATOR: There will be pressures to change ... to create a leaner, more responsive organization, just as we've seen in the commercial marketplace.

There will be new relationships, with old friends ... or 'suppliers', in commercial terminology.

> Visuals show relationships with other 'government' functions like Health, Courts, Police, Probation, Social Security:
>
> Relationships with the private sector, i.e. Housing, Estate Agents, Building Societies, etc.

Relationships with subcontractors to do specific functions, like refuse disposal.

NARRATOR: There will be closer relationships, with new entrants to the government 'marketplace'.

Visuals show 'M.S.C.', 'Technical Schools', 'Voluntary Organizations like C.A.B., etc.'

NARRATOR: If we stay with our commercial metaphor, we can look towards new 'products', too.

Visuals show 'Provision of Economic Development Units', 'The fight for new jobs', 'Neighbourhood Offices', etc.

NARRATOR: Lastly, there will be the new breed of relationship with 'clients' ... the public, in the community.

Visuals show 'Better public information', 'Right of access' (Government legislation), 'New clients, e.g. Estate Agents', etc.

NARRATOR: In all this, there is one very important common denominator which few computer companies have failed to notice.

Information—already a major asset—will become even more crucial to the success of local authorities than it is today.

(Company X), has done much more than merely take notice.

Because (Company X) can see that what is truly important, is not just the USE of that information.

With the new structures that may emerge, whole new approaches to the management and communication of information, will be urgently needed.

Visuals show need for communication among many of the examples already shown: e.g. between two-tiered authorities, with other 'government' functions like Health, Courts, etc. (see above): the private sector (see above): subcontractors (see above): M.S.C., voluntary sector, Technical Schools, Neighbourhood Offices, etc.

NARRATOR: New lines of communication, new needs for sharing information, new types of information, new flexibility, new availability. They all add up to one thing.

Information technology will have a lot of work to do.

Computers will have to be realistic, logically designed, and very, very agile.

Implementation of systems will have to happen smoothly, economically, and incrementally.

To give local government the information technology it needs to succeed in the future, it will take all the experience and knowledge of Britain's foremost computer company.

And this computer company needs to be prepared for the future, long before that future materializes.

(Company X) is ready. Now.

(Product X), the land and property system, is just one of a series of products designed with the long-term future in mind.

Because whatever the future may bring to local authorities in Britain, (Company X) will be there. With practical, workable solutions, whatever the problem.

Together, local government and (Company X) can look forward to that future . . . with total, secure confidence.

To summarize, the key to writing good corporate programmes is to capture the character of the company (or division of the company) as well as convey information. In the example above, for the computer company, very little was actually said about the company itself. But the 'character' of the company in this case lay in the fact that it knew more about local government, and what was in store for it in the future, than any competitor. This was not put across in bald terms, but through the way in which the whole programme was treated.

Rather in the way that you do with marketing/sales programmes and short promos (see Chapters 9 and 11 respectively), you need to find a USP (Unique Selling Proposition) for a company about which you're to write a corporate programme. In this case it is not the fact that it washes whiter or that it is more cost-effective or whatever. What you're looking for is a less definable quality that makes the company unique. And it is only through careful research that you will find such a quality—but speaking from over ten years' experience, I have always managed to find that quality in every corporate project I've undertaken. To say that such a quality does not exist is almost certainly not true. If necessary, you should 'live' with the company concerned for as long as it takes; and, interestingly enough, you may find what you're looking for in the most unlikely place. It could happen in a predictable place like a boardroom meeting with the company's directors, but equally the thought could be triggered in your mind by having a chat with the night watchman or the tea lady. And even if the company concerned is the one for whom you have worked for some years, it may well be that to create a good corporate TV or AV programme for it you need to step back and look at it in a totally fresh light. As always, consider the audience; become one of them, and ask yourself the questions that a prospective customer or investor would ask. Then, answer them truthfully in your script. It sounds simple; it isn't; but the effort involved is always worth while.

Chapter 8

The training programme

Training programmes probably represent the largest group of specific-topic programmes made in the overall corporate field. In many respects, the advent of the audio-visual media in their current cost-effective and easy-to-make form has revolutionized training throughout organizations everywhere. Either on their own or combined with distance learning or classroom studies, video and AV programmes provide the best possible means of demonstrating products, techniques and practices.

Sometimes, they can be even better than the real, live thing. A video describing the intricate workings of a complicated machine can show live action material of the machine being used, combined with lively graphics sequences illustrating its innards. A live demonstration of the machine will allow only a small number of people to see the machine at close range—and to show how its innards work, the trainer will probably have to resort to a boring, two-dimensional blackboard.

The other tremendous advantage video or AV training programmes provide over live training, is consistency of message. No matter how well trained your trainers are, you will always get a certain variance in the way that live training is carried out from group to group. Nor does this need to be a reflection on the quality of the trainers—it is merely the result of human beings not being identical clones of one another. Video cassette copies of a training programme are. And particularly when training is being carried out with large numbers of people over a geographically dispersed area, the knowledge that everyone has seen and heard exactly the same messages provides a great deal of corporate reassurance.

Things to avoid in training programmes

The most common problem with training programmes made by the inexperienced, is a patronizing tone. If you and/or the programme commissioners know your subject backwards, and realize that you must de-tune your knowledge in order to convey it to the uninitiated, there is a natural tendency to 'talk down' to viewers in an adult version of Joyce Grenfell's nursery school. This must be avoided at all costs, as a patronizing tone will alienate viewers and make them lose interest. Here perhaps, even more than in any other category of programme, you must practise what I've preached in earlier chapters about identifying with your audience and 'getting inside their minds'. Research into the audience concerned, and acquiring a thorough understanding of their needs, problems and attitudes, are crucial.

Another problem is too much information. Video and AV are emotional media, and as such are only suitable to convey broad concepts and ideas—not intricate detail. Even though your viewers may watch a programme several times, it is unfair to expect them to memorize a large number of facts and figures. It's far better to use the programme to create a mental framework, so they understand the most important messages, and leave the detail to supporting print material. Having established the framework in the programme, you'll find that trainees absorb the written detail very easily, as they will understand its broad meaning and relevance.

A further problem, connected with the last, is running time. Some years ago a Californian university carried out some research into viewer retention of audio-visual programming, and discovered that 8 minutes is the optimum time. After this, retention drops off slowly at a more or less acceptable rate, to 18 minutes. After 19 minutes, however, the drop is alarming. Of course, broadcast television programmes are usually much longer than this, and people making training programmes often make the understandable mistake of assuming that their material can be remembered just as easily as a 90-minute costume drama on the BBC. But there are two major differences between these two types of programme. One is that the broadcast programme is entertainment only—no one is going to test you afterwards to see if you can recall what Anthony actually said to Cleopatra about the bath in asses' milk. Two is that the overall storyline of an entertainment programme is likely to be much simpler than a new electronics process or sales technique, even if it was a play written by William Shakespeare. Realistically, the optimum running time for any training programme is 10–15 minutes. If you have more material to convey than will fit comfortably into this timeslot, create your programme on a modular basis with defined stops between 10–15-minute sections. This will allow viewers to take a breather between modules, perhaps to hold a discussion, or have a cup of coffee, or whatever, and then return to the next module refreshed and ready to retain a new chunk of information.

The last common problem with badly made training programmes is that they're boring (a problem common to all categories, but especially important in this one). Once again, there is an understandable tendency for programme commissioners to regard their new die-stamping machines that cut production time by 25 per cent as the most interesting thing since sliced bread. But to the factory worker who is going to use it, it's just another piece of kit. As I keep repeating to the point of boring you, always, *always* write from the viewers' points of view, and tell them things about the die-stamping machine that will interest *them*—not necessarily the person who designed it, or the financial director, or the production controller, or the foreman. The fact that you and your management colleagues pay the factory workers their wages does *not* mean that they're going to be interested in the same things that you are. That's human nature. Get on their side; write things that will interest them in connection with their work and your programme will be a success.

Things that work well in training programmes

Documentary style programmes in training work reasonably well, provided that they identify very strongly with the viewer (see above). Here is an excerpt from a video programme I wrote for a large nationalized industry, concerning the introduction of a new computer system throughout the organization's installations nationwide.

....

11 (LOCATION 1)
....

Cut to (Presenter 1) in office.

> *(PRESENTER 1):* So, (Installation X) is a major undertaking, to put it mildly. And now, it won't be long until you'll be seeing (Installation X) equipment arrive at your station. In fact in some cases, it will already be there.

....

12 (LOCATION 2)
....

Cut to (Presenter 2) in control room.

> *(PRESENTER 2):* For a start, (Installation X) will be used by more people ... many of whom won't have used a computer system at work before. Obviously, there'll be plenty of training, whether you've used computers before or not. We'll tell you about that a bit later in the programme.

12a Cutaway to library shots of turbines, etc.

13 (LOCATION 2)

Interior control room. C/V equipment.

> *(PRESENTER 2):* (OOV) Needless to say, (Installation X) won't be introduced all at once. That would take up too much of everybody's time. The equipment will be installed at your plant, and then the system will go in, in stages. That way, everyone feels comfortable with it.

13a Inputting hard copy to system.

14 (LOCATION 2)

Interior, office.

> *(PRESENTER 2):* One of the first really big practical jobs that has to be done, is for all the information held in existing computers and manual systems to be put into the (Installation X) machines.

14a Cutaway to screens.

> *(PRESENTER 2):* (OOV) For example, the large amount of data for equipment, plant and commodities will all be written into the (Installation X) computers, with their own special codes.

14b Cutaway to GV ext. building.

> *(PRESENTER 2):* (OOV) In other words, that means creating a complete new inventory of the whole plant. Now, much of this information is already available, and will be tranferred into (Installation X) electronically.

Interior, office.

> *(PRESENTER 2):* But where this can't be done, a few people from your station will help to do it manually. And once it's all in, you may still need to run both systems for a short time until the transfer is complete.

16 COMPUTER GRAPHICS

Computer graphics to illustrate.

(PRESENTER 2): (OOV) Basically, (Installation X) works on what computer people call a 'menu' basis. Most people in each station will have their own menu on the (Installation X) system, and it will look something like this. The menu is based on the actual jobs, or roles, that you do. And, it has been produced by the site application technique we mentioned earlier. All the activities you're likely to need, will be available on your menu. And through this simple arrangement, you can do most of your important work . . . including many of the tasks you've been doing manually.

17 (LOCATION 2)

Mix from graphic symbol of fuel oil to delivery sequence as live action.

(PRESENTER 2): (OOV) A typical example of that, is recording fuel oil delivery . . . a task many of you will be familiar with. (Installation X) will help speed up this process, because you can directly enter the essential information; the quantities and type of oil delivered, and the tank it's put in.

18 (LOCATION 2)

(Presenter 2) walks into shot.

(PRESENTER 2): Obviously, some people have a wider range of roles, or jobs, to do. So their menus will be more complex. In fact, (Installation X) has five levels of security. That way, each person's level of access to the system can be set out according to their needs. And this method of controlling access is very important, to help run the business efficiently.

19 (LOCATION 1)

Interior, office.

(PRESENTER 1): Another aspect of the business control (Installation X) will provide, is the swipe card. This is a bit like a credit card, with a magnetic stripe . . . and it will be your personal identification when you use the (Installation

X) system. You pass it through the (Installation X) card
reader, and it automatically tells the computer who you are.

19a Screen shots to cover

> *(PRESENTER 1):* (OOV) You'll also have your own
> password. Now I know this sounds a bit like some high
> tech spy movie, but in real life passwords help make sure
> that personal security is truly efficient. By using passwords,
> the system just allows the right, approved people to have
> access to information at any given level. Your customized
> menu only comes up, once you've used both the swipe
> card AND the password.

20 (LOCATION 2)

Interior, control room.

> *(PRESENTER 2):* Okay. Now let's see just how the
> (Installation X) system will work in practice. You remember
> we mentioned how (Installation X) will give every single
> piece of equipment, plant and commodities, a special
> code? In fact, (Installation X) will use two main codes to
> identify plant: plant code, and equipment code.

> (Etc.)

Dramatization and/or comedy drama are extremely useful tools in a
training context, because they provide viewers with the opportunity to
identify with the issue in question, and also to see how things should and
should not be done. I find the best way to make the most of drama is to
combine it with a quantity of documentary material. Not only does this
allow you to get more information into the programme than would be the
case with 100 per cent drama; it also provides viewers with a welcome
gear change in style, which keeps them interested.

In the following excerpt (from a script for the same organization as the
previous example, and to roughly the same audience), the comedy drama
sections ran as a parallel storyline to the documentary material, and it
was not until near the end of the programme that you realized the two
storylines were connected. This gave a little suspense to the programme in
addition to the entertainment value of the dramatized sections. Needless
to say, both the documentary sections and especially the drama sequences
involved the audience by identifying very strongly with them.

PRE-TITLE: EXTERIOR, SUBURBAN STREET   **MORNING**

We open on a pair of terraced or semi-detached houses in an ordinary residential street. One of them is fronted by a fence or wall topped with barbed wire. This belongs to Dave, the most pessimistic man in the world. He has named his house 'DUNHOPING'. He also has bars on the windows, several locks on the doors, and a sticker in the window proclaiming 'THE END OF THE WORLD IS NIGH'.

A postman makes his way to Dave's front door and delivers some letters. As he goes next door to Bill's house, Bill comes out and greets him with a cheery hello, taking his post as he does so. They are distracted by the sound of Dave unlocking his door. First one lock, then the next, then a couple of bolts, and another lock, and so on. The postman shakes his head disapprovingly and Bill shrugs.

The postman goes on his way, and eventually Dave emerges from his house, clutching three letters. Despite the fact that it's not raining, he wears a raincoat and a rain hat. He looks up at the sky and grimaces.

BILL: Hey up, Dave. Nice morning, isn't it?

Dave opens his post.

DAVE: That's what you think.

BILL: Got anything good there?

DAVE: Only a tax rebate.

BILL: Only? Lucky beggar.

DAVE: Probably a mistake. They've just sent me this to get my hopes up. Oh, no. Not again. I've won a free holiday in Spain as well.

BILL: Another one?

DAVE: (WEARILY) Yeah.

BILL: I never win anything. Why is it always you?

DAVE: Yeah, why me? I don't want to get sunburn. Oh well, they say bad news comes in threes. Let's see what this one is.

BILL: Let me guess. Invitation to tea with Samantha Fox, knowing your luck.

DAVE: I'd only get food poisoning. Oh, NO!

BILL: What?

DAVE: Says I should go on a training course. Turbo chargers. Whatever next!

BILL: So what's wrong with that?

DAVE: Waste of time.

BILL: It might not be. You're always saying there's no chance of promotion at the garage. Maybe this'll help.

DAVE: No. Anyway, I don't want to be promoted. Might have to wear a suit. Work in an office. And all that extra responsibility. (MISERABLY) Wouldn't have any fun.

BILL: You might enjoy it.

DAVE: I don't have a suit.

BILL: What a wally. You could get more out of your OWN job, the one you do now. And any road. If you're trained, you'd enjoy being promoted.

DAVE: No, it would just be more work. (RHETORICALLY) I mean, what's the point in me going and training for something I might not enjoy doing when I probably wouldn't get the chance to do it anyway. I'm happy as I am.

> Music fades up, and Dave leaves for work. Bill shakes his head sadly as he watches him go.

TITLES: GRAPHICS   STUDIO

> We roll the opening titles of the programme, with suitable music over.
>
> Dissolve to . . .

---

1 INTERIOR, CONTROL ROOM   DAY

> We see some GVs of operators going about their work. The presenter walks into shot, and sits casually on the edge of a control desk. He speaks to camera . . .

PRESENTER: You know, there are still a few people about who think training's a waste of time. That's because some training in the past, was badly designed. It usually meant you had to work in your own time, and often learn a whole load of theory you didn't need. No wonder some people couldn't see the benefits.

But good training these days is a different ballgame. It's properly designed, so everything you learn is relevant, and necessary. You train in working hours, with no competition. That's POSITIVE training . . . designed to help you succeed, not make you into a statistic.

A good example of that in this industry is what's known as (Scheme X). That's (brief explanation). It all started when the industry took a long hard look at operator training back in the 1970s, and realized that technology was moving forward pretty fast. Training just wasn't keeping up.

Cut to . . .

....

2 INTERVIEW, LOCATION   **DAY**

....

We see mute footage of (Senior Director)

PRESENTER: (Senior Director), (FULL TITLE HERE), tells us what happened next . . .

We fade up sound and watch the first interview.

(SENIOR DIRECTOR): (TRANSCRIPT) Well first of all, once we looked we recognized that there were different training standards throughout the country. We needed therefore to make sure we had a very high standard and everyone was trained to that standard. We needed to make simulators available to all our staff, so in fact they could be trained and experience those conditions without being actually in the firing line straight away. We saw also a chance to increase the skills of a unit operator; increase his standing in the (industry sector) world, and also give him further career opportunities.

(Etc.)

There are a number of different ways in which you can structure the style combination of drama and documentary. In the next excerpt (part of an introductory training programme about the tourism industry), the dramatized sections appeared to be 'real life' examples of people with whom the trainees could identify, describing their work experience.

NARRATOR: Sometimes, it *can* be a bit more difficult to be pleasant to people, though. Tourists, like everyone else, can come under pressure; whether it's from fatigue, from a difference of opinion, or just through bad humour. Business travellers come under even greater pressure;

sometimes their work places great demands on them. And those strains have a habit of making themselves felt ...

> We cut to Keith (character actor) in his restaurant. It is late at night. There are still a few people there finishing their meals, and Keith and his colleagues are discreetly tidying up and resetting tables ready for breakfast. After a few moments, a middle-aged woman walks in carrying a briefcase. She looks extremely flustered and bad tempered. Keith glances at her, at his watch, then approaches her with a welcoming smile.

KEITH: Good evening, Madam.

WOMAN: (IN SCOTS ACCENT) Table for one. Now. (LOOKING HARD AT KEITH) Oh. I suppose I'm too late for dinner?

KEITH: (SMILING PLEASANTLY) No, not at all, Madam. In fact you're just in time for last orders. Would you come this way, please?

> Keith leads her to the table. We then dissolve to the end of her meal. A wine waiter pours the last little bit of wine from a full-sized bottle into her glass. Keith approaches.

KEITH: Have you enjoyed your meal, Madam?

WOMAN: (WITH A SLIGHT SLUR IN HER VOICE) What? Oh, yes, I suppose so. Only good thing that's happened to me all day.

KEITH: Well, I'm glad we could be of help, Madam. Would you like some more coffee?

> The woman nods. Keith fetches her some more coffee and pours it into her cup as she continues to speak, almost to herself.

WOMAN: Honestly, I don't know what's gone wrong with the art world. I travel four hundred miles to buy a painting for my customer in Edinburgh, and what do I find? They'd sold it to someone else. After I'd telephoned, and written to them to reserve it. Total waste of time. Rather like people in your business. Take hotel bookings from you, take your money, then let your room to someone else. It's downright dishonest. (STARING AGGRESSIVELY, AND SLIGHTLY DRUNKENLY, AT KEITH) Isn't it?

KEITH: Well, Madam, I'm very sorry to hear you've had such a difficult day. Such a long way to come. Are you a guest in the hotel?

WOMAN: (HARSHLY) It's too late to go home now, isn't it? (SOFTENING) Yes, I'm staying the night.

> She continues to talk for a moment. Keith excuses himself, then carries on tidying up. This is intercut with close-ups of the woman, who is staring around her, and into her coffee cup, obviously reliving the frustrations of the day. Keith continues telling us the story in voice-over.

KEITH: (OOV) Poor woman; she must have felt really angry and worried. I just hope we helped her to unwind. More often than not, good, efficient service and a pleasant, polite manner will put guests like her back into a good mood. And at the very least, it will stop them biting your head off!

> We now return to our characters in conversation.

KEITH: Would you like me to have a liqueur sent up to your room?

WOMAN: (SMILING) That would be nice. I'll have a Drambuie.

KEITH: It'll be up shortly. And I believe the hotel video system is showing a good film tonight.

WOMAN: Good. I'll have a look at it. Can I have my bill now?

KEITH: Of course. Excuse me.

> As Keith's voice-over takes the story up again, we watch as he brings the bill over, and the woman settles it with a credit card. Then she gets up and leaves, without even saying goodnight to Keith. He grins ruefully as he watches her leave the dining room.

KEITH: (OOV) Heavens, I thought she'd never go! All the other staff had left half an hour earlier. But with people who've had a bad day, as she had, you can't rush them. Mind you, I think she'll keep a good impression of our hotel. And if she's back in the area again, she'll probably come back; repeat business is very important to us, even if they do come from a long way away.

In my job, you can't be nosy or chatty. So it's up to you to be subtle and sensitive, and try to FEEL what their problem is, no matter how disagreeable people are.

The following example (in treatment form) shows how the modular approach can be used, this time majoring on drama with only a little explanatory documentary input towards the end to highlight teaching points. The project was to motivate parts sales staff in dealerships of a major European motor manufacturer, to do a better job—a notoriously difficult goal to achieve in the motor trade.

Style and approach

The style is borrowed from the highly successful comedy school of Eric Sykes/Ronnie Barker/Benny Hill. This introduces a surrealistic feel to the programme, with a minimun of realistic dialogue. The action is not physically speeded up, but edited with a very fast cutting style to progress the narrative. Another advantage of this approach, apart from its humour and piquancy, is that it can be slowed down every now and again to emphasize a point ... with great dramatic effectiveness. Links between modules are in the form of amusing graphics and captions. There is some voice-over narration in Module Three, to help us summarize the main points. The main character—the perpetrator of poor service in Module One, and the 'victim' in Module Two—is a strong character actor capable of assuming a number of different roles. This actor should be instantly recognizable, to help viewers identify with the programme and to trigger a high entertainment level. If budget permits, an actor such as David Jason would add greatly to the memorability of the programme. Alternatives might be Andrew Sachs or Tim Brooke-Taylor.

Module One

In a series of cameos, we see our two parts employees out during their time off. At this stage, we do not know that they are (Company X) staff; the only hint we have is that they both drive (Company X) cars. The module opens with a caption which says, 'DO YOU KNOW THE FEELING?'

Our first cameo is of one of the characters driving into a large do-it-yourself superstore. He has to park miles from the entrance, as the main door area is cluttered with other cars, plus two or three large trucks delivering fresh supplies. He walks in clutching a scrap of paper on which, no doubt, is written the measurements of the items he needs, and pushes his way past a bevy of men in overalls and flustered shop staff.

We next see him fiddling with a large number of wooden planks, trying to figure out which are right for his needs. He has forgotten his own measuring tape, and calls out to a white-coated assistant for help. The assistant turns and says he is stock-room staff, so it's not his job. We then see a series of short cuts where our character tries a number of other shop staff, but with no luck. He waits for some time at the information counter while the attendant there conducts a long conversation with her boyfriend on the telephone. Eventually, the manager appears, and he is played by our main actor. He listens to our character intermittently, being distracted every few seconds by a comment or question from someone else or by being called to the telephone. Finally he understands what our character wants, but brushes him off by saying his measurements can't be right and he'd better return home to check again. Our character, furious and frustrated, goes back to his car.

Meanwhile, we see our second parts employee drive up and park outside a travel agency. He is accompanied by his wife, and they are about to book their annual holiday to Benidorm. They walk into the travel agency; it is quiet, and there is no one around. They shuffle about looking at brochures for a while, waiting for someone to come and see to them, but no one appears. However, we can hear the sound of voices, laughter, then angry exchanges taking place in a back room somewhere. They sit down and wait. Eventually a man appears—our main actor again—nods at our couple, and says he won't be a minute. He then gets into a long conversation on the telephone with a customer, obviously spinning a yarn to the person on the other end of the line about why something hasn't been done. Not only do we know from what he says that he's lying, but he reinforces it by winking at our couple every now and again. Eventually he comes off the phone and asks our couple what they want. Just as they are explaining someone else comes in, bangs on the counter, and announces that he must book three first-class return airfares to New York, right away. This being more interesting business than that of our couple, the man behind the counter drops them like hot bricks saying he'll be back with them in a moment. They stare at him incredulously; he shouts out to them that he must just deal with this urgent request, but that they should come back at lunchtime. They exit angrily.

Now, we return to our first parts employee, who drives up to the do-it-yourself store again. This time he is clutching two wooden planks, obviously hoping to find similar ones of the right size in the superstore. There is a fair amount of bustle in the entrance way, but eventually our character finds the manager again and announces that he has brought the correct size of plank—all he needs now is more of the same. The manager tells him to go back to the relevant department and someone will be there to help him. Needless to say there isn't, so he tries to find the correct planks himself. He gets into a terrible muddle, and winds up with a number of planks tumbling down around him. Sitting on the floor in a heap along with the fallen planks, he sees the manager walk over to him. Then, the manager tells him off—he should have asked someone to help him. Furious, he tells the manager that he'd sooner die than buy his planks from this store; the manager points out that there isn't another similar store for miles around, so he hasn't much choice. Our character retorts that driving thirty miles or so is preferable to taking this kind of abuse, disentangles himself from the pile of planks, and stalks off.

Meanwhile, our second character and his wife are having a furious row in the middle of a High Street. We gather from the short clips of conversation that whereas he doesn't want to go back to the travel agency, she feels that as it is the only one in the town it will be less inconvenient to go back there than drive to the next town. They continue arguing noisily until they reach the door of the travel agency, when they finally stop and the husband capitulates. They push on the door, only to find that it is locked; a sign in the glass of the door says 'Closed 1–2 p.m.'. They stare at the door in amazement; then, the husband remarks that he can't understand how anyone stays in business giving such awful service as that. They walk off.

Module Two

This module begins with a caption that reads, 'NOW WHO'S THE VICTIM?' Our main actor, who is now to be the recipient of bad service (as opposed to the exponent of it, as do-it-yourself store manager and travel agency clerk in Module One), drives up to a garage. In large letters over the showroom we can see the name 'FIASCO AUTO (UK) LTD', in a logo style and typeface which is remarkably like that of (Company X). He can't park, because the 'customer parking' area is full of new cars ready for the showroom. He drives away again, and returns on foot, heaving and panting to suggest that he's had to park miles away.

Our character's next problem is to find the parts department. He hunts high and low, being given complicated and wildly inaccurate directions by a few languishing staff members. Eventually he ends up at the back of the dealership, and carefully squeezing himself between the dustbins and the central heating oil tank he finds himself facing a small, unmarked door. He pushes it open and enters a dingy, dimly lit parts department. As he walks up to the shabby counter, furnished only with a dusty telephone and racks of gloomy, unrecognizable parts, a cat yowls and slinks past him out into the fresh air.

Beyond the counter and the racks, we can see sunlight through a half-open door. Two men in overalls—our two characters from Module One—are larking about, giggling, but they're too far away to notice our main actor. There's no bell on the counter for our main actor to use, so he waits. The lonely telephone on the counter begins to ring, unnoticed. The door behind creaks open and another customer enters; he is large and grubby, clutching an unrecognizable piece of engine in his hand, obviously fresh from working on his own car. Still the phone rings on.

Then, one of our two characters walks up to the counter, and lazily picks up the phone. He grunts into it, but the caller has rung off. Replacing the receiver, he looks at the grubby man, then enters into a highly technical conversation with him, culminating in a request for a part. The part appears, gets paid for, and the grubby man exits promptly. Our character turns to go, with our main actor faintly calling after him for attention. He is interrupted; the phone goes again and our character picks it up and grunts once more. He mutters that he doesn't know, hang on, and disappears into the bowels of the parts racks.

We now cut to a homely front room. A middle-aged woman is holding on to the handset of her telephone, staring vacantly into space. A man's voice asks what the man has said. She replies that he has gone to look. She waits on.

Back in the parts department our main actor waits on, too. A door slams behind the parts racks, and an animated argument begins between our character and the service manager. From the muffled expletives and angry shouts we gather they don't get on too well. Although we don't see anything, we hear the row and intercut between the surprised, shocked faces of both our main actor in the parts department and the middle-aged woman, still clutching her phone in her home, as they react to what they're hearing. Over the row, we also hear the spoken thoughts of both people, underlining the deficiencies of the service and the relationship between parts and service departments. In the final cut of the middle-aged woman, we also see her husband with his ear pressed to the other side of the receiver. They're both shocked at what they hear.

We now come back to our character, who emerges from behind the racks looking mildly dishevelled and picks up the phone. He grunts down it that they're temporarily out of stock and could she call back next week. Finally, putting the phone down, he notices our main actor and grunts at him.

Our main actor squeaks, then blurts out that he wants a certain part for his 1983 (Company X car). Our second character appears from behind the parts rack, and between the two they manage to confuse our main actor totally by asking multiple questions about which serial numbers, what month of 1983, which model, and so on, ending with our second character smiling triumphantly. He points out that without having all this ludicrously complicated information, they can't be sure of producing the right part. He has won. Our main actor sheepishly asks what to do next.

He's told that there's a number stamped on the bulkhead just behind the distributor, followed by a stream of other instructions we can't understand. Our second character then disappears; the phone rings again, our first character answers it, grunts, tells the caller to hang on and disappears as well. The parts department yawns emptily in front of our main actor, who then exits.

We cut to a street where our main actor's (Company X car) is parked. In a series of quick cuts to suggest a time lag, we see his feet sticking out from under the jacked-up front end, the bonnet up and his backside upwards as he vainly tries to see the serial number, him attempting to remove the dashboard to get at it that way, etc. After a while we notice that dusk is gathering, so he reaches into the glove compartment for a torch and continues his search with the aid of the light. Eventually, he leaps out from the engine compartment, shrieking out the number in eureka fashion. He walks back to the dealership, reciting the number over and over again so he doesn't forget it, and finally arrives at the parts department door. He finds the door locked, and a sign hanging off the rusty doorknob saying 'closed'. He slides to the ground, groaning, and we close the module on a long shot of him sitting dejectedly by the door.

Module Three

This module begins with the caption, 'SORRY, LET'S DO THAT AGAIN'. Here, we examine each of the main teaching points raised in Module Two. Beginning with a freeze frame of the 'wrong way', we then show a very short sequence of the 'right way', performed by the same actors. Where relevant, we also go back to the comparable sequence from Module One, not so much to dictate the 'right way' in a do-it-yourself store or a travel agency but to underline the way our two characters *felt* when being given a dose of the same medicine. In each 'right way' sequence we notice that the original name of FIASCO AUTO (UK) LTD has been changed to (Company X) (UK) LTD. The module is linked by voice-over narration, spoken by our main actor. Main teaching points are also reinforced by captions on screen where appropriate.

The last sequence shows the right way in all three examples: do-it-yourself store, travel agency, and parts department. Here, our voice-over makes the point that not only does good service lead to happy customers, but also to increased sales. We see, first of all, our character with his wooden planks in the do-it-yourself store. He is walking towards the check-out, being assisted by a helper and the manager, when he suddenly remembers he's out of varnish. He mentions this to the manager, who leads him to the varnish gondola and then asks him if he's well stocked in brushes, etc. The outcome of this sequence is that he buys quite a lot more than he originally came in for.

Similarly, our couple in the travel agency—having been well and courteously treated, and asked if there's any further help they need—remember that the old lady next door has mentioned that she wants to book a coach tour of the Lake District. Our main actor (as the clerk) gives them a selection of brochures to give to her and helpfully suggests that she can book by phone, etc., to minimize inconvenience. Once again, a value-added sale has been achieved.

Thirdly, we see our 'victim' in the parts department, having bought the required part for his (Company X car), being asked if there's anything else he needs while he's there. He ends up by buying a can of touch-up paint, some spare bulbs, and some seat covers (or other non-essential accessory) as a result of being politely 'sold to'.

At the end of the module, the voice-over sums up, and reinforces the importance of pride and professionalism in performance . . . the significance of the dealership team . . . and the relevance of these points to the overall survival and success of (Company X) (UK) LTD, every one of its dealerships, and everyone who works in them.

Some training programme commissioners feel that programmes should make it very clear to viewers which sections are dramatized and which are documentary. Often I have been asked to write lines of narration saying something like, *'the following section is played by actors, but the stories they tell are based on real life experience'*. I believe that this is a bad idea for two reasons: (1) to make an issue out of the fact that you've used dramatization however 'don't worry, guys, it may be play-acting but it's all true, honestly' . . . could make cynical viewers wonder if it's actually all lies; (2) as mentioned earlier in this book, what matters to viewers is the *message*, whoever conveys it—not whether the message is conveyed by a company interviewee, an actor, a narrator, the chairman, or the tea lady. In the following excerpt I blended drama and documentary content without any visible joins, and the programme worked very well. The project was a store staff product knowledge video for one of the big High Street names, introducing viewers to an entirely new product line.

> The programme opens with a very short dramatization, set in a fairly large bathroom of a Victorian house. We see Fiona, in her late thirties, with her hair in heated rollers. She is lying in a bubble bath, looking somewhat disgruntled. Her husband, Nigel, is obviously in the adjacent bedroom. We assume that they are both getting ready to go out for the evening. We also assume, through the ensuing dialogue, that they have only recently moved into the house.
>
> A rickety shower, hand-held but on a peg, is located within

the same area as the bath, with the shower head directly over the woman. It keeps dripping on to her head. After a couple of seconds, she calls out to Nigel ...

FIONA: Nigel! (SHORT PAUSE) When are you going to mend this wretched shower? This whole bathroom's really tatty!

We hear the sound of man's voice in muffled reply, but can't make out what he's saying.

FIONA: (GRABS A LITTLE OF THE OLD SHOWER CURTAIN AND LOOKS AT IT IN DISGUST, THEN YELLS OUT TO NIGEL AGAIN) Well, it may have done the previous owners for forty years, but I think it needs a facelift.

Again, we hear Nigel's muffled voice.

FIONA: (LOOKING PEEVED. SHE SHOUTS BACK ...) Not me! The bathroom! (THEN QUIETLY, TO HERSELF, AS SHE REACHES FOR AN OLD FACE FLANNEL, AND WIPES IT ACROSS HER CHEEK) My skin's as good as it was when I was twenty. (THEN TOSSES THE FLANNEL TO THE SIDE) Should think we've had that since I was twenty, too.

She reaches for a towel, which is looking very worn. It is of a colour that clashes with the flannel, and both in turn clash with the old shower curtain. Fiona looks at them all, with a disgruntled expression on her face.

Now, we cut to an interview with a senior representative of (Company X) Bathrooms. We see her in a store, chatting to a (Company X) sales assistant. The assistant is the same character who appears in the dramatization later on, but in this context she is acting as the interviewer, although still in character. Effectively, this sequence will appear to be an informal training session, with Mrs X giving friendly instruction to the assistant as to the content and nature of the bathrooms department.

Interview questions will be scripted, and a selection is included below. However, the actress cast in the role will be someone capable of ad lib questions, if the need should arise.

Mrs X's replies to questions must *not* be scripted, to ensure a natural, informal style.

(Etc.)

During this section, we occasionally cut away to Fiona in her old bathroom. Now, she is wearing a robe, and she is shuffling about, combing her hair out, putting on some makeup. With each quick cut, we see more examples of her annoyance with the room ... nothing matches, the cupboard is rickety and hard to open, the curtains at the window are old and tatty, the wallpaper has begun to peel away in one or two places, the towel holder is hanging off the wall. We also notice that the bathroom suite is white, and in good condition.

After the last section of the interview, we return to Fiona in the old bathroom for the last time.

She is nearly ready, but is now struggling to get the last few specks out of a container of (Company X) compressed powder (*or other similar product. Whichever product is chosen, it must have the logo clearly printed, stamped or embossed on it*). Having only just succeeded, she tosses the empty container into an ugly waste paper basket. She mutters to herself ...

FIONA: Must go to (Company X) and get some more tomorrow ... (LOOKING AROUND THE BATHROOM) ... definitely needs a facelift in here... (PEERS AT HER OWN FACE IN THE MIRROR, PULLING THE SKIN UP AT THE TEMPLES WITH HER FINGERS, THEN TAKES HER HANDS AWAY AND LOOKS AT HER FACE AGAIN) Cheeky devil. (NOW SHOUTING) I'm nearly ready, darling!

She exits. The camera then moves to show a close shot of the empty cosmetic container in the waste paper basket, and zooms in on the logo. We then dissolve from this to a (Company X) logo on a product from the (Company X) bathroom range. The camera zooms out again, to reveal that we are now back in the (Company X) Bathrooms Department.

Using a combination of live action in the store, and stills from Company X's Bathrooms' brochure, we then briefly take viewers through the product range, and describe the different looks which can be achieved. We also describe the merchandizing concepts, showing how products are to be displayed, etc.

(Etc.)

Chapter 9

The marketing/sales programme

The most important thing to remember about sales programmes is that they are not advertising commercials, and should never be treated as such. Yet all too often you will see 'corporate' sales programmes that try to emulate television commercials, with disastrous results. This is largely for two reasons.

Firstly, money. Advertising commercials normally cost their creators well into the telephone numbers, whereas the corporate sales programme will only merit perhaps one-tenth or less of that budget. On a budget of, say, £20 000, you simply cannot afford to send a crew and half a dozen sinewy models to the Bahamas to do an opening seascape shot. On a TV commercial budget of £200 000, however, you probably can. Consequently, the creative treatment of a sales programme must be quite different from that of a commercial.

The second reason leads on from the first. One of the reasons why TV commercials must have so much money spent on them is in order to create impact *within a very short space of time*; normally no more than one minute or so. Corporate sales programmes, although they should not run over the magic number of 18 minutes for maximum retention, do have a great deal more time to play with.

TV commercials can do very little other than create a strong (and usually expensive) impression, and implant the name of the product plus its main benefit in viewers' minds. Although viewers are likely to see TV commercials several times during a campaign, and it is possible to create a series of different commercials about the same product to try to expose more about it, sales programmes really score over TV commercials because they are able to demonstrate a product or service in a far more thorough and detailed fashion than a commercial can ever hope to.

What sales programmes are truly useful for, then, is to show viewers what a product or service can do. And, taking a leaf out of most good marketing books, it is important to add to that thought the point that sales programmes should show viewers what the product or service can do *for them* ... stressing only its features and benefits, and leaving out all the high-precision electronic widgets that are of no relevance to a prospective buyer. Once again, it is a case of putting yourself into the viewers' shoes and writing only what will interest them.

Setting the scene

A television commercial does not give you the luxury of time to establish the background to a sales pitch and viewers are normally dropped right into the middle of the action, whereas the corporate programme allows you to indulge in some scene-setting. This is not strictly necessary if the programme will always be seen as part of a live presentation. However, in normal circumstances you will want the programme to be capable of standing alone, even if it is used as part of a live presentation from time to time. So, use the luxury of time to locate your viewers in time and space, preparing them and hopefully generating a receptive attitude for the sales pitch that inevitably follows.

Obviously, all the golden rules of corporate scriptwriting apply to this category of script. Perhaps the most important, after establishing what information will be of interest to viewers (as against what is of interest to the product or service's creators), is to establish viewers' average level of literacy where the product or service is concerned. There is nothing more insulting than watching a programme that tries to teach grandmothers to suck eggs, and this does not exactly put viewers in a receptive frame of mind to accept the sales pitch. However, a programme which assumes that viewers know a great deal more than they actually do will leave them feeling confused about the sales message, which is hardly a useful outcome, either. Careful research of the viewers who will be watching your programme is the key to pitching the information level accurately.

Setting the scene can be done in a purely documentary fashion. In the following excerpt from a multi-media programme about tonometry—a means of measuring pressure within the human eye—which was aimed at hospital administrators, the scene was set using historical information that examined the problems of previous methods, leading naturally up to new product which (of course) solved them all. The programme was illustrated with both stills and motion picture clips, starting with a sequence of slow dissolves of a number of different pairs of human eyes, followed by historical drawings, old photographs, and graphics.

> *NARRATOR:* The painless, unseen threat of early chronic glaucoma ... an eye disease which creeps up on one out of every fifty adults over forty

... usually unnoticed, with no symptoms, until serious permanent damage has already been done.

Nearly ten thousand people in Britain go blind every year as a result of chronic and acute glaucoma ... caused by increased pressure inside the eye. Yet ocular damage caused by this disease, *can* be successfully arrested and controlled ... *if it is diagnosed in time.* So, the need for *prompt and efficient* diagnosis of glaucoma, especially in its early, symptomless stages, is absolutely vital.

For many centuries now, doctors and scientists have been searching for better and more accurate diagnostic methods. And one of the most important advances in this field was the development of tonometry ... measuring the pressure *inside* a patient's eye, by the way in which it reacts to *external* pressure.

Digital tonometry, pressing on the closed eye with a finger, was first practised by the Ancient Greeks. This method continued right up to the late nineteenth century, when ophthalmologist William Bowman introduced the first *machine* to carry out the test, in 1862.

Most modern tonometry in Britain, tests intraocular pressure using a light, fast puff of air on the locally-anaesthetized eye. Notable examples of these tonometers are the Maklakoff ... the Schiotz ... and, particularly, the Goldmann ... probably the most commonly used tonometer in Britain.

However, most systems like the Goldmann have their drawbacks. General anaesthesia is needed for infants and the elderly, with all the associated risks and use of valuable theatre time. And even for patients outside these two groups, local anaesthesia is essential.

The testing procedure requires considerable skill, and can be uncomfortable for the patient. And the tonometer's direct contact with the cornea can pose the risk of cross-infection.

With the requirement for widespread early diagnosis of glaucoma as urgent as it is, there has been a pressing need for new developments in tonometry.

Until now.

Now, a *new* tonometer has been designed, which offers all the accuracy and advantages of earlier systems. But *unlike* its predecessors, this tonometer is totally portable ... small enough to hold in one hand ... automatic in use ... and economically priced.

The (Company X) Tonometer ... developed by (Company X) Technology in conjunction with (Company Y) Design for (Company Z) Ltd.

Etc.)

Another way of setting the scene is to use dramatization. Even if you do not have a large budget, it's sometimes possible to create mood and atmosphere through drama that is far more effective than a documentary representation. The following excerpt is from a programme selling a unique and very cost-effective form of mobile medical unit to health services in Third World countries. The programme could not contain any 'lip sync' dialogue as it was to be translated into a number of different languages. In addition, the English language version had to be kept simple as the majority of viewers seeing this would not have English as their 'mother tongue'. The budget was small, but, with a little imagination and string-pulling on the part of the director, we managed to create the impression of a Third World drama on location in Hertfordshire and Warwickshire.

The programme opens on a small, dingy, but functional room. There are no blinds or curtains at the windows. A single electric bulb lights the scene. The wind blows forlornly. Four tough-looking men sit around a central table. They are wearing functional clothing. We notice that one of the men is of Asian origin.

We cut to a close up of one of the men. The two-way radio buzzes. He answers ... a few brief words. He reaches over for a map. The men pore over it; fingers trace tracks, point to names. They all have a sense of urgency visible in their faces. They talk sparsely and quickly to each other; their remarks are garbled, and unintelligible to the viewer. A sheet of paper is pulled out. It has the names of various pick-up vehicles on it ... Nissan, Peugeot, Land Rover, Ford, Toyota, etc. We see, close up, a finger tracing a very remote track towards a hastily marked red 'X' on the map. Then, we see a close up of a pen hovering over the words, 'Land Rover'.

We cut to the exterior, and see a row of pick-ups, neatly parked. We are in a yard outside the hut. Four men manhandle the '(product name)' onto the Land Rover base. We see shots of front fixings being made fast. When the '(product name)' is secure, the men nod to each other. We cut to a man quickly opening the rear doors of the '(product name)'; he checks that all is secure within—cupboards, drawers, other fixings. We cut to a front shot of all the vehicles.

The Land Rover, now loaded with the '(product name)', starts. Its headlights blaze as it speeds off. We introduce a strong, powerful music track to accompany this sequence. The vehicle bounces over rough terrain, around corners, up and down hills. All the time the '(product name)' sits, secure, on the back of the vehicle. At one point, we notice just how tough the '(product name)' is, when the vehicle drives under a large overhanging branch; the '(product name)' is hit, hard, and yet remains unmarked. The sequence ends with the vehicle being flagged down by two anxious-looking people. The vehicle-borne '(product name)' has made its rendezvous. We freeze as the people wave.

Over this, as the music builds to a peak, we superimpose the '(product name)' logo, wiping on the red and green stripes in a dramatic way.

THESE RED AND GREEN STRIPES, AND THE LOGO, REMAIN ON SCREEN THROUGHOUT THE FOLLOWING SEQUENCES.

Now, we cut back to our original yard outside the simple hut. We see the remaining pick-ups lined up, but there is no sign of life. Then, a further pick-up drives in, loaded with another '(product name)'. The camera zooms in very slowly. The narrator introduces us to the product ...

NARRATOR: It took the considerable medical expertise of the (XYZ) Group to invent the most ingenious development in mobile healthcare this century. And like many ingenious inventions, it is simple, inexpensive, and very, very versatile. The (product name).

We see the logo.

NARRATOR: The (product name) fits on to almost ANY one-ton pick-up vehicle; NO modification is needed.

The names of these vehicles roll, in caption style, up the screen.

NARRATOR: It's light, very strong, and maintenance-free. (Product name)s are designed to go on serving, even after the base vehicles must be replaced.

(Etc.)

A touch of reality

Another useful tool in sales programmes is real, unscripted human voices. No matter how convincing the narration or dramatized sequences, (as I've said before) viewers are not idiots, and they always know that these have been written by whoever is trying to sell them something—or at least someone paid by them. Natural, unrehearsed dialogue and/or unrehearsed interview clips add a touch of reality to any sales programme and give even the most cynical viewers some reassurance that what they're watching is bona fide.

In the next excerpt, taken from a demonstration programme about a very sophisticated vehicle testing service, the people shown in the programme were encouraged to talk normally, as they would if they were conducting a real test. This is not always easy, especially when people are asked to behave and speak naturally while being gawped at by a camera crew, but with careful preparation and priming it can be achieved. The results are well worth the effort.

....

2 EXTERIOR, CENTRE

....

Cut to customer exiting reception with technician. They both look round car—technician looks at interior and exterior, makes a few notes, then hands form to driver who signs it.

> *NATURAL DIALOGUE:* (CUSTOMER AND TECHNICIAN)
>
> (Fade under to background)
>
> *NARRATION:* Then, a (Company X) person goes out and checks the car over with the driver. This is to see if there is any existing damage or other defects on the car. If anything's found, it gets noted down on a form which the driver signs.

....

3 EXTERIOR, CENTRE

....

Closer shot of technician looking underneath car, feeling underbody with his hand, etc.

> *NATURAL DIALOGUE:* (CUSTOMER AND TECHNICIAN)
>
> (Fade under to background)
>
> *NARRATION:* The (Company X) person also checks to see

if the car is clean enough to go through the test. If it isn't,
(Company X) can have it washed for a small extra charge.

(Fade up)

NATURAL DIALOGUE: (CUSTOMER AND TECHNICIAN)

4 INTERIOR, CAR IN MIDDLE OF WORKSHOP

First time we see inspector. He looks round car, poking around at upper
bodywork, panels, trim, paintwork, etc. Technician helps him and also
writes notes on clipboard.

(NATURAL DIALOGUE AND AMBIENT SOUNDS UNDER)

NARRATION: Now, the car goes into the testing bay, and
the independent inspector sees it for the first time. His first
job is to carry out external visual checks, plus the security
and forensic examination, with the help of a (Company X)
technician.

Here, the inspector judges if the upper bodywork, panel fit
and finish are consistent with the car's type, age and
mileage . . . if the weld seams and repair work in the engine
bay are of acceptable quality.

(Fade up)

NATURAL DIALOGUE: (INSPECTOR AND TECHNICIAN)

(Etc.)

In the next AV programme (already described in Chapter 4) I used live
interview clips to illustrate the knowledge, expertise, enthusiasm and
dedication of a number of the company's staff. Having spent quite a lot of
time with these people in my research phase, I believed that they would
come over much more convincingly than any dramatization or narration
that I could write. It required a whole day of audio-interviewing, resulting
in five hours of tape which took the producer and me several days to
wade through and edit, but the exercise was well worth it. Narration was
only used to introduce the programme's various sections, convey essential
information, and link. The approach would work just as well with
videotape, with the interview clips shown as 'vox pops' or as voices over
live action tape. Here's an excerpt . . .

The programme opens with a series of darkened visuals of
(Company X) corporate designs, and interesting historical
shots, plus a montage of general High Street shots.

We hear suitable music, plus an audio-montage of voice clips. These suggest the fact that (Company X) is the most experienced building company in retail. Appropriate sound effects are also included.

Contributors to these clips will include (Company X) staff members, and any clients we may interview. After a short time the voices subside, leaving just the music, and a voice-over narrator begins to speak.

NARRATOR: For over forty years now, (Company X) has been building for successful retail all over Britain.

Visuals, now bright, show a montage of well-known High Street names, all of which are clients of (Company X).

NARRATOR: To almost every household name in our High Streets, (Company X) has become synonymous with building quality.

Visuals show a montage of finished projects.

NARRATOR: It is this kind of experience that has led to the building of (Company X) itself.

Visuals dissolve through to shots of the senior (Company X) people.

NARRATOR: Experience in kind, and experience in person. All board directors have many years in the business behind them ... most of them spent with (Company X). Every (Company X) project has the personal supervision of a board director, all the way through.

Visuals show one or two of the (Company X) directors either on site during a project, or in discussion with a client.

NARRATOR: Experience of this quality, leads to understanding. A deep understanding, that comes from years of practice and firmly-built foundations of excellence.

Visuals dissolve to show a selection of shots that represents the (XYZ) Group, plus all of its significant member companies.

NARRATOR: Such understanding is also greatly helped, by the vast resources (Company X) can call upon. As part of the (XYZ) Group, ALL members have a dedication to the clients of each individual company. It is a spread of knowledge and expertise that reaches the four corners of retail world wide.

Visuals begin to show examples of new build projects, now finished.

NARRATOR: Only (Company X) can truly build on this success.

As you know, building within retail can play many roles.

New build, creating from the beginning, is just one way in which (Company X) experience performs for its clients.

Visuals show examples of new build, both in wide, general shots, and in a selection of interesting close-ups that illustrate the quality of work and attention to detail. Such shots should be graphically intriguing as well as illustrative.

This section is accompanied by voice clips to match; they emphasize not the factual aspects of new build, but the way in which (Company X) understands the full implications of new build. Here, too, comments will be made on the ways in which (Company X)'s experience has permitted greater cost-effectiveness for the client, and on how—where appropriate—the resources of the (XYZ) Group have helped in the same way.

Interviews for this and all other sections will cover the essentials for good building; e.g. quality control, budget monitoring, experience, understanding, resources, time-keeping, etc.

At the end of this section, the visuals will begin to dissolve through to shots of edge of town developments.

NARRATOR: A more recent, and very exciting aspect of retail is edge of town development. Naturally enough, (Company X) has been building on the success of this concept, since its advent in the UK.

We see examples of (Company X)'s experience in edge of town development, and hear voice clips to match. These are the result of the interview objectives as set out above.

The visuals then begin to change into those of fit-out work.

NARRATOR: New build is just one aspect of retail where (Company X) experience is playing a major part. But where a building already exists, (Company X) experience begins at the next stage: in the fit-out.

(Etc.)

Contrast dramatization

Needless to say, dramatization in a sales programme is just as useful a method of demonstrating something as it is in training and other forms of corporate programme. This is on the assumption that it demonstrates in a straightforward manner.

However, dramatization can also be used to provide a contrast to the main sales story, setting up the reasons why the product or service is such a good idea. The next programme was used to promote a group of hotels which specialize in conference and business meeting work. They all have eighteen-hole golf courses and excellent sports facilities, thereby providing conference delegates with a more healthy means of unwinding after work than by propping up a bar. The idea behind the approach was to get this information over in a way that viewers (business executives) could identify with. The following excerpt shows how the approach worked.

> The programme opens with a blank screen. Gradually, a caption comes into view: it says ...
>
> *AN INTRODUCTION TO (COMPANY X) HOTELS*
>
> We hear sound effects of people saying goodbyes at the end of what has obviously been a hectic business meeting. Papers rustle, briefcases are clicked shut, chairs scrape as they're pushed back, etc.
>
> Further captions come up on screen ...
>
> *WHEN IT COMES TO CREATING THE PERFECT BLEND OF BUSINESS AND LEISURE ...*
>
> The sound effects continue
>
> *NOBODY DOES IT BETTER.*
>
> We hear a door close, and then there is silence. We then fade up the picture; two men, in smart suits but with ties akimbo, obviously left behind. They are sitting either side of a boardroom table.

GEORGE: Wow. (SARCASTICALLY) Another lively brainstorming session in the proverbial smoke-filled room, eh? The joys of senior management.

> From here, the following dialogue will be heard largely OOV. Using special effects we will dissolve or mix from the occasional in vision glimpse of the two men, to shots of (X) premises that correspond—or contrast—with what they are saying. The following suggestions for visual input will of

course be dependent on both existing and new footage, and the way in which it is edited. For this reason the following dialogue has been written without stating which lines should be in vision and which should not. The dialogue is easy-going in nature; the two men are staying on behind to finalize the next quarter's budgets, in time to reconvene the meeting the following morning. But, they are tired, hot and bothered, and break from their work to comment and exchange views with each other. The tone is casual. Whenever we see them, they are up to their eyes in paperwork, calculators, even a computer screen, breaking off every little while for a short conversation. In the first sequence, we realize that one of the characters, Bob, is leading up to something, but we're not sure what. George, slightly more senior of the two, is unaware of this.

The first (X) visual should be of a general countryside establishing shot. At this stage, we do not identify the locations as (X); this comes later. Throughout the following sequence, we see an attractive visual montage of (X) shots, interweaving with one another, giving us a flavour of what the hotels have to offer. This corresponds, in an ironic way, with what the two characters are saying.

BOB: Can't remember what fresh air smells like.

GEORGE: I never want to see another dried up sandwich, either.

BOB: It's like a sauna in here.

GEORGE: Open the window.

BOB: Ugh! You can smell the traffic fumes.

GEORGE: That's what I could do with right now.

BOB: Traffic fumes?

GEORGE: A sauna. Unscrambles the brain.

BOB: Hmm. Game of golf. Now that's *really* relaxing.

GEORGE: An hour's drive away. At least. Through the rush hour.

BOB: Oh well. One day soon, perhaps.

GEORGE: Could do with a decent meal, too.

BOB: There isn't time, George. We've got all these budgets to finalize for the morning session. Time we book a table, drive for half an hour, park the car ...

GEORGE: You're right. Ah well. It's takeaways again.

BOB: Marianne's still here, isn't she?

GEORGE: Expect so.

BOB: I'll see if she can pop out and get something. (PICKS UP PHONE AND WAITS)

GEORGE: As long as it's not sandwiches again. I couldn't stand to see another ...

BOB: (ON TELEPHONE) Oh, Marianne? George and I will be working pretty late, so I wonder if you wouldn't mind? Great. Er, no, not sandwiches, thanks. And d'you think you could bring in the, er? Yes, that one. Thanks. (PUTS PHONE DOWN)

GEORGE: We really should have these meetings outside the office, you know.

BOB: What, in one of those conference hotels?

GEORGE: We tried that five years ago, didn't we?

BOB: Trouble with them is there's nowhere to relax.

GEORGE: Except drinking in the bar.

BOB: Can't do too much of that, either.

GEORGE: Not when we're working. Now, exercise. That's what we need to help us relax.

BOB: Some companies go for a quiet old country place.

GEORGE: They don't all have proper meeting rooms, though. Huge great ballrooms with dangling chandeliers. That's no good.

BOB: No good at all.

GEORGE: Two rounds of mini-golf and a game of croquet. Or a tennis court covered in weeds with holes in the net. Hardly proper recreation.

BOB: True. But you're absolutely right, George. Meetings in the office just aren't on. Uncomfortable. Phones ringing. Interruptions.

GEORGE: Nowhere to unwind. And talking of that, we'd better press on. I'd like to get home before midnight.

BOB: What time is it?

GEORGE: Late.

BOB: Perhaps I should ring my wife.

GEORGE: Shouldn't think she remembers what you look like.

BOB: Oh, yes she does. We took a break last weekend. Had a great time.

GEORGE: Where?

BOB: Oh, a really nice place. Lots of things to do, good food, golf, you know. Excellent course, it was.

GEORGE: Your wife plays as well?

BOB: (POINTEDLY) Off a handicap of eight.

GEORGE: (THOUGHTFULLY) Oh. She does play, then. What's your handicap?

BOB: These blasted meetings. And working in the middle of Fun City, here.

GEORGE: (CHUCKLES) Know the feeling.

BOB: Last weekend was the first time I'd played in weeks.

> Marianne enters with some takeaway food. We see close shots of her hands as she puts it down on the table between the two men.

BOB: Thanks very much, Marianne. Kind of you.

> They share out the food, and we notice that there are some brochures which Marianne has brought in at the same time.

GEORGE: What's this?

BOB: Marianne must have brought them in.

GEORGE: Marked for your attention, Bob.

> We now see a proper reveal of the (X) logo, and then go into some specific shots that correspond with what the two characters are talking about. Wherever relevant, we can leave the dialogue for a time to illustrate more involved points. However, the way the dialogue is structured should allow us to convey all the main selling points in a logical order. What we now realize, too, is that the so far unnamed venue of Bob's weekend away with his wife, was in fact a Golf Break at a (Company X) Hotel. So we see shots of Bob, accompanied by his wife at times, in various places around the hotel. From the shots we see, it is obvious that he is not

only there for a weekend break; he is also checking the place out for its suitability for the next quarterly management meeting, unbeknown to George. From time to time, during a gap in the two characters' dialogue, we hear snatches of conversation between Bob and hotel staff, as he's asking questions and getting replies.

(Etc.)

Creating an identity

Once again taking a leaf out of marketing books, one of the most important things to establish in any piece of sales material for a product or service is a USP (Unique Selling Proposition). This is what makes your product or service different from, and better than, anything else. Sometimes this is easy, where the product or service is genuinely unique, but as we all know a large number of products and services are not dissimilar from the competition. Often you can find something to hang the story on—for example, price, convenience, cost-effectiveness, fast service back-up, etc.

In the examples given above, the USPs were fairly obvious. The tonometer (instrument for measuring eye pressure) was more convenient and cost-effective to use than any other previous instrument; the mobile medical unit was the only one of its kind; the vehicle testing service was more sophisticated and thorough than any other in existence; the construction company genuinely was the most experienced in building for retail; and the hotel group was the only one of its kind to offer such extensive sports/recreation facilities within the conference venue market.

What, though, if the product or service not only has no visible USP, but no visible identity, either?

The answer is to look hard, and if you find nothing, look again—but this time using a bit of lateral thinking. The treatment that follows was for a programme for another group of hotels. However, they had very little in common; they were of varying sizes and ages, located mainly in the south-west of England plus one in the Channel Isles, and to round it all off the group in question was new and had no existing trading reputation to work with. The key clue was found to be in the name of the group; and although for reasons of client confidentiality the name cannot be revealed, it had strong maritime connections. The approach was tackled in the following way, which led to a successful programme that gave the group and the hotels the identity they needed.

Programme structure and content suggestions

Introduction

(Company X) ... a name for a collection of hotels, grown from the rich history of islands so strongly influenced by the sea and the many cultural and trading influences it brought.

Hospitality perfected over the centuries

Beginning with MALMESBURY: its particular encounters with the invading Normans plus its other historically important points, including the world's first recorded human flight ... the (hotel name), an establishment offering hospitality for nearly a thousand years ... its connection with the Abbey ... its role today as the centre of the region's beauty spots, and a welcome to guests wishing to relive the richness of the past. STONEHOUSE: mentioned in the Doomsday Book ... and the (hotel name), with its origins also going back to Norman times—a gift from William the Conqueror to his cousin ... the present building originating from the seventeenth century and lovingly preserved today, in its glorious setting that's ideal for both the business person or the tourist. SHERBORNE: known in Saxon times, then later a favourite for the invading Romans living in their 'British Villas' built along the stream ... the (hotel name), more recent, a priceless example of a luxurious home from Georgian times, and still welcoming visitors as an elegant home-from-home. LYMINGTON: a town of immense maritime significance since the ancient Britons, carried forward by the Romans, the Normans and later French invaders ... the (hotel name), an exquisitely preserved building from the days when Lymington was the Georgian capital of the West Solent, and today caring for the town's many sailing enthusiasts as well as land-loving guests. JERSEY: a small island within the British Isles, formerly a part of France—source of considerable maritime trade to New Jersey in the New World ... St Brelades, home of Victor Hugo, and home of the (hotel name)—a private home from the mid-nineteenth century, and developed as a hotel from the mid 1950s ... now welcoming guests in grand style, including Royalty and international celebrities.

Hotels rich in charisma, comfort and courtesy

How modern systems and facilities work discreetly with the comfort and charm of traditional elegance and character. How guests can enjoy the very best of both worlds, doing business, relaxing and enjoying recreation with the latest amenities at their fingertips ... in a setting that faithfully preserves all the best of traditions other hotels ignore. The quality of cuisine, the attention to detail, the personal service that grew from the British people's reputation as the finest inn-keepers in the world. The importance of all (Company X) hotels within their own local communities ... the chance for visitors to experience local culture, over a drink in a relaxing bar ... to spend a night in a traditional four-poster bed, and wake to the sight of a truly English country garden ... to take tea on an English croquet lawn, or overlooking a famous British waterway (Channel/River Avon) ... to lunch on award-winning cuisine (Jersey) that characteristically blends the influences of two neighbouring nations connected by the sea ... to stroll on a gentle sunny evening, overlooking the spires of some of Britain's finest abbeys (Malmesbury and/or Sherborne), or the myriad yachts of a harbour that's moored the shipping of ten centuries (Lymington) ... and return for dinner, a nightcap and bed in a living part of that rich culture.

(Company X) Hotels: caring with character
From crisp, white sheets to a cordial welcome from every member of staff, (Company X) cares for guests with the perfect balance of British hospitality and good manners. This kind of caring stems from the British people's expertise in hotel-keeping, perfected over centuries of entertaining visitors ... with character that's based on centuries of foreign influences and traditions, yet uniquely, delightfully British. Both Britain and (Company X) itself ... invigorated and characterized by the sea, and what it brought to this collection of islands—now brought to a collection of hotels that knows no equal.

Feel the quality

Finally, I would say that the key to writing good sales programmes is to make viewers identify with the benefits they can enjoy from the product or service. With the luxuries of time, visual images and an audio track, plus a comparatively captive audience, the audio-visual media allow you to create the right environment and mood so viewers can *feel* why your product or service is good, as well as see and hear the information. As suggested above, it's sometimes difficult to create that feeling—the identity, and the USP—but with some careful creative thinking it's possible to achieve with virtually any product or service.

Chapter 10

The recruitment programme

Many programme commissioners make the elementary mistake of assuming that a recruitment VT or AV programme can be an edited (or even unedited) version of their normal 'corporate video', with perhaps a few graphics at the end detailing perks and pension schemes. This is wrong because what is of interest to a general audience is not necessarily of interest to people who are contemplating the devotion of the next X years of their careers to your company. Obviously there will be some cross-over, particularly if you are recruiting for graduates and/or management staff who will be interested in last year's turnover figure, the company's product range and other general issues, as well as the career opportunities. But much of that type of information will be totally lost on school leavers, who will probably interpret your eight-figure turnover as a sign that the company is too big to care about them as individuals.

As always, it is essential for you to put yourself into the viewers' shoes and understand what information will be of relevance to them. Let's now look at some of the more common points of interest to potential employees, which should be covered in a recruitment programme.

Who would I be working for?

This may seem obvious but remember to tailor the answer to the audience concerned. If that consists of school leavers or other groups who may not necessarily understand the global overview of business, put the answer across in simple terms. For example, if you want to quote figures, don't just say that Bloggs Machine Tools is a large engineering company that produces 370 000 widgets per annum; bring it down to a more human level by adding something like 'that's more than a thousand widgets for every day of the year'. Avoid lengthy sequences about the company's history, unless it's *very* interesting. The fact that the Founder still came into work every day when he was 94 may be interesting to you as an experienced business person (especially if you plan to retire at 55!) but to a young graduate 94 seems a long way away, and a 94-year-old Founder calling the shots at the office is not exactly an earth-shattering point anyway.

How does this company value its staff?

This does not mean a boring monologue in an interview with the Human Resources Director about all the old clichés like opportunity and commitment. It means showing what the company offers its staff: the canteen (if it's a good one) with subsidized meals, the gym, the recreation facilities, the health centre, and so on. Another good way of conveying this information is to interview existing staff of an appropriate level (comparable to the level of staff you're recruiting for, and about the same age) and ask their views. Don't put words into their mouths, and tell them to be honest. If their responses are terrible you can edit them out, but remember the odd mild criticism—provided that it is accompanied by good points—will make the whole interview appear to be much more natural than if the interviewee is trotting out nothing but praise.

Is there a 'them and us' barrier between workers and management?

Whatever you do, never show the chairman wearing a pin-stripe suit and a constipated smile being served fish and chips in the works canteen. Even if he actually eats there every lunchtime, no one will believe it. Once again, try to answer the question through suggestion and implication, thereby getting viewers to draw that conclusion for themselves, rather than by using a bald visual or verbal statement. As with so many things in life, people are more likely to believe something if they feel they've thought it up for themselves, than if they're told it point-blank.

How does it feel to work for this company?

Once again, don't get the narrator to talk about the exciting, upbeat working environment over wide shots of the factory floor, but show tightly shot 'slice of life' sequences almost as if the camera is a person standing with the other people, as a silent colleague. Interview people at their place of work; get them to talk about their job and how it feels to do it for your company. Get a number of employees together in the canteen over a cup of coffee, and conduct an informal group discussion about the company. Let them say what they want, and encourage them to inject a little humour as well if they want to. Shoot this and use excerpts to punctuate the programme.

What opportunities will there be for me to move upwards?

Rather than state the point about there being good opportunities, let it be seen as implicit through other material—otherwise it will not seem as believable. If you're using interview clips, ask your interviewees to run briefly through their own career progression, and use this if it illustrates the fact that promotion opportunities are good.

What will this company expect from me?

Obviously this question can only be answered in specific terms on a one-to-one basis. But general, overall expectations can be suggested, if only in a subliminal way. If your company values long service, this can be brought out in interviews or case histories. If you're interested in movers and shakers whom you don't necessarily expect to stay for more than a few years, the programme can make the point about how the company looks for and encourages initiative and upward mobility, even if that means losing people to greater things once they've galloped up the ladder. If you want people to use their initiative, you can illustrate the point by describing some individual examples, or show how many ideas from the corporate 'suggestions box' in Reception have been acted on and rewarded.

Does this company have a good future?

This question is more likely to be asked by graduates and other management recruits, but may well be asked by the older and wiser variety of shopfloor worker, too. If you're recruiting for staff at junior management level and upwards, by all means talk about the fact that the company has a beautiful future ahead of it—but substantiate that with information about the past and present as well. Unless someone has done something incredibly stupid, a company whose growth has been steady and regularly consolidated in the past is also likely to be well set up for the future.

What will I get out of working for this company?

To an extent this question may well have been answered by the other points above, and once again can only be answered fully in individual terms on a one-to-one basis. However, general points can be made about the standing of the company within its community or communities (perhaps through a brief sequence about local charity involvement or work experience schemes), the standing of the company within its own industry (not boring statistics, but a proud manager or supervisor saying in an interview clip how his or her group's hard work helped to make the turbo-charged widget the market leader within six months), the team spirit of staff and management (perhaps a 'fly-on-the-wall' sequence shot during a meeting of the works quality improvement committee), and so on. These points and others like them will convey the message to potential recruits that working for your company will give them a good self-image, reflected from the good image of the company.

What about trades unions/industrial relations?

This is not always relevant—it rather depends on whom you are trying to recruit. If it is relevant, though, the last thing you should do is to brush the subject under the carpet, however you and your superiors might feel about it. If your company is a 'union shop', it makes a great deal of sense for you to consult with a suitable TU representative before you write your script. It's often a good idea, too, to involve a TU person in the programme—perhaps in a short interview with their Health and Safety representative talking about the company's good safety record, it's new hazard reporting initiative, or something similar. This way, you do not open up a can of worms, but by implication you make the point that your industrial relations are good and that everyone works within the team. At the end of the day, your company's own policy will probably dictate the way in which you handle the TU issue—but whatever you do, don't ignore it, as this can involve companies in potential misunderstandings and hostility at a later date, usually after the programme has been made and the money has been spent.

Now, for some examples. The excerpts are from, first, the treatment, followed by the script, for a recruitment programme for a major UK construction company. They were seeking management people, predominantly from a civil engineering background.

Treatment

Introduction
In a programme of this nature it would be easy to become blinded by the numerous and diverse nature of the messages we could put over. It is true to say that (Company X) is a huge organization with a vast number of achievements behind it ... many business centres, areas of operation, and so on. But this is not a marketing programme, or even a corporate programme in the strict sense of the term. This programme must excite viewers ... make them want to know more about a company that communicates such a strong, vibrant and positive image ... make them

want to be part of the company conveyed to them on screen. The messages we give must be made up of the right emotions to obtain those reactions from every single viewer. And excessive information, plus excessive running time, are likely to dilute the strength of the more emotional messages that would otherwise attract the right calibre of personnel.

Consequently, we must concentrate not so much on information as we do on inspiration. From a strong framework built around the image of the company, we can provide viewers with enough information to clinch their interest in and commitment to (Company X), without allowing facts to clutter feelings. This is not to say that the programme should be sketchy on facts; merely that facts should not be considered as motivational tools on their own. What we must focus on, is the conveying of facts through the expression of emotions and image ... and, vice versa.

The most important quality to emerge from (Company X) on an emotional, inspirational level is its underlying, all-encompassing feeling of enthusiasm, dedication and team spirit combined with personal commitment to success. So to put over not the details but the scope of (Company X) activities, and the single-mindedness of its philosophies and image, we must look to the company's most valuable asset of all ... the personification of its image ... (Company X) people.

There can be no better example for new recruits to follow, no stronger image for viewers to wish to emulate, and no greater collective or individual success story, than that of (Company X) people themselves.

It is for these reasons that we strongly recommend this programme should paint the picture of the (Company X) image, convey its essential messages and the scope of its tremendous achievements, through the sight and thoughts of a selection of (Company X) people.

But the programme will be far from the TV viewer's idea of a soul-searching documentary. This programme will move swiftly ... concentrating hard on today's (Company X) image, its sophisticated professionalism and techniques ... its lead in the fast lane of the construction industry.

The words spoken by (Company X) people will provide the basic essentials of information, with many remarks that subtly convey the underlying emotions felt by those who work in the world's most successful construction company. The clips of monologue, linked where relevant by a presenter, will provide almost as many unspoken facts as they do spoken ones ... inspiring viewers with a tantalizing desire to become a part of an organization that can breed such strong, responsible and entrepreneurial success ... imparting the qualities of sophistication, professionalism and confidence in the future to which every viewer will want to aspire.

Programme structure

The idea behind this programme structure is to get *a small number of key (Company X) people to recount their own personal experiences and observations* of working for the company, and through their mix of disciplines illustrate the spread of (Company X) activities. As we must focus very strongly on our audience of potential recruits, we do not want to provide a purely factual account of the company's history and operation. So, every fact that we do put across must emerge from one of the individuals and be expressed in terms of his or her own acknowledgement and interpretation of it. Similarly, the philosophies of (Company X) must be conveyed through the individual subjects' enthusiasm and professionalism.

The vehicle for the recounting of these personal experiences will be *one core construction project for each person*, used as a visual and verbal backdrop. These projects should be connected in some way—e.g. a city centre development involving both refurb and new build. As personal 'ownership' of a project is a major part of the dedication and enthusiasm of (Company X) people, our choice of projects must be those which directly involve the subjects themselves. It would be preferable to find construction projects in which more than one of our key (Company X) people are involved, to provide us with an additional link. *Other unconnected construction projects can be brought in* and illustrated as necessary, when our subjects wish to use them as further examples or asides.

Each of the subjects would speak on his or her own experiences of *clearly defined topics*, cross-connecting these with their *individual construction projects* where appropriate. Where the topic is not relevant to a specific project, other illustrative material (such as graphics, etc.) will be used for cutaway shots. Also cross-connecting with the topics discussed, in the style and presentation of each person's input rather than specifically stated, will be *the following themes*:

>   Professionalism
>   Imagination
>   Entrepreneurial attitudes
>   Care and concern
>   Progressiveness and opportunity

Our recommendation for the choice of subjects is as follows:

1 A *senior director* of (Company X) who has been with the company for a long time, and has worked his way up from a fairly modest level. The person should be a lively speaker, and youthful in approach; (name of person) is a good example of a suitable person to fulfil this role. This subject would touch on these topics:

- The corporate story, plus the (XYZ) Group
- Management contracting, fee system, etc.
- International aspects.

2 A senior manager within (Company X), who has strong connections with civil engineering. Someone who actually is a *civil engineer* would be preferable. He or she should emphasize the importance of civil engineering in the (Company X) construction process, and stress the advances (Company X) has made in this area. This subject would touch on these topics:

- (Company X) structure and opportunities for the professions (not just civil engineering)
- The partnership between (Company X) and the professionals
- Technological methodology used and encouraged by (Company X).

3 A representative from one of (Company X) *specialized divisions*, preferably Retail. This person would cover the more operational aspects of working within a particularly fast-moving and demanding sector of the industry, and stress (Company X) ability to lead from the front. Although Retail is probably the ideal sector in which to make these points—not only is it fast-moving, but visually exciting and interesting—the statements made by the subject would be relevant to a broader spread of (Company X) activities. This subject would touch on these topics:

- Partnership with clients at all levels
- Innovation in methods and techniques
- Imaginative concepts
- Flexibility of work processes
- Speed and quality of construction (fast track).

4 A *young, up-and-coming (Company X) staff member*, who is destined to be a successful (Company X) manager. This person should be a fairly recent recruit to (Company X), and should not be a professional or operational specialist. This subject would touch on these topics:

- Personal pride in and ownership of each project
- The team concept within (Company X)
- The team concept externally
- Career progression for recruits
- The opportunities for the future.

Style and approach

The format of the programme is documentary and presenter led. The presenter will introduce the programme, and also be seen to be 'interviewing' the key (Company X) subjects from time to time. However, the main bulk of the subjects' input will be conveyed in the style of 'off-camera' interview, i.e. with just the subject in vision, appearing to talk to the interviewer—and, of course, in voice-over, as we frequently cut away from the subject to show complementary illustration.

The presenter will also link as voice-over narrator where relevant. However, the majority of the spoken words will come from the key (Company X) people, not the presenter; the presenter's role in the main body of the programme is as visual and verbal representative of the audience, probing and encouraging responses from the subjects. Each subject will be interviewed separately, although we may well see two or more of the subjects working together in cutaway shots. The interviews will not be conducted in offices, but in interesting and emotive locations connected with each subject's core construction project. It may be possible to shoot the interviews in more than one place, as is demonstrated below in the description of the opening sequence.

The core construction projects will be secondary to the main subject matter, but will act as a highly relevant underlying 'storyline' through the programme. It is difficult to be more specific on the precise direction of the storyline until such time as the core projects have been allocated. If it were possible to find *one core project common to all subjects*, the underlying storyline can be made that much more powerful; however, separate projects with a strong common denominator, e.g. a city centre development or an edge-of-town shopping centre and business park, etc., will provide us with suitable continuity. Naturally we will leave the storyline much of the time, both visually and verbally, to emphasize the vast spread of (Company X) activities. The storyline will not be explained in any detail, as to do so will detract from the subjects' input. But it will be made obvious in a subliminal way, to underscore the powerful team spirit of the company and also the wide range of professions and disciplines that (Company X) must orchestrate successfully.

Through the use of good lighting and camera techniques, we will create an atmosphere of creativity, visually dramatizing the storyline, the key (Company X) people, and also the warmth and solidity of (Company X) products—the buildings the company creates.

Now, here is an abbreviated version of the script that was developed from the treatment.

Script

The programme opens on a close-up of our presenter. At this point we notice that he is wearing something on his head, but we can't make out what it is. He begins speaking ...

> PRESENTER: You know, it's strange how some people still have the old-fashioned view that the construction industry is about digging holes in the ground.

> The camera pulls back slowly, now revealing the presenter in full length. He is wearing a work jacket, a hard hat, green rubber boots, and is leaning on a shovel. The camera continues to pull back as he speaks, showing us that the presenter is on a building site ...

> PRESENTER: The truth, is that construction today is one of the most sophisticated combinations of engineering, management, technology and design in our industrialized world.

He releases the shovel, which is left standing upright in the ground. He takes off his work jacket to reveal a smart suit underneath, and rests the jacket on the handle of the shovel. The camera continues on its slow journey backwards, pulling out all the time to reveal that the presenter is standing not just on a building site, but on a *huge* site. One or more (Company X) signs are clearly visible. Towards the end of the sequence, we can only see him as a small figure surrounded by a massive structure, machinery, etc. There is no one else around. He continues his monologue ...

> PRESENTER: In an industry worth around 40 billion pounds in the UK alone, there is one construction organization which emerges head and shoulders above the others as leaders in helping to create our heritage of the future. Through its world-acclaimed methods of construction management, this company has turned building, into high-tech *creation* ... constructing the environment in which the business of working and living will be done for a long time to come. This involves everything from ...

He grins and rubs his hands together ...

> PRESENTER: ... working the ground, to generating the vision of tomorrow's landscapes. Civil engineering, technology and equipment are essential tools.

A Range Rover drives up to the presenter and stops. As he is about to get in, he says his final words.

> *PRESENTER:* But the most important asset of this company is the vital link between its tools, and its outstanding achievements of the past hundred-odd years. The company, is (Company X); and the vital link, is (Company X) people.

He gets into the Range Rover and it drives off. We then dissolve from this very wide, long shot of the site, to a similar shot ... but this time the site is fully populated. The presenter goes on to state a few introductory facts about (Company X), out of vision, and we see the opening titles over a fast-moving montage sequence of action shots, illustrating the speed, scale and quality of (Company X) projects ...

> *PRESENTER:* (Company X) Construction began in London, in 1885; today it's the largest company of its kind in the UK, and the fifth largest in the world. As part of the giant (XYZ) Group, (Company X) now accounts for more than one-third of the entire group's turnover and profits; by far its largest autonomous profit provider. With its unique approach to the industry, including the fee management system it introduced back in 1927, (Company X) has left the competition standing. In London alone, (Company X) projects account for an average of 65 per cent of all construction at any one time. The rest is divided among *all* its competitors.

The next shot is of the presenter in the Range Rover, touring around London. With him is another man, of whom we catch glimpses but do not see in full view. They are having a conversation about a number of buildings we examine, including the (name) building and (name), and the unidentified man explains his own personal experience over a number of years of working on the projects involved, at various different levels. He also touches on the fact that (Company X) is involved in 65 per cent of all construction projects in London ... and that's just one practical example of the massive market lead (Company X) has in the UK. At the end of the sequence we see the man in full view, and he comments that he is now a Divisional Managing Director of (Company X); (name of person).

We cut to a general view of (name) and the presenter introduces us to it.

> *PRESENTER:* (name), London; one of the largest developments of its kind, with luxury residential accommodation, small business premises, a hotel,

restaurants, and a number of other leisure amenities. Here, (Company X) combined quality and speed of construction to new heights ... just six months from the granting of planning permission to the topping out of over twenty floors in the (name of building). (Name of person), now Divisional Managing Director of (X) division, has been with (Company X) for over thirty years.

Then, we see the Range Rover drive up, and the first subject emerges from it.

We now continue with (name of person)'s interview, touching on the following topics:

> (Etc.)

(Final interviewee) should speak about career structure and progression in general terms, with any specifics related to his own career rather than to anyone's. This will then provide us with the cue we need to move on to the next module, which is about career structure, training, development and rewards. This will consist of an interesting and tightly edited mixture of graphics and live action, including some general shots of the four interviewees going about their business, with the presenter narrating out of vision ...

> *PRESENTER:* New (Company X) people can enter the organization at a number of different levels. The main management routes are production management, financial management, planning, and engineering, although there are many parallel routes of equal interest.

Captions here should show the following areas: sales and marketing, corporate finance, human relations, personnel, legal, purchasing, estimating.

> *PRESENTER:* From the day a new (Company X) person joins, there is a strong emphasis on continuing education and career development right the way up to the top echelons of management. (Company X) sponsors a number of building and civil engineering places in many British universities, including (names of six). And there are similar sponsorship schemes at a number of UK Polytechnics including (name) and (name). (Company X) also runs one of the most comprehensive staff development programmes in the industry, with over a hundred external courses available for trainees of all disciplines. All levels of management are also offered external training in a number

of subjects. And there's sharp focus on in-house training, too.

Here we show some general views of the training facility at (name), with students on an induction course (mocked up?) being addressed by the Personnel Services management team.

> *PRESENTER:* Internal induction and training takes place at the (Company X) training centre in (name), conducted by the Personnel Services team led by (Company X) director (name).

We show an establishing shot of (name).

> *PRESENTER:* This team also monitors the career development of all (Company X) people, directs the large range of staff benefits, and ensures that the many ancillary benefits—like preventative medicine programmes and screening—are used to their best advantage.

We now go into a short interview with (name), who outlines the aspects of training, induction and career development he feels are appropriate. During this section we can cut away to illustrative examples of what (name) says, including some sort of visual representation of (Company X)'s part in the community, the efforts it makes and the awards it has won in the area of caring for disabled people, etc. These shots should be interspersed among dynamic action shots of our four original interviewees, to show the two extremes. At the end of the interview we show a final selection of cutaways as mentioned above, as the presenter links ...

> *PRESENTER:* One of the greatest strengths of (Company X) people is that they *care* about their success and that of their projects and clients; this can only stem from an organization that cares for every employee's welfare. Caring, both personal and corporate, paves the way ahead for both personal and corporate *success.*

This then leads us to show the more 'human' face of (Company X), but now back into the professional/operational arena. So, to bring the main body of the programme to a close, we see (name of first interviewee) getting into the Range Rover and the vehicle drives off. This forms the last sequence in the montage leading from the career structure/training/ rewards module.

We then cut to the exterior of one of the restaurants (Company X) has constructed at (name). It is in the evening, and a number of people are walking into the dining room (or other appropriate action as determined by the Director). Our presenter walks into shot, accompanied by a woman whom we assume is his wife. He looks at the camera, and concludes the programme . . .

> *PRESENTER:* However much (Company X) has led the construction industry into the space age, the company never forgets that buildings are created *for* people, *by* people. (Company X) isn't just about construction; it's about nurturing, creating, and caring for the quality of life we've got, and the quality of life—both old and new—that we pass on to our children. The buildings (Company X) people create, will last a lot longer than we do. And (Company X) people thrive on the responsibility they have to everyone who works, lives, *and* (GESTICULATES AROUND RESTAURANT) relaxes in those buildings . . . like in the (name) restaurant here, which (Company X) constructed as part of the massive (name) project.

The four key (Company X) people who have been our subjects earlier on, now walk into shot. They are accompanied by spouses. The presenter greets them, and they all move towards their table in the restaurant (or other appropriate action as determined by the Director). As they do so, the presenter turns to camera for the last time . . .

> *PRESENTER:* (Company X) is playing a very large part in constructing *our* future . . . and helping to do the same for a number of other countries all over the world. (Company X) people are people who *care* about that future, and who devote themselves to it with energy, enthusiasm, professionalism, and enjoyment. It's not hard to see why (Company X) itself, and the numbers of (Company X) people, are growing so fast.

He turns away from the camera, and the group sits down at the table (or other appropriate action as determined by the Director). We superimpose the closing titles, over a very fast visual montage of reprises from earlier sections of the programme. As this is an image programme rather than a training film, it is not necessary for the presenter to 'sum up'; it's better to end the programme with a strong visual impression, a few captions superimposed if relevant, and some uplifting music.

Dramatization is a useful technique in recruitment programmes, provided that you're careful not to create characters that in any way insult or patronize the audience. In the following excerpt from a script for a quasi-government body trying to recruit graduates, drama was used to bring home to viewers how the body's seemingly bureaucratic and distant work was closely related to the average person in the street. A fuller background on this particular project appears in Chapter 4.

....

1 INTERIOR, SITTING ROOM OF STUDENTS' FLAT   DAY

....

We open the programme in the sitting room of a typical students' flat. The room is comfortably furnished, though some of the chairs are a little threadbare and the other furniture has seen better days. Everywhere we see the accoutrements of student life; books, ring binders, files, an ageing typewriter, plus scarves, jackets, woollen gloves, and an assortment of dirty mugs, empty crisp packets, and other rubbish. Obviously, no one here has a lot of time for domesticity.

There are three students in the room, sipping steaming coffee, lolling on the sofa and chairs, relaxing at the end of the day. They are Peter, Melanie, and Nerys. There is also a fourth student in the room; John. But he, unlike the others, is busily at work, going through papers and scattering them about him in untidy piles. Occasionally, he takes a calculator in his hand and punches figures into it, busily scribbling information from it on to a notepad. He glances up from time to time, seeming slightly irritated at the others' lethargy.

JOHN: (LOOKING UP AT THE OTHERS) It's alright for some. Aren't you going to contribute *anything* to rag week?

PETER: (IN WEST COUNTRY ACCENT) Next week, John. Next week. Right now I'm looking forward to a weekend down where I belong.

JOHN: Wandering around Portsmouth harbour by moonlight, I suppose. Gazing at the ships and pondering the mysteries of the sea. Very romantic. While I'm here, working all hours to raise money for charity.

NERYS: (IN WELSH ACCENT) Oh, stop nagging, John. We're all having a tough term. I haven't seen my Mum in ages. And I've got the queues to look forward to on the Severn Bridge tomorrow.

PETER: (CHUCKLING) Well, your car is perfectly suited to slow traffic. Only does ten miles an hour downhill, doesn't it?

> Melanie looks depressed, and is still silent. The two young
> men chatter on. Nerys turns to Melanie, looking concerned.

NERYS: (QUIETLY, SO THE TWO MEN CAN'T HEAR) Are you alright,
love? Worried about your exams?

MELANIE: (LOOKING WORRIED) Not just that. I've been called up to
the hospital on Saturday.

NERYS: What for? Surely it's not about your broken arm. That was
months ago.

MELANIE: No. It's the Well Women Clinic. They think I should have a
smear test. You know, to check for, er, abnormalities. (WITH AN EDGE
OF PANIC TO HER VOICE) It's becoming more common among women
our age. Oh, why does the Health Service have to scare me like this?

NERYS: Thank Heavens for the Health Service! Screening women. Catch
it early, if you've got any trouble. I wish *every* National Health authority
called women in for testing ... mind you, I expect they will soon, now
there's been so much in the press about it. (CHEERFULLY) But there's
nothing wrong with you! You'll see.

> The conversation returns to all four once again.

JOHN: (TAPPING HARD AT HIS CALCULATOR, THEN PEERING AT IT)
Four thousand seven hundred and sixty-two ... that's the target to beat,
folks. And that was up nearly eight hunded on the year before. (TO
OTHERS) Think we can improve on that this year?

NERYS: On what?

JOHN: Four thousand seven hundred and sixty-two. Pounds. Raised for
charity in last year's rag week. Not bad, was it?

PETER: Very good for a small town. But with you running things, we
should double that this year.

JOHN: Yes, well we'll need to get moving next week. Once you're all
back from your weekends off ... (HE GLARES MEANINGFULLY AT THE
OTHERS)

MELANIE: Where does the money go, John?

JOHN: Oh, a selection of local and national charities. Changes every
year.

PETER: Think of the millions and millions that get raised for charity each
year. I wonder who checks it all out? How it's spent?

NERYS: Oh, the Government, I suppose.

MELANIE: Well I certainly hope *somebody* does it. Someone we can count on to get the *real* facts. Make sure everyone's getting value for money, in return for what they collect. I should think we need that for other public spending too. You know, a watchdog.

NERYS: That would be fascinating work, wouldn't it? Being a watchdog for the nation's money. Getting behind the scenes and finding out what *really* matters. I'd like to see them check our roads. See if the fortune they spend on them gives value for money. They never seem to repair the pot holes in Cardiff.

PETER: You can certainly feel *all* the pot holes in that car of yours. Each and every one. (HE LAUGHS)

JOHN: Just like the holes in your boat, Peter. (THEY ALL LAUGH) Hard to tell if you're rowing or swimming. (BECOMING SERIOUS) Stick the box on, would you, someone? Should be time for the news.

> Peter languidly leans forward and switches on the small, colour television set. As it bursts into life, we see Black Rod approaching the door to the House of Commons, at the State Opening of Parliament. The four students stop chatting, and watch. The camera zooms in until their television screen fills our full frame, and we mix through to actual footage of the Opening of Parliament as Black Rod hits the doors of the House of Commons, after they are shut in his face.

(The next section introduced the body concerned in a documentary style, with the narrator stating the main facts over library footage of Parliament plus graphics, etc., to back up the information.)

(Then there were a couple of very short interview clips with a Parliamentarian, and the head of the body concerned, both underlining the importance of the body's role, and briefly outlining what that is.)

(Next, the narrator linked as follows, over introductory footage of the case histories that were to ensue.)

NARRATOR: It's easy to imagine that the activities of the (body concerned)—interesting though they are—consist largely of paperwork, and take place behind a desk. But, this is *not* always the case.

Money is spent in order to achieve things. And to check out how well things are achieved, the (name) must frequently *see*, for itself, what happens on the ground. Money spending programmes directly affect members of the public.

And if you must audit spending on social services or the health service, for example, you've got to get out and see for yourself *how* the unemployed, the elderly and the sick are actually benefiting.

6 EXTERIOR, SUBURBAN STREET   DAY

We now move into the case studies section of the programme. We begin, by returning to our students' home. They are outside the building, loading up their vehicles in preparation for their weekend journeys. We watch as Nerys puts her case into a dilapidated old car: Peter packs the bags on his motorcycle; and Melanie gets into a taxi which we assume is about to take her to the railway station. John, still clutching a notepad, stands outside the building to see them off. It is obvious that he is not going anywhere.

7 EXTERIORS, SEVERN BRIDGE, AND INTERVIEWS 3/4   DAY

We see a variety of shots of Nerys in her car, approaching the Severn Bridge, waiting in a queue, paying the toll, etc. Over this, we hear from one or two (name) staff members—preferably young assistant auditors (who refer frequently to their superiors). These people should be within one or two years of joining, and should of course be graduates. These (name) staff members should be members of the team which carried out the report on the Severn Bridge, and should describe the story to us briefly and in a conversational style. They will be responding to questions and guidance from an interviewer, so will be unscripted.

Also through skilled interviewing techniques, it will be possible to bring out in the interviews the occasional reference to working conditions, training, and prospects for promotion within the body concerned. These will be described later in the programme in the graduate recruitment module; but passing references, in conversation and in context with the case study concerned, will serve to bring the points home in a subtle way.

Now and again we will show the interviewees in vision, talking to the off-camera interviewer, as well as showing any relevant stills and/or documentation that accompanied the study. Combined with this, we will keep cutting back to Nerys in her car, to retain the feeling of identification with and relevance to an ordinary member of the public. Any 'gaps' left in the telling of the story can be filled in by links from the narrator: however, it is not possible to script these until the interviews have been conducted and edited. In this way, we can be sure that the story will be told accurately.

(The following two case studies were conducted in the same way.)

10 INTERIOR STUDENTS' FLAT, AND INTERVIEWS 9/10   DAY

For our final case study, we return to the students' flat as our linking device. John, the only one of the flatmates to stay behind, is busily at work on preparations for Rag Week. Right now, he is going through correspondence from the various charities to which the proceeds from the week are due to go. As we listen to and watch the interviews (and narration as necessary)—conducted, once again, in the same way as before—we are aware that John is studying the charities' literature. He also makes a telephone call or two, discussing the events of the following week with colleagues, and also discussing the funds to be raised. This case study is, of course, that of the Charities' Commission.

11 INTERIOR STUDENTS' FLAT   EVENING

John is still busy, working on the administration of Rag Week. The time is Sunday evening, and one by one the other flatmates have reappeared, ready to begin another week. We see a few exterior shots of the other three arriving, then bustling into the flat laden with carrier bags of food and clean washing from home.

JOHN: (LOOKING AROUND AT THE OTHERS, WHO HAVE MADE THEMSELVES YET MORE STEAMING COFFEE) Good weekend, was it?

PETER: Wonderful. I feel at peace with the world again.

JOHN: How did you get on, Melanie?

MELANIE: Get on? Oh. (BLUSHING SLIGHTLY) I didn't realize you knew. It's all okay. It was just routine. Apparently they're calling up all women my age in the area. They said the result would be through soon—but I'm as fit as a fiddle, they reckon. I'm not to worry about it. (SHE SMILES AT THE OTHERS)

NERYS: See! I told you. The Health Service really does care about preventative medicine. I'll bet I get called in for a test soon, too.

MELANIE: Expect you will. And you're right; the Health Service really *is* getting its sums right these days.

JOHN: (EMERGING FROM BEHIND A LARGE PILE OF PAPERS AND NOTEPADS) Oh, by the way. Talking of sums. Do you remember what we were saying on Thursday night? About how somebody should be checking on public spending?

PETER: Yes. An independent body who can find the real facts and report them.

JOHN: Well, I did a bit of digging over the weekend. There *is* an independent body like that. And they're recruiting graduates, provided they come up to expectations.

> Nerys and Melanie both perk up.

NERYS: Really? Who are they?

> John pulls some (name) graduate recruitment brochures out from under the large pile of papers, and places them on a low coffee table. The camera zooms in to show a full frame image of the cover of the first brochure.

(There now followed an optional module that described training and career progression with the body concerned.)

....

13 EXTERIOR AND INTERIOR OFFICES OF THE BODY CONCERNED   DAY
....

> The following section *can* run straight on from Scene 11, or it can run after Scene 12, depending on which version is being used.

> We see a following shot, beginning with the full exterior of the building, then travelling in through the main doors and culminating in the reception area. As the camera travels in, we are aware of a young man sitting or standing in a suitable place.

NARRATOR: The (name) ... the taxpayers' watchdog ... guardian of public expenditure ... monitoring and investigating *thirty* per cent of Britain's gross national product. Accounting to Parliament ... and serving the entire nation ... *this* is the (name).

> The camera zooms in on the young man we have already noticed: he is John, one of the four students. We see him go to the desk, sign in, and then be met by a senior (name) representative. We end on a tight shot of the (name) logo in the reception area. We then 'freeze frame', and superimpose the closing titles.

Chapter 11

The short promotional programme

This category of programme is perhaps wrongly named (although usually this is how it is known in our business). It would be better known as the short demonstration programme because, in my experience, and in that of a number of other professional corporate scriptwriters I know, the vast majority of such programmes are used for demonstration purposes.

In many ways they are similar to sales programmes, in that they show how a product or process works in the best possible light. The obvious difference is that they are short—no longer than five minutes or so—and this is because the 'promo' programme is normally used for one very specific category of audience: a moving one. That breaks down into two subgroups: people watching the programmes in a store or shop, and people watching them on a stand at an exhibition.

For these reasons, there are a few important points to remember when you are writing for promo programmes.

Firstly, the fact that the audience is transient means you need to grab their attention and hold it for as long as you can. But even three minutes is quite a long time for people to stand around watching a TV screen. So it is a good idea, particularly if the programme is to be shown at an exhibition where your competitors are also shouting for attention, to keep the name of the product/service/company in prominent view at intervals throughout the programme. In this case you need to 'brand' the promo programme rather more than you would need to do for a corporate or sales programme which is to be watched by a seated audience. This can be achieved either through some sort of graphic device, which is up on the screen for all or most of the time, or through regular glimpses of the product's packaging, or through mentioning the name in the narration or dialogue. But beware the audio track . . . and this leads on to the next point.

Invariably, promo programmes are played back on some form of continuous loop tape, or are recorded over and over again on three- or four-hour video cassettes. This way, as soon as the programme finishes there is a short pause, then it begins again, and so on, so that the use of one tape can allow the programme to be shown forty or fifty times. Human nature being what it is, staff working on the exhibition stand or in the department of the store in question become heartily sick of the same soundtrack being played over and over again, and often sneak over to the playback machine when the supervisor isn't looking and turn the sound down. Most managers will deny that this happens, but the number of times I have watched people do it (and not always to one of my programmes, either!) has convinced me that this can be a serious problem.

In fairness, if you or I were to work for eight hours or so with the same soundtrack running continuously within loud earshot, we would probably be tempted to do the same. No matter how good a programme is, the novelty wears off after you have heard its soundtrack eighty-four times in one day.

In addition to this, there is also the point that at exhibitions and in stores there is usually a lot of ambient noise, so even if the programme's soundtrack is at full volume it is still competing with other sounds for the audience's attention.

There is an obvious solution to the problem, defeatist though it sounds, and that is to ensure that the programme is written and produced so that it can, if necessary, get the message over on the strength of the visuals alone.

Both main points mentioned above affect your choice of style and approach when writing for promo programmes. The fact that the audience is transient means programmes must be memorable but simple; complicated, dramatized sequences will not grab attention, and will require too much of the precious time to get the message across. Similarly, wide establishing shots or factory views have far less meaning; interviews will not necessarily be perceived in context; and anything surreal or 'arty' will be lost, unless it is highly relevant to the subject matter. The fact that there is a good chance the soundtrack will be turned off altogether, or at least will be competing with ambient noise, means that you are restricted to an approach which is visually led. So, what is effective?

This is obviously a subjective question, and to a great extent you must judge the answer for yourself. In theory, the whole range of styles and approaches is available to you, and the restrictions I suggest above are only the result of my personal opinion and experience. If you are to write a short promo programme, it is a good idea to take a trip round your nearest shopping centre (large department stores are the most fruitful) and watch some of the promo programmes on display. Also, if possible, attend an exhibition or two. Then ask yourself which of the programmes you have seen not only attracted your attention and made you stop to watch, but also made it abundantly clear to you what the message was, in spite of the din of ambient noise and other distractions.

My feeling is you will find that the best programmes are simple, clear and uncluttered, inviting the viewer to watch on and identify strongly with the message, and showing close and well-shot sequences of the product or process in question. The promotional stand at an exhibition or store is *not* the place for the whistles and bells of the rock video, or for the glitzy but often vague and emotive glamour of the TV commercial. Even promo programmes about cosmetics should not be written as long TV commercials. Viewers at cosmetics counters don't want to see exotic sequences of svelte 20-year-old models on beaches; they want to see how a particular product is best applied to a face not unlike their own. When they watch the TV commercial they are likely to be at home doing the ironing, so the models on the beach will allow them the opportunity to fantasize for 30 seconds and hopefully remember the feeling (and the name of the product) next time they're in a department store. But when they're actually at the counter, dressed up and out on a shopping trip, they're in the mood to contemplate a purchase—not trying to escape from the drudgery of real life while wrestling with a pile of crumpled clothing.

Promo programmes should be without gimmicks, and should focus viewers' attention on the product or process very quickly, very effectively, and very thoroughly. Naturally, in the few minutes you have before the viewer walks on, you don't have the time to expand on the technical widgets or the intrinsic exponential factors. Those are best left to the sales programme, if they're relevant to the audience. Here, we can take a leaf out of the advertising book and say that promo programmes should concentrate on the *benefits* of a product or process, not the features. And in case you're not aware of the difference, features are what a product or process is, and benefits are what the product or process does for the person who uses it. As suggested elsewhere in this book, viewers must be regarded as utterly selfish, and will only be interested in your programme if it focuses on 'what's in it for them'.

In the following examples—from a series of twelve programmes that were written for the kitchenware section of a major High Street retailer, shown as promos in the department concerned—I focused not just on what the product or products were, but showed the benefits of using them and/or buying them as gifts. They were all very nicely shot with good lighting at close angles, so you could see clearly not only what they were but what they did. The style was straight demonstration (documentary) with the minimum of frills. Once these programmes were made and running in the stores, I called in from time to time to see them. Surprisingly, I didn't find the sound turned down once; and each time a number of customers were watching the screen with interest. I also understand that the resulting sales of the products concerned were very encouraging, so it is reasonable to assume that the approach was successful.

The first focused on the benefits of economical, healthy and easy cooking using a pressure cooker.

> (Name and department) logo.

> Tight shot of pressure cooker, gently hissing on hob. We hear a woman's voice, humming contentedly. Quick cutaway to a wall clock, which shows 6:55.

NARRATOR: How *do* busy people manage without a pressure cooker? Modern, safe, quiet pressure cookers like this save so much precious time and money, they could be worth their weight in gold. And here at the (Name and department), you can invest in one of many pressure cookers; a small investment in really big help for your family meals.

> Graphics and live action to illustrate method. (Show automatic model.)

NARRATOR: Pressure cookers work by cooking with steam. You simply put your food, with some liquid, in place; bring the pressure cooker to boiling point, then reduce the heat for a short time. Some cookers even tell you when it's time to lower the temperature. Using the locked in pressure of high-temperature steam heat, food cooks much faster and better—sealing in all the goodness and vitamins, in a fraction of the time it takes with other methods.

> Show examples . . .

NARRATOR: Soups that would ordinarily take an hour, are done in just 8 minutes in a pressure cooker. Beef casserole is juicy, tender and beautifully cooked in only 20 minutes; in the oven, it would take two hours. On almost any dish, you can save up to 75 per cent on time—and costly energy as well.

> Brisket beef being taken from freezer and placed in pressure cooker. Wipe to suggest passage of time, then cooked dish being decanted into serving bowl.

NARRATOR: It's not just with fresh food that cooking times are greatly reduced. Food straight from the freezer can be tastily cooked in a pressure cooker; two pounds of brisket beef, frozen solid, takes just one hour to be tender and delicious. Any other cooking method would take two and a half hours.

> Show crisp, colourful vegetables being taken out of pressure cooker.

NARRATOR: Pressure cooking really is healthier, too. With all the goodness locked in by the steam heat, you can cook fresh, wholesome foods in less time than it takes to heat up a convenience package.

> Show whole meal being prepared, then served from the three compartments.

NARRATOR: And because all the flavours are individually locked in, you can cook entire meals together, in one go. Fish, poultry and most meats take no longer to cook than potatoes and green vegetables; a complete, balanced meal done to a turn, in minutes.

> Tight shot of price label of packaged meat; low price. Then show same meat being served.

NARRATOR: Cheaper cuts of meat are superbly tenderized in pressure cooking; yet another way in which these ingenious cookers save you money.

> Show range shot of food described.

NARRATOR: And there are so many different dishes your pressure cooker can prepare! Apart from meats, fish, poultry and vegetables, you can turn your hand just as easily to many other creative ideas. Jams, preserves, chutneys, pâtés, soups and desserts are all made simply and easily, in a fraction of the time. The choice is yours; creative cookery has never been healthier, tastier, or more economical.

> Range shot of pressure cookers and spares. Woman can be heard humming again.

NARRATOR: Modern pressure cooking is one of the safest, fastest ways for busy people to make tasty, healthy meals. And you'll find a large range of economically priced pressure cookers, plus all the spare parts and accessories you'll ever need, here—at the (Name and department).

> (Name and department) logo.

The next programme was about quite a large range of products from all over the world. Obviously with so many products and only a short time, there was no room for expansion about what you could do with each one. So, I created a culinary travelogue, and emphasized the scope and variety of the range.

(Name and department) logo.

General music. Globe turning.

NARRATOR: There's a whole *world* of exciting cookery equipment and gifts, here at the (Name and department).

Dissolve to crabbing shot of boxed products.

NARRATOR: From the far corners of the globe, (Name) have gathered together a delightful range of products to give your cookery a delicious foreign flavour. And if you're looking for something really different to give to friends and family, these are gifts that will be treasured for a lifetime.

Chinese music and props. Show products.

NARRATOR: From the exotic Orient, there's an amazing selection of Chinese woks and accessories, for quick, easy stir-frying and lots of other recipes. There are Tempuras, from Japan, with all the accessories you need along with a huge selection of dishes and utensils to create a truly Oriental occasion.

Indian music (sitar) and props. Show products laid out; boxes in shot.

NARRATOR: India is our next stop. A five-piece chapati set is the ideal accompaniment to many meals. And a complete Tandoori oven lets you cook a range of spicy, savoury delicacies in the traditional Indian way.

Italian music (Neapolitan folk songs or light opera) and props. Show product range, ending on wine carafe and coffee cup.

NARRATOR: Travelling west, we arrive in sunny Italy ... home of the pastas and pizzas that are everyone's favourites! Here at the (department) there's everything you need to bring some tasty Italian sunshine into your home; even for your robust Italian wine and rich cappuccino (PRONOUNCED CAPOOCHINO) coffee.

Austrian style folk music (accordion) and props. Show fondue sets and accessories.

NARRATOR: A brief journey north, and we're in the breath-taking Alps. Rediscover the healthy, bracing mountain air and delicious flavours of the fondue, with these comprehensive fondue sets and accessories. Perfect for parties with a true Alpine atmosphere.

General music. Dissolve through stills of countries concerned, then show relevant product in each case.

NARRATOR: And there are lots more treasures from afar, at the (department). A quick hop over to France, and you can try your hand at sweet or savoury crêpes. Down to the Iberic peninsula, and you can bring back sunny memories with a Spanish paella set ... or marvel at the rich taste of food cooked in a Portuguese Cataplana. From across the warm Mediterranean, more exotic treats can be cooked in a Moroccan Tajure. And for another jet-setting journey, we can fly west to Mexico ... and create some spicy treats with a real Taco set.

> General crabbing shot of whole product range. Prop with flags of countries concerned.

NARRATOR: Foreign cookery is fun, creative, and so delicious! And for tasty gifts that everyone will love, there's nothing more original. Every item comes neatly boxed, with full instructions. There's everything you need for creative cookery and gifts from around the world—right here, at the (Name and department).

> (Name and department) logo.

The next example was selling two somewhat unusual products; equipment for smoking your own food, and for making sausages. As these products were so out of the ordinary, I had to sell the concept and the methodology rather than the hardware, showing viewers how to use the kit, and what the end results were like.

> (Name and department) logo.

> Selection of prepared smoked dishes—expensive food.

NARRATOR: There's nothing quite as delicious as a lovely piece of smoked salmon ... or tasty smoked meat.

> Dissolve to someone smoking food in kitchen (or outdoors).

NARRATOR: And now, thanks to the (Name and department), you can smoke your own food, at home.

> C/U Smokit kit.

NARRATOR: Smoking your own food, with this compact, easy-to-use Smokit box, is really easy.

> Pull back to include leaflet in shot.

NARRATOR: All the instructions you'll need are enclosed with the pack.

> Open leaflet to show recipes.

NARRATOR: And smoking food at home opens up a great many

possibilities to save money, and create appetizing new recipes of your own.

Selection of home-smoked foods.

NARRATOR: Hot-smoked foods, like these, retain most of their vitamins and minerals for extra goodness.

Cheap food being placed in smoker. Herbs and spices in shot.

NARRATOR: And you can experiment with herbs and spices for superb new flavours; not only with the more expensive meats and fish but also with economical foods.

Show finished products emerging from smoker.

NARRATOR: The smoking process—plus your own creative imagination—can turn the most modest meats and fish into tasty delicacies.

Cut to sausages being removed from smoker.

NARRATOR: Smoked sausages, for example, can be truly mouth-watering. And because there's everything for creative cookery at the (Name and department), you can even buy all you need to *make* your own sausages, too!

Show bought packet sausages.

NARRATOR: The sausages you buy in the shops are often expensive for what they are.

C/U on contents label; fat, additives, etc.

NARRATOR: And apart from the fact that they can contain a lot of fat and additives . . .

Dissolve to shot of home-made sausages.

NARRATOR: . . . they can never be as special—or delicious—as your own creations.

Show selection of sausages and raw ingredients, plus kit.

NARRATOR: Making sausages at home is so easy! With this simple kit, you can create sausages of many different sizes; fresh, wholesome and full of nutritious goodness. And you're by no means restricted just to meat; you can use vegetables, nuts, and even fruit, as well as fish and poultry.

Show sausage-making process.

NARRATOR: All you do is prepare your ingredients, then load the correct quantity in one end of the machine. At the other end, you place the sausage casing—made of hygienic, safe protein material. Now you just operate the lever so your sausage casing fills, then detach your finished sausage. And it's ready for cooking, smoking or freezing, straight away.

> Show selection of products in sausage-making kit, plus main book.

NARRATOR: Needless to say, the (Name) Sausage-making Kit contains everything you need to start you off—including a large selection of mixers and seasonings. The leaflet tells you how to make basic sausages. And there is also a comprehensive book that includes dozens of different recipes.

> Quad split of stills showing barbecue, party, bonfire, etc.

NARRATOR: Creating your own sausages—and smoking food—at home is fun, healthy and economical.

> Range shot of both sausage-making and smoking kits.

NARRATOR: It's a perfect family treat for barbecues, bonfire night parties, Christmas and birthdays, or just any time you want a tasty, wholesome meal. And there's everything you need to create your own delicious sausages, and smoke your own food, here—at the (Name and department).

> (Name and department) logo.

The last example was for the company's chocolate-making range of products. Here again, in order to sell the products I had to sell the concept and the methodology. But with such photogenic and visually attractive material, this was an easy job! I attended the shoot for this programme, and watching the company's food experts prepare the sweets and chocolates made me want to roll up my sleeves and have a go. I gather the finished programme had a similar effect on customers, and the range sold very successfully.

> The programme opens with a crabbing shot of made-up chocolates in commercial boxes, and on plates.

> Dissolve to shot of customer in sweet shop, handing over a £5 note.

NARRATOR: Beautiful, delicious chocolates make wonderful gifts ... and a lovely treat for your family. But buying them, can be expensive; and a little bit impersonal, too.

Cut to shot of woman, in own kitchen, setting out finished chocolates on worktop.

Warp dissolve to graphics animation of range design and logo.

NARRATOR: It's so much nicer to use your skills at creative cookery—to make your own, with '(Name) Chocolate Making Range!'

Mix through graphics back to woman in kitchen.
Tight shots on chocolates.

NARRATOR: Think of the pleasure you can give, and the money you can save. And home sweet-making is very simple, and great fun—as well as being economical.

Shots of simple chocolates, made up and being prepared.

Show moulds being turned out.

NARRATOR: If you like you can start on the really easy, one-colour, one-flavour chocolates, with the professional touch—using moulds.

Shots of various different types of fillings and fondants, being prepared. Some in shot are already made up, as are a selection of items for wrapping and packing.

NARRATOR: Then you can progress to more creative sweet-making with cream, fruit and nut centres, liqueur and other flavours. It's all made simple and straightforward, with everything you need right here at the (Name and department).

Shots of chocolate buttons in packs; then being melted in double boiler, slow cooker, and microwave oven.

NARRATOR: The method is very easy. First, you melt your chocolate—available in three flavours as chocolate buttons. You can use a double boiler, a slow cooker, or a microwave oven; the choice is yours.

Tight shot of chocolate being 'painted' into mould. Quick cuts of different shapes (HOLD). Quarter-screen window over previous shot (HELD) of shapes on fancy cake.

NARRATOR: Then, you paint the chocolate directly into moulds. There are lots of different shapes here at the (department): numbers, animals, letters, classic chocolate shapes, and even mice! And by the way, these shapes are perfect for making fancy cake decorations, too.

Woman takes moulds out of fridge, puts fillings in, and 'paints' final coat of chocolate on.

NARRATOR: Once the moulds are set ... just by putting them in the fridge for a short time ... you then choose your filling, put it in, and finish off with a final coat of chocolate.

Cut to range shots of flavours, fillings, fondants, etc.

Woman puts fillings into finished moulded shapes.

NARRATOR: Within the (Name) range, you can make your selection from a wide range of flavours and types of fillings.

Woman prepares fresh fruit and nuts.

NARRATOR: And, you can use your creative talents to develop your own ... like fresh fruit, nuts, dates, and many other delicious ideas!

Show fresh fruit, nuts and fondants being dipped in melted chocolate.

NARRATOR: If you prefer, you can dip your prepared centres in the melted chocolate. This gives you natural, bon-bon shapes.

Crabbing shots of range. End on kits.

NARRATOR: All the tools and ingredients you'll ever need are available right here, in the (Name and department). You can pick individual items from the range, or choose one of our all-inclusive kits, with prices starting at less than five pounds. They make great gifts, too!

Tight shot of pretty box; hands open it, to display ribbon, inner papers, etc.

NARRATOR: And so you can give your chocolate-making a professional finishing touch, we've included a comprehensive range of packaging.

Pull back to show range of packaging, including some assembled with chocolates in place. Also show some in silver and china dishes.

NARRATOR: With all you need here, you can make your chocolates into beautiful gifts that could have come from the finest shop in town.

Cut to woman wrapping chocolates and putting them in a box. Then she writes a card by hand: 'To Gran, with love from Janet'.

NARRATOR: But there'll be two important differences. First, they'll have cost a fraction of the price. And second, they'll be gifts with a priceless quality ... personally made by you, for someone very special.

Range shot of special occasion packaging and cards.

> Include child's gift—and show animal shapes being
> wrapped and inserted into box.

NARRATOR: Chocolates are perfect for so many gift occasions . . .
Mother's Day, Easter, Christmas, birthdays, and lots more.

> Previous shot ends on one pack, with card written out 'To
> Jack and Maureen, with love from the Simpsons'. Then,
> warp dissolve through to exact same pack being opened
> on elegant dinner table. SFX conversation and music.

NARRATOR: And what better gift can you give to your hostess, when you
go visiting . . . or, to say a really special thank you?

> Crabbing shot of range.

NARRATOR: So make a start today, with the (Name) Chocolate Making
Range.

> Warp dissolve to graphics animation of chocolate-making
> range design and logo.

NARRATOR: It's fun, simple, and very economical. And, as always, you'll
find everything you need for creative cookery . . .

> Horizontal cross wipe to (Name and department) logo.

NARRATOR: . . . here at the (Name and department).

Chapter 12

Interviews: the voice of the people?

In any kind of documentary programme, interviews can be a very useful tool to create variety and added interest.

Michael Barratt is one of the UK's most experienced newsreaders, broadcasters and interviewers, and now employs his skills in the corporate TV field as well. He is a firm believer in the effectiveness of interviews:

> I think they're probably the most effective way I know of putting across the facts about controversial issues. If the interviewer is playing a sort of devil's advocate role, it is somehow a very effective way of getting the positive answers across that you want.

> There's something, too, about the interview, that gives more variety—visual variety. There are two heads to look at, there are cuts in the camera shot and all that sort of thing, some kind of rapport developing between the two which helps the communication process. Pieces to camera—straight pieces—will be often stilted as well, whereas the fact of a conversation developing helps the understanding.

From a psychological point of view, no matter how cynical viewers of a programme may believe they are, properly conducted interviews or interview clips have a ring of truth about them and viewers find them believable. And this is for good reason. A natural, unscripted and unrehearsed interview comes largely from the heart, and viewers know this; but some programme makers attempt to script interview responses so interviewees say 'the right things'. Apart from making the interview look ridiculous, this is downright dishonest. No matter how nervous interviewees are, you will never make them less nervous by asking them to read out answers to interview questions. And no matter how well an interviewee reads the script, even if you use a trained actor, a scripted response sounds scripted; it's likely to be too good, too perfect, without the natural 'ums' and 'ers' and pauses people use in unrehearsed speech. All that you achieve with this is a Mickey Mouse performance which convinces no one of anything other than the fatuity of your whole programme.

Michael Barratt agrees:

> I believe for any interview to work it must be truly ad lib, it must be
> thought through, worked on—you've got to do a lot of homework—and it
> is very, very hard work. But, if you rehearse the actual words, you'll find
> that when you come on to do the job, a question will be asked, and the
> chairman in setting out to answer will suddenly stop and think: 'Have I
> just said that to him?' or 'Was that in the rehearsal before?' The other
> danger in the rehearsal of that kind is that he will say to himself: 'Now, I
> put this rather well in rehearsal, let me try and repeat that', and he will
> fail to repeat it.

So, interviews must be real. And if you're Sir Robin Day or a Dimbleby,
interviewing anybody from the office cleaner to the Prime Minister is no
problem. For the rest of us, this isn't always so.

In a corporate context, the politics of interviews are likely to get in the
way of a good result if you're not careful. If you interview someone much
more senior than yourself, you may be tempted to be too formal, too
hesitant, and just a bit grovelling . . . it's hard to pressurize the person
who signs your salary cheques. If you interview subordinates, the
responses you get to your questions may be what the interviewees think
you want to hear, rather than the naked truth. And the whole process
may scare the pants off them, too, which hardly makes for
natural-looking and sounding interview clips; very nervous interviewees
talk in squeaky voices and look as if the cameraman has a sawn-off
shotgun aimed at their kneecaps just out of the viewfinder frame.

For these reasons it is sometimes wise to get someone else to do interviews
for you; preferably someone who is not a company employee, who doesn't
depend on the interviewee for more than a day's fee, and who can chat up
factory floor workers without reminding them of that bonus you might
award them next week. But if you can't get someone else, or don't want
to, take heart; good interviewing techniques can be learned and can be
used without affecting your future place on the Board or your extra
chocolate biscuit with morning coffee.

Types of interview

Interviews can be used to achieve a number of jobs within a programme.
They can be used to break up long sections of information which are hard
to illustrate visually, rather than doing the whole lot with captions and
narration or one presenter frantically trying to keep viewers' attention.
They can be used to emphasize points, endorse policy, resolve negative

issues, and many more useful purposes. Let's look at the main types in detail.

The endorsement from the top

This is the type of interview where the chairman or other senior figure endorses the message being put over by the programme, and encourages the troups to do whatever it is they're supposed to do. High-level endorsements are fine provided that they don't take over from the main body of the programme, that they don't go on for too long, and that the senior figure comes over as a real human being—not Robocop reading a teleprompter. The trouble with interviewing senior people is that they are likely to be very busy, or at least the people directly under them will tell you that they are very busy. This leads on to a request for a script for the very busy person to read to camera, because very busy people are far too very busy to think about what they're supposed to be saying beforehand. Usually, you'll find that this is nonsense. In my work I'm often led to believe that the chairman or managing director of the given company is a venom-spitting ogre, and perhaps that's true in 1 per cent of cases. The rest of them, when I'm finally allowed into the inner sanctum, turn out to be nice, normal, logical people who fully understand the need to speak naturally and well in an interview, and allow enough time to do everything properly.

Michael Barratt recounts this experience:

> I was doing a conference for a very, very well known firm, on a stage, audience of 300 sales reps. This guy came on and I put the first question to him about what did he have to say about the year that had just gone by? And he said, above all else, what a splendid bunch of people he had, they were a wonderful team, and he went on for about twenty seconds. And I interrupted and said: 'That's enough of the bullshit, can we get down to the real facts of the case?' Now the roof came off. And the reason the roof came off was because everybody suddenly relaxed, all the tension had gone out of what the managing director was saying, and suddenly here was me representing them, being able to use that sort of language. He smiled—he knew it was part of a game, of course, but it meant that from then on as it developed I was seen to be being convinced by him, and being persuaded by him and what he was saying. So that at the very end of the interview when he announced that for the year ahead they'd got a new product that he thought was going to go through the roof, there was I accepting that. And because of the attitude I'd taken in the first place, that was much more convincing to the audience.

If you're an in-company interviewer, though, the path to the top person may be riddled with political booby traps. All sorts of individuals who have the chairman's ear guard their privileged positions with fiendish ferocity. If you're not one of them, you've got to use all your political skills to hop over the booby traps and see the person you want to interview in plenty of time to have a relaxed chat about the project. This way, you not only stand the best chance of conducting the interview the way you want to, but you also avoid the Chinese whispers syndrome. That's where you tell someone you want the chairman to give an interview on the new incentive scheme, and by the time the message has worked its way up the grapevine to the man or woman in person, he or she thinks you want to do an interview about hiring a Swedish masseuse to work in the company gym.

Picking up a telephone may sound a little obvious, but it can be a useful alternative. Realistically, you may not have the time or opportunity to see the person before you do the interview, especially if you're in two different cities or countries. Even so, don't rely on letters or telephone conversations with secretaries; phone the person direct. If he or she is out, ask when he or she will be available to receive a call, and then keep trying until you're successful. Direct personal contact saves a lot of hassle in the long run.

The key to getting good senior endorsement interviews is time; allow plenty of time to work your politics, somehow get through the barrage of his or her lieutenants, and discuss what you want to do with the person concerned. Once the two of you understand each other, the road to the interview ahead is clear.

The oil on troubled waters

This one needs very careful handling if it isn't to bring the house down in hysterical laughter or create a mass walkout of the audience. Programmes are sometimes made when there has been a major problem in a company —like redundancies or a potentially unpopular relocation announcement. Sometimes, too, certain programmes—particularly training or motivational programmes—have to get over cynicism or hostility among viewers, while at the same time selling the good news very hard. Often there is one particular sector of the audience that is likely to take a negative view. In any of these instances, it's very useful to include an interview with someone who is easily identified as representative of the cynical/hostile/negative view, but who essentially sees the good side and can express it. This is far more convincing than saying it through 'voice of God' narration or a presenter whom everyone knows is saying it simply because he or she is paid to.

Whereas the key to successful senior endorsement interviews is time, the

key to troubled waters interviews is honesty. It's no good picking on a
person who is, or appears to be, a paid puppet. If your interview is going
to work you have to get someone who is known to be his or her own
person without any vested interest in making nice noises. When you
approach that person, don't lie; make sure he or she knows that you're
aware of the real problem on both sides, and that the programme is
genuinely trying to solve it. Don't make suggestions as to how the
questions should be answered or try to put words in the person's
mouth—they'll only be spat out, all over you. When the time comes for
the interview, let that person answer your questions in a natural
way—don't use pressure. And let the interviewee say his or her piece,
warts and all. Honesty in addressing viewers' real or perceived
problems—even if it means the interviewee saying how totally unfair the
new bonus plan was thought to be—can only strengthen the argument
when the interviewee goes on to say how he or she subsequently
discovered that the plan wasn't so unfair after all.

Michael Barratt believes that this sort of interview should be tackled
head-on:

> One of the key things here—absolutely crucial if the whole exercise is
> not to backfire on you terribly—is to make sure you do not avoid the
> embarrassing issue. Because if you do, you'll finish up with the audience
> going away, or into the bar, or going home or wherever, and saying, 'well
> that was alright, but you notice they deliberately missed out so-and-so'.
> And all that's left is the bad taste in the mouth because of the issue you've
> avoided.
>
> So it's very important to bring that out—it's like leeching almost—but get
> it out into the open and air it. And most times—in my experience—having
> done that you will find it's not all that difficult to tackle the problem. It
> clears the air wonderfully, and you have therefore achieved credibility
> and trust, and all those things you're striving for.

Although I agree with Michael Barratt that addressing the issue head-on
is by far the best approach in an ideal world, there are times when for
political or other reasons it just isn't possible. However, there is a more
subtle way of doing it. That is, to use an interview with someone who is
known to be from a cynical or hostile group, to talk about something else
... something other than the problem.

This then becomes a cross between the troubled waters interview and the
senior endorsement. Let's say you're introducing a new training scheme in
your company. Previous training schemes have been met with a
resounding raspberry on the part of staff who feel, with some justification,

that the old schemes were irrelevant, out of date, and participation in the schemes robbed staff of overtime potential. The new scheme, however, has addressed all those problems and is genuinely good news. Although the trade unions have been noisily underwhelmed by the previous schemes, they have been involved with the new scheme from the start, endorse it, and have even helped to develop it. You interview a senior trade union figure—not the one the lads snigger about in the gents because he wears a toupee—one whom they genuinely like and respect. But instead of getting the union person to talk about how useless the old schemes were and how good this one is, you simply get the person to describe the new scheme—or one aspect of it—in a normal, factual manner. This way, the very presence of a union figure in the programme tells viewers that the unions must be in favour of the new scheme ... without any controversial issues being discussed.

The technical wizard

Real experts, interviewed in order to describe a process, piece of equipment, etc., can be a lot more interesting to viewers than a narrated graphics or live action sequence describing the same thing. Provided they are genuinely enthusiastic about the brass widget in question, experts can bring it alive in a way that no one else can—especially if they have been involved in its development from the start and regard it as their own little brain-child. Technical wizards can also be used to demonstrate the brass widget in all its glory, giving a running commentary as they do so, in a way that comes across far more genuinely than if it's done by a professional presenter whom the audience knows has never seen the thing before.

There is only one potential problem with technical wizards, and that is their technical wizardry. Their idea of a simplified explanation might be perfectly understandable to final year astrophysics students, but to an audience of salespeople it's about as understandable as Arabic backwards. In the main, a very thorough briefing on the audience's true level of comprehension will make sure the technical wizard keeps it simple. But beware the odd one who slips back into his or her native gobbledegook, having forgotten that the audience only wants to know how it works, not the square root of its exponential uprating factor. Careful and firm interviewing technique is required here, and through asking the right questions at the right time a good interviewer can keep nudging this type of technical wizard back on course at the first hint of untranslatable jargon.

The sparkling salesperson

Sparkling salespeople sometimes give interviewers a nasty surprise. I have found that the big, ebullient, extroverted non-stop talker who is the life and soul of the sales conference dinner dance often turns into a shrivelled, monosyllabic mouse when faced with the cold eye of the camera and the director yelling 'action'. The reverse is often true, too; shy, mousy types in real life can turn into eloquent, precise and well-spoken interviewees on camera.

Michael Barratt's experience is similar:

> In my own profession of television, we often find someone—perhaps a journalist, a Fleet Street journalist—who looks good, is forceable, has a good use of language, all that sort of thing, brash, extrovert, etc. etc. But put him in front of a camera, or put him on a stage in front of an audience and he just collapses on you.

> So to find the person for the job in-house, you've actually got to do a proper audition. You really have got to set them in a situation which is finding out whether they are able to cope with talking to an audience, or in front of a camera, or whatever it might be. You get a lot of surprises, and you are most likely to find that the best performer is the quietest, most introverted, and shyest person on your staff.

Why these sudden personality changes take place is hard to tell. But there is something very clinical, very sobering, about trying to convey your thoughts to an unknown interviewer with a small piece of glass and a strange crew of people and equipment peering at you over his or her shoulder, when you're used to communicating face-to-face with a live punter. Sparkling salespeople of the extroverted type depend very heavily on exuberant body language to get their messages across. Once you rob them of the chance to leap about and wave their arms (the camera exaggerates gestures like these even further, and the finished programme looks like a video nasty), it tends to have a deflating effect. Also, salespeople are often closet actors, who can perform only when in their usual environment with their usual props. Take them out of that environment, take away the props, and they fluff their lines.

Having said all this, though, sparkling salespeople are very useful as interviewees in corporate programmes—provided that you do *not* ask them to sell what they normally sell for a living. In other words, you do not ask them to try to recreate their selling role in an unfamiliar and faintly hostile environment; you ask them to drop the role and be interviewed as ordinary human beings. This way, they can add a great deal to a programme in terms of motivating other members of the sales force, describing their work for a recruitment or induction programme, demonstrating a new order-processing system to other members of staff, etc.

The happy customer

Customer endorsements or testimonials are very popular in corporate programmes, especially where there is a marketing or sales message to be put over. There's nothing like expressing a strong corporate statement which is then backed up by a few customers or clients nodding in agreement like those dogs you see in the back windows of people's cars. But, as with testimonials in the advertising world, there are drawbacks. Viewers are not idiots, and the fact that it is illegal to stage false testimonials (in the advertising world, at least) does not obscure their view that you're hardly going to interview hostile customers who want to tell everyone that your product or service is a pile of manure. So beware of the straight endorsement; no matter how genuinely enthusiastic your customer interviewee might be, viewers will tend to be cynical about it.

The way to make customer endorsements stick is to be subtle. Don't ask customers to give an interview about what they think of a given product or service; ask them to describe a process they utilize that just happens to use one or more of your products or systems or metal boxes or backhoe loaders, etc. You can even create a whole programme around your product's role in customers' businesses: Bloggs Backhoe Loaders at Work in Industry. As I intimated above, never ask the direct question 'What do you think of Bloggs backhoe loaders?', because even if the response is positive, you will get groans of cynicism from your viewers. Ask questions about the jobs the backhoe loaders do for the customer: how long they've had the machine; why they needed a backhoe loader (not yours, but the generic) in the first place; etc. These questions will elicit positive replies that sound natural, and endorse your product in an indirect way. Even if you don't ask any questions about backhoe loaders at all—let's say the programme or programme section is just about the customer's business operation—the very fact that your product is seen in use, making a valuable contribution, is an endorsement in itself.

The factory floor factor

One of the main pitfalls with interviews with factory floor people is the intimidation factor, as suggested above. If these are conducted by an in-house person, particularly if he or she is 'management', there is bound to be a certain amount of nervous tension present in the interviewee even before the camera starts to roll. In this case, perhaps more than any other, it is far better to employ an outside interviewer who has no company profile and is perceived as a neutral party. But if there is no alternative and the interview must be conducted by an in-company person, careful preparation work is needed.

Michael Barratt has this to say about factory floor interviews:

> The first thing is that the guy on the shop floor has got to trust the middle management guy. If there isn't that trust then he'll never get anywhere. So that's really quite a big thing to be asking in the first place. If there is that sort of trust, then the management man needs to talk to him beforehand and say 'look, we're doing this piece for this purpose, we're going to use it in the following way'. He really must be honest about that and straight about it and spell it out exactly so the guy knows he's not going to be misused for devious management purposes. And he must then be given a total and absolute assurance that whatever he says, however critical it may be, will have no effect on his job, and he won't finish up getting rapped for it or sacked for it or anything like that. He really must be absolutely assured of that.
>
> Then you've got to work on the man, as you have to work on anybody, to get him at his ease. Doing that depends on each individual and the kind of people they are. Some people are very nervous, some people are less so, but you need to know your man—you need to get him at his ease. Maybe the first question needs to be very simple or jokey almost, to put him at his ease. You've just got to work on him as you would in any other circumstances.

Factory floor interviews are very useful, especially in large organizations, for in-company communication programmes. They help to balance programmes that would otherwise appear rather management-heavy, and they also help viewers to feel part of the team—particularly when the various divisions and departments of a company are scattered all over a country or continent and there is little or no contact among them. These interviews can be used to put over employees' views on a specific issue like a new training scheme or incentive plan, or they can be used for general motivational purposes.

As with the oil on troubled waters interview, you need to pick your interviewees carefully. You'll often find that politics creep in here, and the head of department or personnel manager will want you to interview specific people for the wrong reasons. Whether you're an in-company person or not, you must be very firm in choosing the people yourself, for the right reasons—i.e. that they're articulate talkers and have something to say that's original and interesting, not repeating company policy like caged budgerigars.

Street interviews and vox pops

These interviews end up as very short clips—perhaps one or two sentences or less—and are usually used to create a mood, perhaps at the beginning or end of a programme, or as a link between main sections. Although the sections you select in the edit are going to be very short, the actual interview you do might be quite long by comparison. I find that in order to get some good, succinct lines from an interviewee, you often need to ask the questions in full first (you discard the full replies in the edit) and then ask each interviewee to summarize what he or she has just said. That way, interviewees will have had a little time to think about what they're saying, and will often come up with a nice, crisp response. With the first question you ask on each topic, no matter how much you stress the fact that you want the answer to be short, you'll find that people usually drag their replies out too far.

You also need to think on your feet with this type of interview, rather more than you do in other types. A prepared list of set questions is fine as a guideline, but to get snappy answers you'll find you often need to grab hold of something that has just been half suggested or said and press the interviewee on that particular subject. For this reason, quite a lot of interviewing skill is required.

Michael Barratt agrees:

> Well, they could be tackled by an amateur, except that he's got to understand that to get half a dozen vox pops, he's got to interview thirty or forty people—possibly more. Because in the street or wherever, going round a factory, you just don't get people giving you immediately exactly what you want. You've got to work at it. And you perhaps record quite long pieces from people, and take out a word—that's one of the techniques of the vox pop, is just to take out the word; 'smashing', 'great', 'awful', or whatever, just as a single word—which gives pace to the way you cut the thing together, and gives it a lift, and then you go to somebody else who you take a couple of sentences from. But to get what you want—and this I say, if you want six people in this vox pop, you've got to interview thirty or forty people, at least.

The secret of successful vox pops is some very sharp editing. But if you know what you're looking for, and you think on your feet as you're interviewing, you can usually guide interviewees through your questions, towards giving the sort of answer your programme needs.

AV and audio interviews

Many people in industry, and even in production companies and in-house production units, don't consider using interviews in AV or audio programmes. They feel that because there is no 'lip sync' (in other words you can't watch people's lips move as they speak) you shouldn't include interviews in an AV soundtrack.

I believe that this is nonsense, and have created a number of very effective AV and audio soundtracks using interviews. In some cases, entire programmes have consisted of interview clips and nothing else—no narration at all. As I said in Chapter 1, one of the things I always tell scriptwriting workshop participants is to think of AV as illustrated radio, and audio programmes as having the same scope as radio. And as you know, interviews work perfectly well on radio programmes.

Unless your whole soundtrack is to consist of a variety of interview clips, isolated interviews should be flagged up somehow. If there is also narration, the narrator can announce the interviewee. In the case of AV, another way is to show a selection of stills of the interviewee as his or her voice is playing on the soundtrack, and place a caption over the stills stating the person's name and rank. If the interview clip is quite long, don't keep the person's face in view too long; cut away, as you do with videotape, to other illustrative material and return to the mugshot every now and again.

Audio interviews are easier to organize because you don't have to trail around with a large crew and lots of cumbersome equipment—just a sound engineer, tape recorder, and one or two decent microphones. Contrary to what you might believe, I find that interviewees are just as nervous—if they're going to be nervous—of audio interviews as they are of the on-camera type. So you must go through the same motions of warm-up and discard question (see below) as you would with a videotape version. Another helpful tip is to make sure the engineer and tape recorder are located behind the interviewee, out of his or her sight. This is useful for two reasons: (1) the interviewee is not faced with an unfamiliar person and unfamiliar machines while he or she is answering your questions; (2) if there is a technical problem requiring a stop in the interview, the engineer can signal to you unbeknown to the interviewee. This way, you can bring the interview to a halt at a natural pause.

Live interviews on stage
These are very difficult to do well unless you are a trained, professional interviewer. Some companies and producers get the idea that in order to create a change of pace, it's better to interview the chairman at the annual sales conference than it is to have him or her stand at a lectern and make a conventional speech. However, the same problems of hierarchical and political positions apply here as they do in the case of endorsement from

the top interviews—only now, because they are live and cannot be spruced up by some editing, you really do run a serious risk of making the whole thing look like a well-rehearsed puppet show.

Interviewers like Michael Barratt can get away with a certain amount of pre-planned *bonhomie* when interviewing a senior company figure, as he said in his example above:

> ... And I interrupted and said: 'That's enough of the bullshit, can we get down to the real facts of the case?' Now the roof came off. And the reason the roof came off was because everybody suddenly relaxed, all the tension had gone out of what the managing director was saying ...

However, the truth is that for an in-company interviewer to speak to a senior figure like this, even if he or she is more senior than the interviewee, would normally be seen as politically undesirable. As a result, most on-stage interviews conducted by in-house people appear to be dull, predictable and sycophantic. With videotape or AV, the fact of the message being conveyed through an artificial medium distances viewers enough for them to believe that the interview is realistic and natural. In addition, the similarity in style to broadcast TV, where interviews usually come across as reasonably credible, benefits the credibility of the corporate interview. Put the interview on stage, though, where the audience can see the whole thing, warts and all, and you'll find it very difficult to make it look and sound natural. Careful preparation—*note*: preparation rather than rehearsal—on the part of the interviewee and the interviewer can help. This is Michael Barratt's thinking:

> In a live interview the advice is—as it is in so much else—it is simply 'work at it, work and work and work'. When I do training of people, after I lecture them, I then do some interviews which we record and play back. They expect my criticisms to be reasonably sophisticated, but they hardly ever are. I would say that, nine times out of ten, I say to people 'you are not working hard enough'.

> The great danger is that people look at television, for example, and they're watching pro's, and pro's make it look easy, that's their job. And if somebody comes to me and says 'Mike, you love it in that studio, don't you? You're absolutely in seventh heaven'. They don't know it but they're paying me a very high compliment, they're really saying to me, 'you worked your butt off to do that programme, to make it like that'. And that's what everybody's fundamentally got to do; work and work, think and think.

On-camera and off-camera interviews

These are not so much categories of interview as they are different techniques. An on-camera interview is where you can see and hear the interviewer ask the questions, as well as the interviewee responding. Normally, in the corporate context you will only be using one camera, but for variety and interest you will need to enhance the interview by shooting a number of different angles, adding in 'noddies' and, sometimes, cutaways as well. This means shooting some sections of the interview twice or even three times. First of all you will shoot the whole interview right through, with the camera pointing over the interviewer's shoulder straight at the interviewee. Then, you might shoot some of the questions and answers again in a wide two-shot (where you see both interviewer and interviewee together from a side view). Then you'll shoot the interviewer's questions with the camera pointing at the interviewer this time, and finally you'll shoot a short section of tape of interviewee and interviewer in turn, 'listening' to the other's words and nodding in comprehension, concern, or whatever. Hence the term 'noddies'. If you don't do all this and just shoot the interview straight from one angle, it is going to look exceptionally boring. And if there are sections you want to remove in the edit, you're going to be very hard-pushed to do the cuts without making the interviewee look like a gibbering automaton. A good variety of shots means that in the edit you can make a cut in the interviewee's response (easy to do on the soundtrack only), and cover it, say, with a shot of the interviewer doing a 'noddy'. Moving around from a wide two-shot to a close-up of the interviewee to a noddy of the interviewer and so on, keeps up the visual interest of an interview without detracting from the verbal content.

For shorter interviews, or for interviews where there isn't a lot of time (shooting all the different angles of a proper on-camera interview can take a couple of hours or more), you're better off using the off-camera technique. This is also useful if the interviewer is inexperienced or doesn't look very handsome on camera. Basically, it means that the interviewer is not seen or heard on the final version; all you have are short sections of the interviewee talking. There are two important points to remember here.

The first point is that the interviewee should be told *not* to answer questions directly, but to make his or her responses as positive statements. That means no responses beginning with 'Yes' or 'No', no reference to the interviewer (e.g. 'as you know, Donald') and no direct dialogue between the two. Obviously, a good interviewer will know how to phrase questions so that the answers come out in the right way—see below.

The other point is that you, as interviewer, must not clutter up the soundtrack with any speech. That means that you ask your question and then keep quiet. You should never prompt an interviewee with words like 'really', 'I see', 'quite so', or anything else, whether the interview is on or off camera. But with the off-camera interview it is essential, as a strange unseen second voice creeping into the interviewee's statements is very distracting to viewers. When you're doing an off-camera interview, it's worth warning your interviewee that you will not be responding with monosyllables as people tend to do in normal conversation. If they're not warned, they can find it a bit off-putting. What you can do, however, is to encourage the interviewee by nodding, smiling and using other facial expressions as encouragement.

Setting the scene

Preparing your questions

The questions you prepare before doing an interview should be not so much questions, as a list of fairly thorough bullet points. And although you can play around with the order of the interview in the edit after you've shot it, it's preferable to put your 'questions' in the order in which the final interview should flow.

What you need to do is analyse first of all the person whom you're going to interview and the contribution he or she is capable of making, as against the information, views or opinions you would like the interviewee to put across. Let us suppose that you're making a retail staff recruitment programme for a large chain of stores, and you're to include an interview with a typical store manager. First of all, form your analysis of the person and his or her potential contribution:

1 Experienced store manager; knows what's expected of store staff, and the types which are most successful.
2 Has good experience of customers and what they expect from staff.
3 Has worked his or her way up through the management hierarchy, but started at the bottom as a sales assistant.
4 Is a good leader, and encourages staff to go on training courses and seek promotion.
5 Is an ambitious person him or herself, and is likely to come across in 'management speak' rather than in the terms potential store staff will identify with.

Then, look at what you want to get out of the interview:

6 The viewpoint of someone who is 'management', but still works at the sharp end dealing with customers.

7 How it feels to have started from the bottom and worked up to store manager level.

8 The opportunities for career progression within the stores.

9 The qualities needed by store staff if they are to be successful.

Here, then are the bullet points you develop out of those points, in a logical flow.

- Description of how he or she started, and how his or her career progressed.
- What sort of training he or she had.
- Why he or she chose to work towards being a manager.
- What it is that makes a good sales assistant.
- What the customer expects from sales assistants.
- What advice he or she would give to anyone thinking of joining the company as a sales assistant.

We know that the interviewee concerned is very experienced and competent, but if left to his or her own devices is likely to aim the answers at the senior managers who will see the programme—to get noticed—rather than talk in terms the main target audience will appreciate. So what we do here is to prepare 'questions' that will ensure that the interviewee makes a contribution that's valid for potential sales assistants. Posing questions about the person's own career progression will impress the audience, because of the obvious success that's possible from a similar starting point. The answers about what makes a good sales assistant and what the customer expects are likely to elicit 'management-speak', but in this case that's acceptable because we want the audience to know that the standards are high. Finally, the advice the interviewee could give the audience is probably going to come from the heart; people love to give advice, and in this instance statements about it being good fun but hard work are probably true (good for the audience) and likely to impress senior managers favourably (good for the interviewee's promotion prospects).

How you should actually phrase those questions is dealt with later in the chapter. Once you become more experienced at interviewing, you'll probably find you choose not to convert those bullet points into questions but use them as guidelines only. That way, especially if the interviewee knows you're not reading the questions out but ad libbing them, the whole interview will sound much more natural. I never 'script' my questions for that reason; I try to conduct interviews more as guided conversations, using the bullet points to remind me how to do the guiding.

Michael Barratt agrees:

A good interview should be a conversation. It should not be a case of somebody coming with a list of questions, asking the first one; totally ignoring the answer, and striding on into question 2. And so, I always say that the art of interviewing, just as the art of being interviewed, is fundamentally about listening, rather than about talking. You've got to listen with a total intensity to what the guy is saying. And then couch your second question in a way that indicates that you have heard what he's said, you have taken on board what he's said, and that your question flows from that. So that it's an intelligent conversation. Very, very important, that is.

Listening is considered in more detail later. Meanwhile, another good reason for leaving the questions loose is that sometimes interviewees will pre-empt your next question, or answer a question that's well down on your list, in connection with the answer to an earlier question. If this happens, you have to do some fast revision of your question list if the interview is to continue running smoothly. Also, if you're counting heavily on the questions and the interviewee upsets the apple cart, it can unbalance your concentration and rattle your confidence. And remember, in most cases the interviewee is much more nervous than you are, and looks to you for reassurance. There's nothing more nerve-racking for a twitchy interviewee than to find that the interviewer has lost the place and is scrabbling around looking for the next question, muttering and swearing. However, for the inexperienced interviewer fully written questions will, if nothing else, make you feel more confident . . . so for your first few interviewing experiences, it's worth taking the chance that you may have to re-order your thoughts in a hurry.

The warm-up

This is where you meet your interviewee shortly before the interview is done. You may or may not have met the person before; if you have, the following advice may not be quite so important, but you should go through the same motions all the same—if in shortened form.

There is one golden rule about interviewing, in the corporate context, which every interviewer must have inscribed on his or her heart. Here it is.

From the time you first begin the warm-up, through the interview, until you and the interviewee part company:

THE INTERVIEWEE IS THE MOST INTERESTING AND IMPORTANT PERSON IN YOUR ENTIRE LIFE.

There is also a secondary clause to that golden rule which is almost as important:

The interviewee must BELIEVE that he or she is the most interesting and important person in your life. Therefore,

YOU MUST BELIEVE IT TOO.

This means you concentrate on the interviewee ... you listen attentively to everything that is said ... you hang on his or her every word ... and become that person's greatest fan. There are very few people in the world totally devoid of an ego; even the most apparently reticent interviewee will eventually warm to genuine, heartfelt attention.

If you have prepared a formal list of questions (not necessarily a good idea, see above), you should never show this or read it out to the interviewee, no matter how much (or by whom) you are pressurized to do so. If you do—in effect 'rehearsing' the interview—you open yourself up to potential problems in the interview itself. To begin with, if your interviewee has already responded to the questions, he or she will not answer spontaneously when you come to do it for real. Secondly, you run the risk of the interviewee responding with lines like 'as I said earlier', or 'as you know', etc., which will come out as nonsense in the final programme. So the answer is to talk *about* the questions ... just outline the subjects you will be touching on, and discuss with him or her the general idea of the responses needed. This way there will be no nasty surprises in the interview itself, but at the same time you will retain a healthy level of spontaneity.

If your interview is to be 'off-camera' (see above) you should tell your interviewee not to answer any of your questions with a 'yes' or a 'no'. Now, obviously you will structure your questions so that a 'yes' or 'no' is never called for (see below), but some interviewees will start with a 'yes' anyway, out of nerves or to give themselves a beat before answering. That's why it's important to impress on them that they should answer in statements, and explain why—that your questions will be cut out of the programme.

Another point to impress upon the interviewee during the warm-up is that he or she should always look at you at all times, not at the camera. Again, explain why—interviews are conversations between interviewer and interviewee, and the camera—representing the viewers—is just an eavesdropper. If the interviewee glances at the camera and then back at you, it makes him or her look shifty, and confuses the viewer—even if it is an off-camera interview. For the same reasons, if you're doing an on-camera interview and it's your turn in front of the lens, always look at your interviewee (or at the wall where the interviewee would be—see 'noddies' below) when you're asking the questions. You only look at the camera if you are doing an introduction or a closing piece.

One of the most important points of the warm-up, especially when this is the first time you've ever met the interviewee, is for you and that person to establish a good rapport. Naturally you'll need to talk about the interview, so that your interviewee knows what to expect. But once you have accomplished that, it's a good idea to *stop* talking about the interview and use the remaining time to get to know the interviewee as a person. Remember, he or she is the most important person in your life at that moment, so don't start telling them about your problems or your pigeon racing or your golf. Ask the interviewee questions about his or her job, hobbies, children, local area, or anything that gets a response without, obviously, intruding on private matters. A friendly chat like this certainly helps to break the ice and, provided that you're a good conversationalist, will make the interviewee feel that he or she knows you quite well (even though you've talked largely about the interviewee, and not about yourself). This helps a lot in making the interview come across in a relaxed and natural manner.

Sometimes you will be obliged to do your warm-up in the place where the interview will be shot. If you can, though, try to keep away from the set-up as, for all but the most experienced interviewees, the sight of a crew of people hauling cables around their ankles, waving heavy lights over their heads, pointing cameras at their faces, shoving a white sheet of paper under their noses ('doing the white balance'—part of the process of adjusting the camera), etc., will have them running for the nearest Valium. Try, if you can, to take the person somewhere quiet and do the warm-up over a cup of coffee, only taking them to the set-up when the crew is just about ready to go. Then, introduce the interviewee to the crew (knowing that all these weird-looking people have names and voices can help lessen the interviewee's tension), and sit him or her down in the correct place to settle in.

If a lapel microphone is being used the interviewee will have to be 'wired up', a job usually done by the sound recordist. Basically this involves clipping the microphone in place and running a wire down through the person's clothing, either directly to the recorder or to a radio transmitter which is attached somewhere at the back of the person's clothing out of sight. Some people find this process a little invasive, but normally you can make a joke about it to smoothe the way.

Another potentially touchy issue is make-up, although for corporate interview purposes you're unlikely to need to go to the expense and trouble of having full professional make-ups done. However, bald patches or sweaty foreheads can gleam like aircraft landing lights when seen through the camera lens, so someone on the crew should provide some translucent compressed powder to cover up the shine. As by this time you should be the person who knows the interviewee best, you're probably the best person to do the business with the compressed powder. I always carry some when I'm doing interviews—and once again, a smile and a joke will help smoothe over any resistance even from the most macho, tattooed, six-foot-six construction worker.

While all this last-minute fiddling is being attended to, you should use the time to explain to the interviewee just what will happen. You should tell him or her what the director will do, and what will be said; here is a rough guide, although obviously this can vary according to the director and the size of the crew. The following is based on a videotape shoot; film will be slightly different, but the difference is of no great significance.

- Director checks that all crew members are ready.
- Director says 'turn over' (this tells the VT recordist to start the tape rolling in the machine).
- VT recordist says 'turning over' or 'running up' (to confirm that he or she has switched the machine on).
- There is a time lag of about ten seconds when there should be absolute silence. This allows the tape, which has started to move in the machine, time to stabilize.
- VT recordist says 'stable', to tell the director that the tape has stabilized.
- Director says 'action'. Now this does not mean you have to leap straight in with your first question—never appear to rush, even if there is a reason to hurry; if you do, it could spook the interviewee. Just smile, say you're going to start, leave a beat (for later editing purposes) and then ask your first question.
- If for any reason there should be a problem in the taping (e.g. the tape cassette runs out or Concorde flies overhead), the director will say 'cut'. You should then chat casually to the interviewee while the problem is being solved. Once it is, you'll go through the same total process again before restarting.

The interview itself

Okay. The director has called 'action', and you're ready to start. The first thing to do—at least this is what I normally do—is to ask a 'discard' question. This is because no matter how experienced and well prepared the interviewee may be, he or she may well still be a bit nervous and unsettled at the beginning. So, you ask a general question (the response to which you don't really need for the final interview) which is then discarded when the tape/film is edited later. Sometimes you might be pleasantly surprised, of course, and find that a very interesting point emerges from the 'discard' question. But make sure that the first question is *not* crucial to the interview.

In the warm-up, you will have told the interviewee not to answer any questions with 'yes' or 'no', especially if the interview is of the off-camera variety. As I mentioned above, some interviewees will reply with a 'yes' even if the question does not beg it; but, in fairness, you must phrase your questions so that a 'yes' or 'no' is not called for in the first place. The key here is to take a tip from newspaper reporters, and start all your questions with words like:

```
... what
... who
... where
... why
... when
... which
... how
```

There is no reason why you shouldn't start the question with a preamble, to give the interviewee a little time to think about the answer, and to encourage or prompt him or her into the subject matter (or angle of the subject matter) you've discussed during the warm-up. Let's say you're interviewing the training manager of a large company about a new in-house training course for retail staff. During the warm-up you've discussed the need for trainees to be motivated by seeing how the training course will benefit them, as well as benefit the customer. If you ask the question straight off, the training manager might revert to management-speak and emphasize the wrong thing, e.g.:

INTERVIEWER: How will the training course benefit your staff?

TRAINING MANAGER: By showing them how to serve the customer better and more effectively. After all, that's what we're in business for.

Not the response you wanted to that particular question. Here's how I would lead the training manager into the question, so that he or she has no doubt as to the response required:

INTERVIEWER: Now obviously, Mr Bloggs, the main objective of the course is to help your staff give better service to the customer. But how exactly will the course benefit the staff themselves?

TRAINING MANAGER: The course will help staff to do their jobs better, which means they get more satisfaction out of helping the customer. And by doing their jobs better, of course, they'll be in a stronger position if they happen to be looking for promotion.

Although a short preamble to the question can ensure you get the response you want, you must avoid anything too lengthy or involved. The total question must focus on one issue. And never ask more than one question at a time; this may seem obvious, but believe me it happens frequently and confuses the interviewee so much that in the end he or she doesn't know whether you've asked about staff benefits or the train times to Manchester Piccadilly. Michael Barratt agrees:

> Well, he's got to ask questions that his interviewee can understand, first. And he's got to ask one question at a time. Now these seem like very simplistic things to say, but they're rarely followed. In my experience, interviewers very often ask long torturous questions, so when he's finally finished, the poor interviewee is having to sort of struggle through all those words and think, 'Well, what was he really asking me?' He may indeed have to say, 'I'm sorry, I don't quite follow', or 'You've asked me three questions there', or whatever it might be. So you ask one question at a time, and you ask the question as succinctly as it is possible to be.

> I often say if I'm being interviewed, and I were given the choice of who was to interview me, I'd go for Robin Day every time. People tend to be surprised by that, because Robin can look fairly fierce, but the great thing about him is, you understand exactly, there is never any doubt whatsoever, what he's asking you. And that makes life easy for the interviewee. So, you've got to be succinct, you've got to use simple words so that there is no doubt about what the question is, and you don't ask more than one question at a time.

Sometimes you will want to build up enthusiasm in your interviewee, so that the response will come over as inspiring and motivating. No matter how much you have prepared the interviewee in the warm-up, usually you will still need to generate enthusiasm in your preamble. Let's suppose you want a shining endorsement of the new training course from the training manager. The wrong way would be as follows:

INTERVIEWER: Why is this course so good?

TRAINING MANAGER: It's good because it has been designed by some of the best retail experts in the United States, and uses all the most modern training techniques.

A little tepid, perhaps? Try this:

INTERVIEWER: (SMILING ENTHUSIASTICALLY) Mr Bloggs, I understand this new course really is revolutionary, and is going to make a tremendous difference to the way staff perform out there with the customer. But, briefly, what would you say makes it so very special?

TRAINING MANAGER: It uses all the new training techniques. They're fantastic—proven by some of the top retail training experts in the States, who designed the course in the first place. It's miles more effective than anything we've done before. Truly outstanding.

There may come a time when an interviewee tries to evade an issue. Usually, you'll have had a hint of that possibility during the warm-up. But sometimes the harsh reality of an active video machine recording the interviewee's words for posterity can make him or her think twice about making a commitment to something that may not necessarily meet with the chairman's approval—or may make him or her look a bit less than perfect. However, you may need a definitive statement to make the programme work for the viewers. If a straight question does not elicit a good response, you should try a pressure question. Let's now return to our interview with the training manager:

INTERVIEWER: Why is this new training course so much better than anything you've done previously?

TRAINING MANAGER: Well, of course, I didn't mean to suggest that previous training courses weren't very good. They were all excellent. It's just that this one is more up to date. You know, it uses more modern techniques.

INTERVIEWER: Of course, I appreciate that, Mr Bloggs. But you did say that this new course is much more effective than anything your company had done before. Now, just why is that?

TRAINING MANAGER: It's more effective, because it's based on customer needs that are right up to date. The whole face of retail has changed a lot in the last few years, and I suppose earlier training courses were based on customer needs that existed a few years ago—rather than those of today and tomorrow. This new course prepares staff not only for customer service now, but for the future as well.

By pressurizing the interviewee a bit, you've allowed him or her to wriggle out of a potentially embarrassing clinch and actually make a very valid point. If you hadn't pushed, though, the previous statement would have been made to look rather silly. In the final edit, you simply cut out the first question and first answer, and if the interview is off-camera, you merely include the interviewee's last response. QED.

Another often necessary job is to return to a question. This may be for a number of reasons: the interviewee's response may not have been very good, or a bit garbled; there might have been a technical problem or a stop half-way through; even things like the fact that the interviewee's nose began to shine during the response. The one thing I believe you shouldn't do, unless the interviewee is very experienced, is to tell him or her that you're going to repeat a question. (If the boot were on the other foot, you'd find this very off-putting.) The answer is to start the next 'take' and then briefly tell the interviewee that there are one or two more questions you would like to ask. If time permits, it's worth starting off with another 'discard' question before you get back to the question you really want to ask, just to get the interviewee rolling again. Then, ask the question, but rephrase it so it sounds different. For example:

(Original question)

INTERVIEWER: How much time and effort do you expect staff to put into this training course?

(Return question)

INTERVIEWER: As I understand it, Mr Bloggs, the company provides all the audio-visual and printed material staff need to complete the course. What personal input do you need from the staff themselves?

Sometimes you'll find that an interviewee will wander off the subject matter at a tangent, into an area that you've either not included in your list of main points, or that you're planning to discuss later. Most inexperienced interviewers will be sorely tempted to interrupt or stop the interviewee. My advice is, don't—for two reasons. One, an interruption, no matter how polite, may well make the interviewee nervous. For this reason alone it's worth letting the person finish his or her thought, and then come back to the main point with a return question (rephrased, as above). The other reason is that although the interviewee may have wandered off the main point, the new information that is given may turn out to be very useful for the final edited material. So don't be in any hurry to stop interviewees; listen carefully to what they say, and respond accordingly.

Once in a while you may find yourself up against an interviewee who either is more experienced at interviews than you think, or suddenly finds fresh confidence and responds to a question in a way that takes you totally by surprise. Some people may say one thing about a particular issue in the warm-up, and then say something completely different in the interview itself. Some might even do it to catch you off your guard. If you get an unforeseen response, whatever you do, don't falter. Remember, as Michael Barratt says (see above), listening carefully to what the interviewee says is probably the most important part of interviewing skills. Listen to the unforeseen response and, if you can, develop the next question out of it. If you can't, move on to the next question on your list, provided that it isn't likely to cover the same ground as the previous response. If that is likely to happen, jump to the next question after that, then go back to the earlier issue with a return question. Although interviewing for corporate purposes isn't as much of a tennis match as a journalistic interview can be, it's still important that you—as the interviewer—appear to keep control of the whole thing. If the interviewee feels you have lost control—whether he or she has given an unforeseen response deliberately or by accident—it will in the end make him or her lose confidence, and the interview won't work.

At the end of some interviews, you may need to pose a summary question or two. This may be for a number of reasons—perhaps you're thinking of producing a shortened version of the main programme for some purpose, or you may have wanted a brief answer to a question you put earlier and received a long-winded response. It could also be that you use the excuse of a summary question to act as a return question, if the first response was a bit garbled or vague. The one thing to remember here is that interviewees aren't stupid; if you just ask them the question without a suitable preamble, they'll probably remember that you've asked them that one before and wonder why you're repeating yourself. So be upfront. Here's how it might work out, using the example of our new training course; first, the wrong way:

> *INTERVIEWER:* So, briefly, what is it that makes this training course so different from previous courses your company has run?

> *TRAINING MANAGER:* Well, we've already covered that point earlier on. I think I outlined the main benefits then.

Wrong! Try this:

> *INTERVIEWER:* Mr Bloggs, earlier on we went into the advantages of the new course in some detail. But very briefly now, in summary, what would you say is the *main* benefit of the new course?

Don't worry, by the way. Although you've asked for one main benefit, in these circumstances you'll almost certainly get more than one, but only the important ones. If you ask for all the main benefits, you'll get a long answer, which at this stage you don't want.

> *TRAINING MANAGER:* The main benefit is that the course is designed to help staff meet the needs of customers both today, and tomorrow. And it helps staff to perform their jobs better, which is good for them—more satisfaction, and better promotion prospects.

Although I touched on 'noddies' earlier in this chapter, it's worth remembering here that you should use facial expressions and encouraging nods throughout the interviewee's responses. For reasons described earlier, you mustn't grunt or comment during responses, because whether the interview is off-camera or not, your musical tones creeping into responses will mess things up in the edit. However, the interviewee must know that you are listening intently to everything that is said, and this you convey by smiling, frowning, looking incredulous, etc. This, of course, doesn't mean that you have to turn into a Marcel Marceau or learn to grimace like those chimpanzees in the teabags commercial—that can be as off-putting as no expression on your face at all. Just react in a normal, albeit mute, manner. And keep your eyes on the interviewee at all times—don't glance over at the director, your watch, the monitor, or whatever. That's not only off-putting, it's also rude. However, you do need to be aware of any activity, like the director or VT recordist waving to signal an impending stop or technical problem. What I do here is use my peripheral vision—easy with a little practice—and I usually manage to keep abreast of almost everything going on around me without taking my eyes off the interviewee's face.

Unless your interview is really dogged by technical hitches or persistent low-flying aircraft, you should attempt to let it flow right through to the end without stopping, and with as few retakes as possible. Even when you use return questions to get a better answer, if you fail, give up gracefully. If you ask a question a third or fourth time you're extremely unlikely to get a better response—normally the best, most spontaneous responses are the first. Going over the same ground will irritate and probably unnerve the interviewee, which hardly provides the right basis for an improved response. So no matter how tempting it is to go on shooting the interview until you 'get it right' (as you might well do with drama or pieces to camera by a professional presenter) try to keep the whole thing fresh, and get it right first time. Here's what Michael Barratt has to say on that subject:

> The problems of recording are many; and one of them is that you become sloppy because you think to yourself, 'this is only a recording, I can do it again if necessary', all that sort of thing, and therefore you do not think with the same sort of intensity that you should give to the interview. You think you can edit, and of course, editing distorts what you're trying to say, and all sorts of other problems arise from that. And if you're going to do six takes at a recording, by the sixth time there is no chance at all that you will be fresh and that the thing will sound in any way spontaneous.
>
> So I'd always go—if possible—for the live thing. I mean, you can't do that

if you're making a video, but if you are making a video, my advice would be to strive to do it in what we call take one, first time, you know, really try to get it right first time. And if there's a fluff, first time around, leave it in, that's what I say. Then people know that it's real and it's genuine.

Editing an interview

Although some people—especially secretaries—think it's a huge bore, you should always begin your editing process on paper, with a full interview transcript. This can be done by dubbing the complete, unedited sound track on to audio cassette or mini cassette, and then giving it to some poor unsuspecting typist who will curse you, but dutifully input it into the word processor.

No matter how pressed you are for time, using a transcript is a lot faster and more convenient in the long run than spooling through all your videotapes trying to make up your mind which response to use where. The typist should be briefed to note down any places where there is a stop, a plane flying overhead, a response that sounds as if the interviewee has a finger up his or her nose, or any unacceptable stuttering or slurring, so you know if a particular passage is usable or not. You then make a preliminary selection from this document.

Of course, when you come to look through the videotapes, you may find that certain parts of your paper selection are unsuitable for whatever reason. Also, remember that it is unwise to suggest the use of half sentences, or to cut short phrases together. (If the interview is audio only, you can sometimes get away with these.) The editing side of sound is easy, but when you're editing pictures as well you must think in terms of reasonably long chunks, otherwise the interviewee will look like Max Headroom. Also remember that you may not be able to make consecutive use of sections that were shot some time apart, as the camera length or angle may have been changed in between times. If the interviewer is in vision (on-camera) then you can paper over these cracks by using a cutaway to a 'noddy', or if you're including cutaway illustrative material you can show some of that to get you from one response section to the next. However, these are all issues you will need to discuss with the post-production team, who will guide you on the suitability of your initial paper selection.

There is a very understandable, though usually erroneous, temptation to select only the sections where the interviewee is making the best, most visually and conversationally perfect noises in the light of corporate policy. But, depending on your audience, this can be counter-productive.

As Michael Barratt says (see above), the odd fluff here and there makes viewers realize that the interview is real, not scripted and rehearsed. Also, in certain circumstances it actually helps to include sections which are not necessarily verbatim quotes from the corporate brochure, as long as they're not too controversial. This makes viewers realize that not only was the interview real, it was also given by an intelligent human being who was speaking from his or her own opinions—not repeating policy like a high-salaried mina bird.

Overall, the key to good interviews within programmes is 'short is beautiful'. Make your initial selection from the transcript, and then see if you can cut it by half—not by halving the sections, necessarily, but by halving the number of sections. Never leave a 'talking head' up on screen for too long—cut away to a 'noddy' from the interviewer if that's relevant, or to some illustrative material, and keep doing it at comfortable intervals throughout the interview.

Very often, in the programme script, there is narration before and after an interview. In broadcast television documentaries, the whole programme's narration is seldom written until after the visual material has been collated and edited. In corporate programmes, though, we are often obliged to write the narration first, so that the script can be approved before shooting begins. Provided that everyone knows what material is to be shown where, draft narration can be written beforehand without too many problems. But when it comes to the links in and out of interviews, it really isn't possible to do this unless the narrator's words are extremely bland and general. To avoid this, you should make a note in the pre-shoot script that narration links will be adjusted after the interviews have been shot and edited. This way, you can write or rewrite the links so that they lead directly into and out of the chosen interview sections—much more interesting and relevant.

Also, you may well use narration to set up questions to each of the responses given in an off-camera interview. This works well, provided that you don't try to pretend that the narrator is actually *asking* the questions directly of the interviewee. That comes over as phoney, because viewers will wonder why the sound of the narrator's voice doesn't change between narrating and interviewing. Viewers may not actually realize *why* that sounds phoney, but it will jar them, if only subsconsciously. Here's how to avoid the problem, by writing the narration in a different way, based on the interviewer's questions (taken from the transcript):

INTERVIEWER'S ORIGINAL QUESTION: Now obviously, Mr Bloggs, the main objective of the course is to help your staff give better service to the customer. But how exactly will the course benefit the staff themselves?

NARRATOR: We asked Joe Bloggs, the company training manager, to tell us just how the new course will benefit the staff themselves . . .

Or, like this:

INTERVIEWER'S ORIGINAL QUESTION: Mr Bloggs, I understand this new course really is revolutionary, and is going to make a tremendous difference to the way staff perform out there with the customer. But briefly, what would you say makes it so very special?

NARRATOR: It's clear that the new course is going to make a tremendous difference to the way in which staff perform—to the undoubted benefit of the customer. But exactly what *is* it that makes the course so special? Joe Bloggs explains . . .

Chapter 13

Writing speeches

Executives, managers and other corporate speakers have a natural tendency to overwrite their material when preparing a speech for a presentation. Often they don't understand the difference between spoken speech and written speech (see Chapter 6) and generate a presentation in exactly the same language as they would use for a company report or business plan. The result is stilted, boring oratory that's extremely two-dimensional. At the same time, because these people often seem to hide behind corporate jargon and 'business-speak', they don't make use of their own personality to bring life and interest into their presentations.

In addition, one of the most common problems you encounter with speeches is that they lack structure—inadequate form, cohesiveness and theme—so that members of the audience do not come away with any particular message afterwards, and feel that the speaker might just as well have been reading out a shopping list.

The first two problems have been dealt with earlier in this book: the principles of using spoken speech and avoiding unnecessary jargon are just as relevant to live presentations given by in-company people as they are to the audio-visual media. However, more about 'corporate-speak' later.

First let's look at the third problem in more depth, as this is probably the most logical place to start.

Structure

Every now and again you will come across a speaker who can get up in front of an audience and deliver a rousing, motivating and interesting speech that is well structured, well balanced and cohesive in message and content. These speakers are rare; in fifteen years of writing speeches I have only met one such person. He was the sales director of a huge organization, and was such a wonderful speaker he could even ad lib a ten-minute piece to camera for a sales training video programme in one take, with no slips or mistakes. While working for him I soon began to wonder why he needed a speechwriter; but he was such a perfectionist that he wanted my input in addition to his own remarkable ability, to make doubly sure that the structure and content of his speeches were effective.

However, as I said, speakers like this are extremely rare. The vast majority of speech-givers—whether they're company staffers, politicians, actors or professional after-dinner speakers—all have to put a great deal of thought and work into their scripts. Rather than re-invent the wheel, I've included a very useful section in this chapter written by John Butman—a fellow scriptwriter from the USA who is one of the top corporate writers there, and a writer whose ability I respect enormously. This is his advice, with which I agree wholeheartedly:

The opening

The old adage about telling the audience what you intend to tell them is another way of stating the importance of locating the audience. You know what you're going to talk about, or at least you should. Your audience doesn't. So the opening needs to attract their attention, and locate them in time, subject and space. This is only polite. It allows the mind to select the proper file, to locate itself, to prepare itself to listen. There is simply no way around the need for a clear opening. You wouldn't approach someone you'd not seen for some time in the street, and simply plunge into whatever topic you had on your mind. Neither should a speechgiver. Have a little sympathy for your audience.

This doesn't mean that the opening must be dull. It should have a bit of humour, a touch of mystery, a personal note. You're attempting, right at the start, to make contact with the audience. You don't want them to sit placidly, performing the role of audience, as the speech is read out—the speaker dutifully peforming the role of speechmaker. A strong opening that makes contact will have a positive effect on the audience. They will join the event. If you fail to make contact at the start, it's very difficult—if not impossible— to make it once you're into the heart of the message.

One speech began like this ...

'Tonight, I'm going to talk about the operating results for the year, the introduction of the new ZX90 CMU ... and the knees of a young boy.'

What? What do the knees of a young boy have to do with the operating results? The effectiveness of this opening was that it accomplished its two tasks so elegantly—it announced the topics to be discussed and made contact, by intriguing the audience. (It turned out that recent corporate fortunes were like the skinned and scraped knees of a young boy in summer—they hurt, but were indications of experience that would help the corporation/boy grow.)

Talk in scenes/tell a story

The principle of chunking—breaking the writing into small units—is as appropriate to speeches as it is to most other types of writing. It's perhaps even more important in a speech—because not only does it focus the attention of the audience on one current thought, but it focuses the attention and energy of the speaker as well. It's best if the scenes are, in general, quite short—2 to 3 minutes long for each scene. You should be able to state the point or key message in one simple sentence.

Each scene should flow into the next. People are extraordinarily logical (although each in his or her own way) and have a natural desire to make connections between one thought and the next. The goal of the speechwriter is to get everyone mentally nodding their heads as each scene rolls by, so that when you reach the final scene, which contains the summary message—it will seem to be the inescapable result of a closely reasoned argument that they've been agreeing with all along.

The flow should really be reducible to a series of simple statements that closely follow your outline. For example, let's suppose that the MD is making a speech to all the employees of a large company. He has some difficult news to deliver. The flow might go like this:

1 We're going to talk today about some exciting new prospects for our company.
2 We know that business today is changing rapidly.
3 We know that the growth of electronics, in particular, has had a major effect on the nature of Component Module Units.
4 This has led us to develop the new ZX90-E CMU which incorporates a special systems element for electronic connections.
5 We are so excited about the potential of the ZX90-E that we have decided to expand into new markets.
6 The most exciting market for the new electronic style Flange Covers happens to be in Southern Greenland.
7 We believe that, by concentrating on the Southern Greenland market, we shall double our growth in the next three years.
8 It we can achieve this goal, we will be in an excellent position to expand, raise salaries and offer profit-sharing opportunities to all employees.

9 That is why we have decided to relocate our corporate headquarters and all manufacturing operations in Southern Greenland.

10 Because you are so important to us, we wanted you to be the first to know about this change.

11 This change of operations does not mean that there will be mandatory redundancies. We would be delighted to move the entire staff to Southern Greenland.

12 Naturally, for those of you who do not wish to relocate we have a generous redundancy scheme.

13 For those of you who can make the move with us, we look forward to a great new period of prosperity and growth.

14 We believe that, in this changing business world, we are making the right move at the right time.

15 Thank you very much.

In short, the hidden agenda here was to break the bad news that the company is moving to Southern Greenland. The MD might have chosen to start off by saying something like, 'I'm sure you've all heard the rumours that we're moving to Southern Greenland. Well, they're true'. This is a very difficult opening to recover from.

Perhaps one of the most important concepts to remember in any form of speech-giving is that there is nothing but good news. No matter what. And with a little thought and planning, you can turn almost any potentially negative issue into a positive (or at least positive-sounding) speech.

Transitions

Although audiences like scenes, they like them to form a flow; a train of thought they can follow, that begins at the beginning and sweeps—with occasional peaks and valleys—inexorably towards the end.

Many speakers mistake flow for 'making smooth transitions'. They make these so-called smooth transitions by writing such things as, *'Now, let us turn to the all-important subject of . . .'* This is, in effect, a device for locating the audience partway through the speech. The trouble with it is that it is tedious. And no one, except an enormous bore, speaks that way 'in real life'.

The great advantage of speaking before an audience, is that many transitions or changes of tone or thought can be made in ways other than words. A pause. A breath. A slight shift of the body. A new tone of voice. A quickened or relaxed pace. These are the most effective transitions. Announcing your intention of turning to whatever, does the trick, but it's pretty lame.

Styling

Assuming that we're all aware of the need to write and deliver speeches in spoken speech, it is also important to create a style in a speech.

This is relevant for two reasons. Firstly, the style of the speech should reflect the nature of the subject matter; lively and snappy for the announcement of a new product, serious and hard-hitting for the discussion of a major corporate change, emotional and uplifting to motivate a sales force, etc.

The style of the speech in connection with its subject matter must then be aligned with the style of the individual speaker. It's very important that speeches should match the speaker's individual style, because this allows the speaker to make the best of his or her personality. Yet time and time again people get up and make a speech, the style of which bears absolutely no resemblance whatsoever to their personality. For audiences who do not know the speaker, this usually comes over as a stilted, awkward presentation. For audiences who do know the speaker, this can generate anything from suspicion to hysterical laughter. If the speaker is known to be an easy-going, jovial, humorous person in real life and gives a serious, humourless presentation, the audience will be confused. They might even suspect that there is some terrible hidden agenda lying behind the bland words, and that poor old so-and-so who is normally such an agreeable chap must be very worried about something if he hasn't smiled or cracked one gag in the whole speech. Another speaker, normally unfunny, who attempts to make weak jokes in a presentation to colleagues and staff will have the audience wincing with embarrassment within minutes—hardly the impression he or she would want to create.

So, how do you go about assessing and interpreting someone's personal style?

Writing for yourself

If you are writing a live presentation for yourself, you obviously know the personality concerned and so can bring this out in the material. But be careful. Many people have a 'generic corporate' style and a 'personal business' style, which are very different from one another. The 'generic corporate' style is what the person thinks he or she should sound like when speaking in a business context; the 'personal business' style is how he or she actually speaks when talking about business on an informal basis (not necessarily as relaxed as the social persona, but informal nonetheless).

You must concentrate on bringing out your personal business style in speeches, because resorting to the generic corporate style will make you look as though you're hiding behind it. It may sound easy, but it often isn't easy to be honest with yourself and assess what your personal style really is. What *is* easy is to hide behind 'corporate-speak' business jargon and clichés (as discussed earlier in this book), but this sounds about as sincere as Adolf Hitler telling an audience he would never dream of invading Poland. The real you may be a lot more open, frank and genuine than the generic corporate style; it may not use such long words, or such efficient sounding statements; it may not be as grammatically correct; but it is a lot more believable than any other style you could use. And remember this: it is *your* personality in business that got you where you are today—not some grey, faceless style and vocabulary dreamt up by the Harvard Business School.

If you are in any doubt about your own personal business style, try tape recording a small meeting you have with close colleagues. Then listen to yourself on the tape. What you hear is likely to be the real you, in a business context of course, but you as you are, informally. Then, you can write your speech around the way in which you express yourself on this basis. No matter how big your audience, and how important certain members of it are, the informal 'business' you is the style that will be the most convincing and effective.

Writing for others

If you're writing for colleagues, make sure you understand their 'personal business' styles, as described above, plus their own capabilities where public speaking is concerned, and write around those. Basically, you should apply the same considerations in this context as you would when writing for yourself. Once again, the tape recorder can be extremely useful, if you use it to tape an informal business conversation between yourself and the speaker concerned—preferably when you're discussing content for the speech in question (this way you kill two birds with one stone, and learn how the person informally phrases points about the subject of the speech; useful background).

The key points on speechwriting
1 Start all speeches with a strong opening that locates the audience and prepares them for what's to come.
2 Create an order of content out of short 'scenes', and make one 'scene' flow logically on to the next.
3 Tell a story; start at the beginning, work through the middle, and finish

at the end. Slot important facts and points into the flow of the story in the most logical places— don't jump about from subject to subject, or try to write the main points in order of their importance if they don't follow logically.

4 Make transitions between 'scenes' interesting, and don't labour them; often just a short pause is enough.

5 Assess the subject matter and write in a style that suits it.

6 Within the limits of **5** above, write the speech to suit the 'personal business' style of the speaker concerned—not to some preconceived idea of how an important business person should speak.

Once the speech is written
There is only one useful point I can make here; in fact I can summarize it in one word: REHEARSE.

Often I have written very good speeches for people only to find they are delivered badly, because the speaker concerned hasn't found time to rehearse properly—depressing for me, and such a waste of not only a good script but a valuable opportunity for that speaker to make a worthwhile presentation. Some very senior people feel it is beneath their corporate dignity to rehearse, especially in front of their less elevated colleagues and staff. Others have such busy schedules that rehearsing for the presentation falls off the bottom of the priority list, until the last minute. Whatever the problem, though, it is only the highly accomplished, very experienced speaker who can get by without rehearsing—especially when the presentation includes slides which must be cued, handovers to other speakers, and other stage management issues. For the vast majority, no matter how busy you are or how inhibited you feel, you *must* rehearse your presentation within plenty of time of the event in question, with the other speakers if there are any, as well as doing a 'dress' rehearsal shortly before the event. This ensures not only that your section runs smoothly, but that the whole presentation looks professional and polished. Remember, *all* presentations (internal and external, large and small) make a strong and memorable statement about your company or organization to the audience concerned, so they must be good—every time.

It's also useful to rehearse your speech privately: read it into a tape recorder and play that back. The playback will often point out areas that could do with improvement, sections that sound repetitive, plus any potentially awkward sentences and phrases that you could stumble over. When you do this, shut your office door and stand up—deliver the speech as you would to the audience, not mumbling it into the microphone. This way you can also practise your body language and stance, and see how the words and moves work together.

How to give your speech

Many business people now attend courses on presentations, and you'll find that doing this helps a great deal to overcome any nervousness you might feel about 'getting up in front of an audience'. An experienced coach will tell you how to stand, how to use gestures, how *much* to use gestures, how to move, how to hold your hands, etc. If you haven't attended such a course and feel you probably won't, here are a few tips.

First of all, remember that your audience will see you from much further away than is the case in a normal, one-to-one conversation. If you're a theatre-goer you'll have noticed that stage actors exaggerate their movements as well as their voices, to express themselves to the entire audience—'performing to the people in the last row of the gods'. To a more moderate degree, presentation speakers need to do this as well, although in modern business theatre you will have microphones that cut out the need to practise a booming voice. You'll probably be delivering your speech from a lectern, using cue cards, notes, teleprompter or whatever, so you can't stray too far. But at the same time you don't need to remain static before the audience as if your shoes had been stuck to the stage with super-glue; this makes you look nervous and unsure of yourself. You can use your arms and hands to emphasize points—and remember to move them more than you would when talking across your desk to someone. When you're not using your hands, rest them gently on either side of the lectern or loosely by your sides; never put them in your pockets.

You can also move the rest of your body around a bit—a subtle sway to one side or a short step backwards can be useful to emphasize a point or create a transition (see above).

When speaking, try as far as possible to retain your normal conversational voice (if you have a microphone you can do this even if you're talking to 3000 people in London's Albert Hall). But always speak clearly and succinctly, and if your natural way of speaking tends to speed along at a fast trot, slow it down a little. The speed at which sound travels is actually very slow, and if you're speaking at a large venue the people at the back will not hear your words until a split second after you've said them. If you speak too quickly, the sound quality may become distorted, especially over the distance it must travel from the sound speakers, which are usually placed near the stage at your end of the presentation area.

Perhaps most important of all, remember that you're speaking to real people—not a sea of featureless faces, although it may seem that way. Try to get eye contact with members of your audience, and move from person to person around the space. Speak to them as a number of individuals, not as one anonymous group; if you concentrate on this point, it will help you to be more believable and convincing.

Cueing systems

Very few speakers have the learning time, ability or confidence in their memories to speak totally without any means of reminding themselves of what comes next. This means that most people resort to some sort of cue—cards, notes, reading from a script, or a teleprompter system.

If you're an experienced speaker, talking from notes or cards is usually good enough, although if you're using slides cued by someone else this is going to make it difficult for them to know exactly when to put up the next slide.

Reading from an actual script is very difficult to do well, unless you're a professional newsreader from the old school before teleprompters were invented! If you must use this method, it's very important that you rehearse the script thoroughly so that you know it extremely well. This way, you can 'forward read' (memorize and say two, three or more lines at a time without looking down) so that you can at least look up occasionally and have some eye contact with your audience.

By far the most effective system is a teleprompter—widely used by politicians and other speakers. If you haven't used one before, you may feel apprehensive about it. But I can promise you, I have trained scores of speakers to use teleprompters and no matter how twitchy they might have been beforehand, once initiated they *all* have wondered how they ever managed without one.

Basically, a teleprompter works like this: your speech is typed on to a roll of paper (almost obsolete now) or (in modern times) on to a system similar to a word processor. It is then relayed to a monitor lodged in the base of the lectern. In front of you there is a glass screen, which is totally transparent from the audience's point of view. However, the glass is specially treated so the image of your script is bounced up to it from the monitor, allowing you to read the script from your side of the screen.

The beauty of teleprompters is that they free you from any need to look down, to worry about losing your place, or any other problem. The system is run by an operator backstage who can hear you, and who follows your pace and speed—you don't have to follow the machine. However, you should remember that teleprompters are just that—prompters—so they should remind you of what you're to say. This means you need to rehearse just as much as if you were to read from hard copy of the script. If you don't know your speech, you may appear to be squinting at the screen as you try to read unfamiliar words. If you know your material, though, and use the machine as a prompter, you can project yourself, maintain eye contact with your audience all the time, and even move about- as long as you can still keep one eye on the screen.

Writing for professionals

Other speakers at live presentations usually fall into the professional categories of either actors or professional presenters (e.g. newsreaders). If you're writing for a straight actor, remember that these people tend to dramatize everything they read whether it's an Ibsen play or a shopping list, so avoid too many glowing adjectives. Keep their scripts simple and less emotional than would be appropriate for a non-professional, as usually the extra emotional emphasis and delivery will be added into it by the actor whether you like it or not. This is on the assumption that you're using actors to present documentary material—but in a business environment, even dramatizations need to be realistic rather than over-acted.

Personality speakers, such as newsreaders and TV presenters, nearly always have their own style of speaking. When writing for them you should always study their style and write around it, rather than try to make them change their approach. If you do write something that isn't in their style, you'll find they either present badly or change it to their own style anyway.

The reality

I thought very long and hard about whether to include examples of speeches in this book. In the next chapter, you'll see a few examples of humorous speeches, but showing you these has the specific point of demonstrating how to create themes or storylines and how to personalize jokes and gags. In this case of non-humorous speeches, though, so much is dependent on the circumstances and the personality involved that to give you examples of speeches given by people you don't know, in circumstances unfamiliar to you, would be unproductive.

However, I have included the following speech in full, partly because it is one of my favourites, and partly because—suitably adapted—its style and content are universal enough to be useful for your own future speech-writing purposes. It was given by the chairman of an extremely large and cumbersome organization that was undergoing dramatic reorganization and decentralization of its two main areas of business, with the resultant unease and cynicism you would expect among certain members of the team. The occasion was the annual sales conference, and this was the keynote speech. This particular chairman had just taken over and was something of an unknown quantity to the sales force, so he had to get them on his side before he could impart his messages. I wrote his script on the strength of one tape-recorded meeting with him, and tried to convey his unstuffy, extremely pleasant personality through the words. Although I didn't attend the show, I gather from the production company concerned that the chairman delivered the speech virtually verbatim, and got a very long, loud round of applause afterwards. Here's what he said:

(CHAIRMAN): Good afternoon, everybody.

Before I go on to talk about our business in hand, I would like to start by assuring you that I'm *not* the kind of chairman who smiles down on his flock, and trots out the platitudes. My involvement with your activities is much closer to home than that.

It might interest you to know that I started my career as a salesman. My first job was as a management trainee with (previous company 1), fundamentally working in sales. And my first management job, was as a district sales manager, followed by that of Northern divisional sales manager, sales controller, general sales manager, and sales director. I also ran one of the largest sales forces in the country, at (previous company 2) ... with over fifteen hundred sales people in my team. To this day I firmly believe in the old adage that *nothing* happens until somebody, somewhere, sells something.

And although it was a while ago now, I can still remember very well how it *feels* to be out there at the sharp end. So, I admire the work you do and I am a strong supporter of the sales force.

But now, to business. And *our* business in the past has been an operational culture, not a marketing and sales culture. That is changing. (previous chairman), in launching decentralization and bringing in a dedicated sales force, set us off in the right direction. His considerable efforts began this vital process of making (Company X) customer-driven, concentrating on service excellence and dividing the business up into its pieces, so that problems could be attacked more vigorously. We still have a long way to go. But my intentions are to make certain that these necessary changes are firmly imbedded, and that we move even faster to get ourselves reorientated for our improved way of doing business.

What I'm definitely *not* intending to do, is to try and change the course (previous chairman) set out on, as I agree with what he was trying to do. Perhaps the best way to describe my role following on from his is that, if you like, he managed to get the Jumbo Jet out of the hangar and moving the first difficult few yards down the runway ... that time when you wonder whether it will ever take off. My job is to keep the throttle wide open, get the Jumbo off the ground and up to cruising altitude, and pilot it successfully on to its destination.

Decentralization is a key part of my piloting role. One of its major benefits has been to introduce stronger management accountability throughout all the disciplines of operations, finance, sales and marketing, to ensure that we recognize the needs of our customers far more clearly. And, that we tailor our products and services to meet those needs. We're far from perfect at it yet, but we must get better every day.

Now, I remember when I was a salesman thinking, 'are those buggers up at the top *ever* going to come up with some new products?' Well, you'll be pleased to hear that this is *still* a question that I'm asking today. Only now I'm in a stronger position to give good answers as well as ask the questions. And there will be some very good answers emerging over the coming months, as you have heard indicated by the managing directors of the two businesses. This is both in terms of product development, and the ways in which it is being put across to customers ... crucially important in my view as a former salesman ... because this, at the end of the day, is what you have to sell.

Although you represent the dedicated resource, if you like, I am making it clear to *all* management in both businesses, that *they* have got to get alongside the customer as well. I am expecting *them* to have close contact with customers, as well as with their teams.

If we are going to be truly customer-driven, we can't achieve that with just a narrow band of contact. It has got to be a matter of *everyone* participating with equal enthusiasm, and equal visibility.

Of course, you will remain the 'shock troops' of that, but I know from personal experience that you need support and help from the whole organization. And it is only if the whole organization thinks more about the customer, and becomes more customer-driven all the way through, that you will have the right environment in which to be the most successful. So as I see it, it is my responsibility to help you in this way, and make sure each one of you gets the support and help that you need, all the way up to the top.

And needless to say I am totally committed to making sure this happens now, in a number of ways ... through raising the profile of sales within the organization, reducing the hierarchical structure, creating more open, more flexible management, and generally giving positive signs for change. I even get time to talk to the media occasionally, as you might have noticed, to let *all* our customers know that we're a healthier, fitter, and more responsive animal.

So I stand squarely behind decentralization. I know that many people still feel uncertain about this. However, there was no doubt whatsoever that the job had to be done. We were just too big and cumbersome to manage as a monolithic whole. Now that we are committed to decentralization, we must do it thoroughly. I don't believe in being 'half-pregnant'.

Whilst we shall all continue to be part of (Company X), and draw strength from that, each business will be run as much on a stand-alone basis as possible. That means carrying through the process of separation, to give us a sharper cutting edge. And this is going to work to everybody's advantage; particularly yours. Rather than lose the impetus of our business in a diluted effort involving (name) and (name) together, running the risk of falling between two stools, during the course of this year the two individual businesses will receive a much sharper focus. You will have totally dedicated management. And for the first time in the history of (Company X), sales will be represented at the top, in both (name) and (name). This will obviously give sales much greater prestige within the organization, with all the benefits that are then bound to follow.

This is a definite and positive step forward; it's going to make your roles more clear cut, and more successful. These new roles will be something you can really get your teeth into; roles which will give you more scope, and more straightforward commitment to your own personal career development.

Of course, you could accuse me of giving you a perfectionist view of life; saying too much of how things should be in an ideal world. And we all know that real life is never as perfect as that. But we must have some *vision* of where we're trying to go, and some concept of what is the ideal. Now, obviously we're going to fall short of that ideal, so we need to set ourselves the greatest possible vision, and the most stretched objectives that we can. This way, we can unlock people's creative talents, *your* creative talents, to help drive us on towards the most demanding goals ... something that's badly needed in (Company X). And I'm encouraged to hear that you have already made an impressive start by forming your own mission statement; I'm pleased to see that once again, a sales team has set the good example for the rest of the organization to follow. But as you know by now, I am a little biased where sales teams are concerned!

So far, I seem to have been placing a great deal of emphasis on how much work there is yet to be done. But I must point out to you that I am enormously gratified to see just how far the operation has actually progressed so far. Giant steps have been achieved in what, for an organization the size of ours, is a very short time. Having seen this, I have tremendous confidence that through continuing change, we will go on successfully to new and greater heights.

But as you've already heard at this conference, change is a word that can generate mixed emotions ... especially amongst the faint-hearted. However, as experienced sales people, you are well used to working within a background of change. Up until recently, though, the reality has been that (Company X) *hasn't* changed. And that was a major problem. What is happening as we speak, is that there is more of a coming together; because (Company X) *itself* is beginning to change radically. Now, this may worry some people, but in no way should it disturb you. You, as sales people, are used to working within a changing environment, as I just said. In fact, that is all part of the stimulation and challenge of sales in the first place. What's more, most of you will have already felt the *benefits* of the change which is taking place within our business; and there is more to come.

Of course, you won't be surprised to learn that recently I've heard a number of rumblings here and there, to the effect that things are changing too fast. However, I make no secret of the fact that I don't believe it's fast enough.

Reorganization is a positive, productive part of our lives. And speaking as a former salesman, I've been reorganized more times than I've had hot breakfasts. Consequently, I know that deep down, good sales people *enjoy* the upward motion that change brings about, provided of course that adequate support is available in terms of resources and training. And as you've heard during this conference, all the support you're going to need, is already well in hand.

Alright, we may complain about change from time to time. But the truth, between these four walls, is that we are all far more likely to be bored by *lack* of change, than we are to be temporarily inconvenienced by fast-moving progression.

So, my final commitment to you here today, is this personal promise: you will *never* be bored again, in (Company X).

The way ahead may not always be easy, but it is the *only* way ahead for us. And it is the right way ... positive, exciting, challenging ... the right way for us all to create a prosperous, secure, and successful future.

Thank you all very much indeed.

Chapter 14

Humorous speeches

Every so often I'm called upon to write humour into speeches, and the chances are that at some stage you might well need to do this either for yourself or for someone else. Most good comedy writers will tell you that (a) writing humour is actually rather an unfunny pursuit, and (b) there's no such thing as a new gag. Both of these observations are true, in my humble opinion!

Even the most talented and experienced comedy gag writers seldom spend much time on dreaming up completely new jokes. Most jokes and gags you hear are not fresh; they are 'switched', or adapted, from earlier ones. Obviously, in a corporate context you may well have a fund of 'in-jokes' you can draw on, and in this respect writing a humorous speech to be given after dinner at your annual sales conference can be a lot easier than writing one for a general, non-company audience.

Naturally, all the rules of writing around the personality concerned, and in a style suited to his or her own speaking style, apply as much to humorous speeches as they do to the straight speeches. In addition to this, you must ensure that the nature of humour you use is suited to the person who is to give the speech (never write the sort of jokes that the person would find unfunny) and, of course, to the audience concerned. It's always best to stay away from blue humour, unless you're certain that the audience will appreciate it. Similarly, always avoid racist gags, and also sexist jokes—even an all-male audience these days may well contain a few chaps who no longer find mother-in-law jokes very funny.

Having opened this chapter with some rather pessimistic thoughts, I should now put your mind at rest. If you understand the principle of 'switching' (adapting existing gags to new circumstances) it is not that difficult to put together some funny material for speech. The way I normally tackle such projects is to focus on two important concepts: 'theming' the speech so that it follows a storyline, and 'personalizing' the humour. Let's look at those concepts in a little more depth.

Creating a storyline

Often, the theme or storyline for a humorous speech will be suggested to you by the event or the circumstances. In the two examples below, you'll see that the first speech was themed around the fact that the assembled party (the sales force of a major UK life assurance organization) were attending their annual conference in the Caribbean. The brief from the speaker (the sales director) was that he wished to send up his fellow directors, so I created a story around their activities during the conference on the island. In the second example, the occasion was one of a regular series of lunches for a group of retired businessmen in a local community, and the storyline was to be the speaker's experiences in running his own business.

Creating a storyline gives shape and structure to humorous speeches. Without this, they tend to turn out as a number of funny gags just strung together, which—unless you're a professional stand-up comic—lacks strength. A good, relevant storyline also offers you opportunities to make use of in-jokes in the corporate context; not necessarily funny to an outsider, but capable of bringing the house down when the audience knows the people concerned and their individual foibles.

Personalizing gags

Gags (or jokes) can be found in a number of places. In-jokes, as I've mentioned before, can be used either as they stand or can be rewritten/ adapted for the specific purpose. But what if you need to source your material from elsewhere?

I find the best source of jokes is my local bookshop. In most good ones, you can buy a number of collections of jokes on various different themes, often in paperback. Although I shouldn't suggest that anyone plagiarizes material, you'll find that a number of gags in these books, suitably adapted and personalized, are ideal for your own purposes. Here's an example of how a basic gag can be personalized; first, the original:

> When John graduated from Cambridge he applied for employment in the Civil Service. At his interview he was asked, 'What can you do well?'
>
> John thought for a minute and then replied, 'Nothing.'
>
> 'Excellent!' said the interview panel, as one. 'You're just the sort of person we want—and we won't even have to put you through an induction course!'

Now, let's suppose that the speech you're to write is to motivate staff of a used car business. Your competitors up the road have a much larger showroom and a lot more stock, but you as a company pride yourselves on the fact that you only deal in quality vehicles, and that your staff are very knowledgeable. The competition have a reputation of just trying to sell any old banger to any customer, irrespective of whether or not it is suitable for the customer's needs. The storyline of your speech may well be something along the lines of 'a day in the life of Bodgit and Scarper Motors' (the competition) which provides you with the opportunity to work in a number of motor trade jokes. But here's how you could use this one, suitably adapted:

> 'And do you remember old Henry, who used to be the night watchman here a few years back? Well, I ran into him the other day, and he was telling me that his grandson had just left school with no GCSEs or CSEs or anything, but was looking for a job. Apparently he went along to Bodgit's for an interview, and the sales manager asked him if he knew anything about cars.
>
> The young lad thought for a few minutes, and then, being an honest kid, said no.
>
> 'Great!' said the sales manager. 'That means we don't even have to put you through our training course!'

Basically, personalizing ('switching', as comedy writers call it) gags means rewriting them, using the same basic idea. It is not a difficult technique to learn, with a bit of practice.

In the first example—an after-dinner speech by the sales director of the life assurance organization, to the assembled sales force in the Caribbean—I have indicated which gags were original (based on in-jokes) and which were 'switched' from other contexts.

> *(SALES DIRECTOR):* Thank you, (NAME PERSON WHO HAS INTRODUCED YOU IF RELEVANT), and hello again; I hope you all enjoyed your dinner. Actually (fellow director 1) was asking me earlier on why we didn't have Ian Botham curry on the menu, as he claims it is a local speciality here. You know how keen the West Indians are on cricket. Anyway, Brian tells me an Ian Botham curry is just like many other curries, really, except the runs take longer to come. (switched)
>
> But before we get into some light-hearted entertainment this evening, I would like to say a few serious words. And those, quite simply, are to express my very sincere thanks to all of you here, for the enormous contributions you have made to this excellent year. Everyone here ... and that includes spouses and partners as well ... everyone has put in a

tremendous effort. And the result of this is that we are now in an extremely strong position.

(EXPANSION ON BUSINESS RESULTS, ETC. HERE)

I'm especially glad, therefore, that we've been able to come to this beautiful island for our conference. As most of you probably know by now, (island in question) is also known as Little England, and it even has its own Trafalgar Square complete with a statue of Lord Nelson on the top of a huge column. Or at least that's what (fellow director 2, a keep-fit buff) told me after he climbed up there to take a look on our first day. (original)

He was actually a little worried this morning, though, as (island) only has about thirty miles of sandy beaches and he'd already jogged along the whole length four times since we arrived. And for a man who jogged round the entire circumference of Australia three times while he was living there, I can understand that (island) must feel a bit small to him. (original)

It's funny how by observing seemingly insignificant things, you learn a great deal about the ways in which people enjoy themselves at conferences. By the second morning, I noticed that the hotel shop had sold right out of Alka Seltzer, although that may well have been because of the Gordon's Gin conference they held here last week. (switched)

Interestingly enough, (fellow director 1) mentioned to me this morning that this year more than ever before we've been functioning according to 'conference syncopation' ... a term coined at Harvard Business School in America, that means 'making irregular movements from bar to bar'. (switched)

In fact this was borne out by (fellow director 3), who was spotted clutching his briefcase stumbling around the roof of the hotel at three o'clock this morning He thought (fellow director 4) had said that drinks were on the house. (switched)

But of course he had mis-heard. What (fellow director 4, a keen gardener) really said was that he was looking for the hotel's greenhouse, so he could keep all his sugar-cane cuttings safe before he takes them home tomorrow (OR WHENEVER DEPARTURE IS SCHEDULED). I gather he's going to start growing sugar-cane on his allotment back home, so perhaps we can look forward to some (Company X) Rum at next year's conference. (original)

This island really is a delight for the keen gardener, isn't it? All those luscious flowers and exotic tropical plants are so tempting. Poor (fellow director 4) has been getting up at the crack of dawn every morning to forage for avocado pips and mango stones in the hotel's dustbins, and drying them carefully on the balcony of his room. Let's hope they all germinate well back in England, so his family will enjoy a pleasant change from the more mundane fruits and vegetables normally grown in (NAME COUNTY WHERE (FELLOW DIRECTOR 4) LIVES). (original)

Some of us have been indulging in sports, of course. I was really looking forward to a spot of sailing while here, as the warm water of the Caribbean is such a pleasant change from the Solent. I was quite lucky, as it happens, and I managed to hire a delightful small craft which really does test one's abilities as a sailor. I was out for nearly two hours yesterday, single-handed, fighting with the elements and braving the strong currents and other challenges that face the true sailing man. It was tough at times, but very invigorating, particularly as the craft I hired was a little smaller than I'm used to. I believe the locals call it a 'pedalo'. (original—the speaker was known to be a very keen sailor, and owned a beautiful yacht in the UK)

(fellow director 2) was keen to take a break from the more usual keep-fit activities and try his hand at parachute jumping. Unfortunately, though, he discovered that the (island) government have banned parachuting, since a recent incident when a director of (Major Company X competitor) jumped from an aircraft over (island's capital), pulled the cord, and nothing happened. As he was plummeting down towards the town at very high speed, he met a (island) man travelling upwards, equally fast, clutching a large spanner. The (competitor) man yelled out to him, and asked if he knew anything about parachutes. All the (local man) could say was, 'No. And I don't know much about gas cookers, either'. (switched)

But of course, it hasn't all been recreation while we've been here, has it? We achieved a great deal and heard some extremely interesting presentations. On the whole they were brief, explicit, and full of very important messages. You may have noticed, however, that (fellow director 5)'s speech ran three times as long as scheduled, although it was an excellent speech anyway. I had a word with his secretary on the telephone from London this morning and asked her why this was. She couldn't understand it; she said she typed out the speech very carefully, and attached two photocopies to it just as (fellow director 5) had asked. (switched)

I gather my presentation went over quite well, too. I even overheard someone talking about it in the bar last night (OR WHATEVER TIME WOULD HAVE BEEN APPROPRIATE). He said he thought my speech was rather like an ox's head: two good points and a lot of bull in between. (switched)

(ANY FURTHER COMMENTS ON EVENTS DURING THE CONFERENCE HERE)

Sadly, though, we're due to leave here tomorrow (OR WHENEVER DEPARTURE IS SCHEDULED) and it's always too soon, isn't it? It would be nice if we could have all spared the time to stay on for a while, take it easy, watch each other's noses peel, and give (fellow director 4, known to be an avid computer systems boffin) the chance to explain computerized irrigation techniques to the sugar-cane growers. (original)

(fellow director 2) finally could have had his chance to go jogging along the top of the reef at low tide. When he mentioned this I did point out to him that he might slip and fall into the jaws of a passing shark, but he said he does that every time he goes to a (NAME OF MAJOR INDUSTRY EVENT) anyway, so he's used to it. (original)

I could have enjoyed a little more sailing but this time with a two-man crew. In fact I very nearly persuaded a local fisherman to let me have a go with him in his boat, but he flatly refused to let me set up my 'I love (island) T-shirt as a spinnaker. He said oars have done the job perfectly well for several hundred years, and anyway all this fancy sailing stuff is about as much use to a fisherman as a one-legged man at a backside-kicking party. (both: the first part was original, but the last line was switched.)

If only we could stay on, (fellow director 1) finally could have taught the local chef here how to make a decent shepherd's pie, and (fellow director 4) eventually would have persuaded the hotel manager to computerize (OR TOTALLY REORGANIZE: WHATEVER WOULD BE TYPICAL OF HIM) his laundry facilities. However, there just isn't time; and tomorrow (OR WHENEVER) most of us will be at the airport, ready to go home. (original)

Talking of the airport, I had to laugh when we landed here on Tuesday (OR WHENEVER YOU ARRIVED). While we were waiting for our luggage I bumped into an old school chum of mine—a chap called Jeremy—who was just leaving (island) on some important official visit, in full uniform. He joined the navy soon after we left school, and he's an Admiral now. Anyway, we were having a quick drink as he waited for his flight when who should walk into the bar but our old school chaplain, whom we both hated. He's a large, overweight bishop these days, and coincidentally was also dressed in his full regalia. The bishop hated us just as much, and to our surprise, recognized us straight away. He couldn't resist making a bitchy remark, especially as my chum was looking so smart in his dress uniform. He looked straight at Jeremy and said 'I say, steward, when is the London flight due to take off?' Well, Jeremy always was a quick thinker. He looked right back at the fat old bishop and said, 'Madam, if I were in your condition, I wouldn't travel at all.' (switched)

So, we'll be back there at the airport tomorrow (OR WHENEVER), with most of us heading back to the UK and another year, which I feel sure will be every bit as successful as the last. And at roughly the same time next year, I hope we will all meet again in (new venue).

Obviously we'll be seeing a lot of each other between now and then, but in case I don't get the chance to wish you well for the coming year when we're back home, let me do it now. Good luck, every success with your tremendous efforts, and once again—thank you all very much.

In the next example—the retired businessman at the luncheon, describing his experience of running a local newspaper—all the gags were switched from a selection I gathered from books, and also from the speaker's own collection, which runs into hundreds. He made the point to me that most of the after-lunch speeches at this gathering were serious, describing the experiences of local bank managers, company directors, etc., which tended to have a soporific effect on the audience. He wanted his speech to be funny, in the hope that the audience would still be awake at the end. The following is what I wrote for him, and it created the desired effect. Interestingly, my research into the personality and style of the speaker had already been conducted over many years—he is my father!

(SPEAKER): Thank you (whoever has introduced you).

As most of you probably know, before I retired I was a newspaper man —I owned the (County) Standard, which I finally sold, and it has now become the (new name). These days the paper gets put through your door for free, but in my time it was not a freesheet. In fact when I sold it, it was probably the last paid-for local newspaper in this area.

I first took over the Standard when I first arrived here from Canada, back in 1960. In those days we still used hot metal typesetting, with huge Linotype and Monotype machines that made one hell of a noise and worked well but very slowly.

These days all that sort of work is done by computer, and the most noise you get is the occasional bleep from those small plastic boxes which now replace the human brain, as far as I can tell!

Although the old-fashioned printing processes were slow and dirty, there was quite a lot of romance and atmosphere about the whole industry that just doesn't exist today. Sure, there were Union problems and disagreements, and that's something that hasn't changed ... even though the technology has. But running a local paper for all those years brings back a lot of happy and funny memories, and I'd like to recall a few of them now to share with you.

I originally bought the Standard through the first Lord Thomson. He was a fellow Canadian, and was one of the first 'media barons', as they call them. He started the process that's now being carried on by guys like Eddie Shah, Rupert Murdoch, Robert Maxwell and so on—trust a Canadian to show them all how to do it!

Anyway, when old Lord Thomson was on his death bed not many years after I met him, he called his son over and said,

'My boy, I've done everything I could to give you a good start in life. You've had a first-class education, university, nice cars, everything. But I believe a man should make his own money. Promise me you'll bury all my money in my coffin with me.'

The son promised, the old boy died, and at his father's funeral a few days later, just before the coffin lid was screwed down, the son wrote out a cheque for ten million pounds and put it in beside his father's body ...

As you can imagine, a local paper like the Standard comes across some very interesting and often embarrassing stories, sent in for publication by well-meaning local people. In my job as editor, it was actually very difficult to decide which to publish and which to keep out.

A good example is this one about a local MP at the time, who was driving his new white Rover car at around a hundred miles an hour and suddenly saw he was being followed by an identical white Rover. He'd had a few drinks, of course, but still noticed that the other white Rover also had an orange stripe down the side and a blue light on the roof.

Of course he got pulled over and breathalized. Then two cars on the other side of the road crashed, so the policemen rushed over to help. The MP, meanwhile, decided to sneak off home in the confusion, so got in his Rover, drove back home, parked in the garage and went to bed.

At three in the morning, the police knocked on his door. He answered, with a terrible hangover, and they asked him if he'd been stopped earlier on. Of course he denied it. So the police then asked if they could inspect the MP's white Rover, and he could hardly refuse. But he was a bit shocked to find when he opened the garage door, bleary-eyed, that his Rover was parked there with an orange stripe down the side, and a blue light on the roof ...

Well, would you have published that story, or not? I always felt that the press should be unbiased, but when you get prominent politicians doing silly things, you have to use your judgement and decide whether to publish it as serious, or as a joke. Of course, that's the trouble with political jokes ... half of them get elected.

Of course some prominent locals really do have a sense of humour. I remember going to a press conference in the sixties, given by the new Chief Constable of (County) who'd just been appointed.

As the Standard's representative, I asked him what changes he had planned for the County Force. He said there was only one—to have all the gents' urinals in local police stations raised by six inches.

Thinking this was a bit strange, I asked him why. 'Oh,' he said, 'I always believe in keeping my men on their toes.'

That reminds me of another incident in (local town) not long afterwards. We reported a case where a young rookie police constable had single-handedly tackled a burglar, who eventually got away. Meanwhile the young cop was in a lot of pain with a dislocated shoulder. When assistance arrived, his sergeant took him straight across the street into (name) Maternity Home, as it was then—well, it was the quickest way to get a doctor to put his shoulder back.

The doctors in the Maternity Home were very nice about it, and put his shoulder back right away. But the poor guy was screaming with the pain. One of the doctors said, 'My God, you're making more noise than women do when they have a baby!'

The young cop looked up and said, 'Yes—but when they have a baby at least you don't try to put THAT back!'

One of the most difficult parts of taking over any business, as you know, is in dealing with employees who've been there for years and don't like the idea of the new boss making changes. I'm sure most of you've experienced that one.

I was pretty lucky with the Standard, because the staff there were very good and appreciated the need to make changes. But of course there was one exception, and that was old Bill Bennett.

He had been a reporter on the Standard since before the War, and although his local knowledge was good he had a big problem with writing headlines. Some of them were very embarrassing, but how do you tell an old hack journalist like him, politely, that his headlines have to be changed?

I first got a hint of his problem when I looked through the archives at some of the wartime issues of the paper. There were a number of his mistakes in that, but I think the worst one was in his report on the Battle of the Desert in 1942, which he'd titled 'Eighth army push bottles up Panzer division.'

Well, that should have warned me of what was to come. The next classic one was when we reported a nasty case where an inmate had escaped from the old Mental Hospital at (local town), and run into a launderette where he'd raped three of the women in there before eventually being caught.

Bill's headline for that story read like this: 'Nut bolts and screws washers.'

But perhaps the most embarrassing headline Bill ever came up with was when we reported a story about the famous explorer Sir Vivien Fuchs, who actually had relatives near (local town) and was in the area quite a lot in those days.

Bill had been a keen follower of Sir Vivien's travels, especially when he took his famous trip to the Antarctic in the late fifties. And around 1962 when Sir Vivien departed again, Bill reported the story with the headline, 'Sir Vivien Fuchs off to Australia'.

Bill's problem went beyond the headlines sometimes, too. Shortly before he retired, he covered a story about another new local MP in the old (County) constituency, which was quite large then. That was before the government changed the boundaries around, and long before (local new city) came along. Anyway, I can't remember this MP's name, but he was Scottish and got in by a slim majority at a by-election. Bill wrote a long piece about him, and because we were very short of space that week I told him to cut the story down to a few lines.

But I had to send him back to the drawing board when he came back with the final copy. It read, 'The new member wears a kilt. It takes him three weeks to cover his large constituency.'

The next gag comes from the same original as one I used in the previous example. In that speech, if you remember, it was set up in the context of a speech given by one of the speaker's colleagues earlier in the event. Here it is set up quite differently, but the gag is identical.

Of course in my work as editor of the Standard I got invited to a number of functions, some of which were very interesting, and some weren't.

I remember going to a Chamber of Commerce dinner back in the seventies, and the after-dinner speaker was a local lawyer who was known to be boring as Hell for five minutes, never mind a whole speech.

Anyway, the guy went on and on for a whole hour, after which we were all pretty well asleep.

When he'd finished, as you can imagine what with the wine and all most of us were in a big hurry to get to the gents. I happened to be standing at the urinals next to this lawyer and his assistant, who were arguing over something, and being a newspaper man I listened.

The lawyer was obviously trying to blame the boring speech on his assistant who'd written it. 'Smith,' he said, 'what the Hell were you doing? I told you to write me a twenty minute speech and the bloody thing went on for an hour!'

'Well, sir,' said the little guy, 'I did write a twenty minute speech. And just like you told me, I attached two photocopies as well.'

The following gag also appeared in the previous example, set up in a different way.

Another time I was invited along with the other local press over to (local airport), for the launch of a new Cessna plane. The organizers had also invited a lot of VIPs, including an old Admiral, and the Bishop of (city), both dressed up in their full regalia, and we knew they absolutely hated each other.

After the ceremony we were waiting to say goodbye to the VIPs, who were being flown home. But the weather was bad and their flight was delayed. The Bishop and the Admiral were glaring at each other, when the Bishop decided to be really bitchy to the Navy man. He said, 'Tell me, steward, how long will this flight be delayed?'

The Admiral was pretty quick. He looked back at the fat, old Bishop and said, 'Madam, if I were in your condition I wouldn't travel.'

Funerals were another part of my official duties, I suppose, and whenever a prominent local figure died I would put on the dark suit and go along to represent the Standard. This particular time it was old George Sampson, who had run a Ford dealership in (local town) for many years and had a pretty colourful reputation.

After the burial I was standing looking at the gravestone with my old friend, Henry Mason. He was manager of the (name) Bank in (local town) for years. Anyway, Henry read out the epitaph, which said 'Here lies George Sampson, a motor trader and an honest man'.

Henry turned to me and said, 'You know, (speaker's name), it's funny. That's the first time I've heard of two men being buried in the same grave.'

Mind you, although Henry and I were good friends we had our moments, especially over cashflow. I'll bet you remember the feeling! Anyway, one time he phoned me at the office and said, '(speaker's name), I've got a complaint. You're a thousand pounds over your overdraft limit this week.'

I thought that was a bit much, so I asked him how I'd stood the week before.

'Oh,' he said, 'you were two thousand under your limit.'

'That's right,' I said. 'So how come I didn't phone YOU up to complain?'

But I suppose that kind of thing is just part of running any business, isn't it. Running a newspaper did have its unique parts, though, and I think the most amusing part of all was some of the court cases we'd report on.

In the sixties, if you remember, this part of the world was still very rural. We didn't have (local new city), and the (motorway) only went as far as (location). Nowadays most of the local characters have died off or been put into Old Folks' Homes, but back then they still used to get up to all sorts of mischief.

There was one funny case about Paddy O'Halloran, who had a run-down farm near (local town) then. Everyone knew he couldn't make a living out of the farm, but he did pretty well on brewing up the old potheen and selling it to the local Irish community.

Eventually the police couldn't turn a blind eye any longer, so they raided Paddy's farm and found the stills and all the other equipment sitting there. He was taken to court and fined, and afterwards he said to the judge, 'But they never found any potheen, your Honour. How could I be convicted?'

'Ah,' said the judge, 'it doesn't matter. You had the equipment.'

Paddy thought for a minute, then said to the judge, 'So what about my rape case, then?'

The judge looked at him and said, 'But there is no rape case.'

Paddy looked back and said, 'Ah, but there must be, your Honour. To be sure, I've got the equipment.'

The other classic case I remember was a dispute over boundaries between two neighbouring farmers. It got reported in the Standard in about sixty-four, I think. Anyway, one of the farmers was defended by my friend Bob Henderson, who had a small legal practice in (local town) around the corner from my office. He was horrified when his client announced he would clinch the case by sending the judge a brace of pheasant from the farm. Bob was very concerned and strongly advised his client not to do anything of the sort.

Anyway, Bob's client won the case, and afterwards Bob asked him if he had sent the pheasants after all. The farmer smiled and and said, 'Of course I did, Mr Henderson. But I sent them in the other man's name.'

Well, as the Scottish Lord Killearn once said, 'A good speech is like a woman's dress—short enough to be interesting, but long enough to cover the subject.'

I've enjoyed recalling some of my experiences in my business—and I hope you've enjoyed sharing those memories with me.

Thank you all very much.

Both the above speeches were designed purely to entertain. However, many speakers like to include a few gags in an otherwise straight speech, either to warm the audience up at the beginning or else to give them a smile at the end. Here are two examples of how this can work; and in the first, see how many gags you can recognize from elsewhere in this chapter!

(SPEAKER): Well, I hope you enjoyed last night, and that you're all feeling fit today. I did see that the hotel shop had sold out of Alka Seltzer by seven o'clock this morning, but then that's probably for the Gordon's Gin conference next door. However, don't worry, I drank six bottles of Perrier water and I feel much better. You'll just have to excuse me if I pop out every now and then while you look at my slides.

Actually, what we *were* suffering from last night was what (name of colleague) calls 'conference syncopation'. That's making irregular movements from bar to bar.

In fact, I overheard (NAME SOME SENIOR SALES PERSON WHO WORKS IN BRIGHTON AREA) saying to one of his colleagues in the lounge last night, 'Look, (NAME OF OTHER LOCAL SALES PERSON HERE), I really wouldn't drive home tonight if I were you. Your face is getting all blurry.'

And the barman agreed. He used to work at the Grand Hotel, just along the front. And apparently after the reconstruction work from the Conservative conference bombing, it very nearly didn't get its drink licence back. The local council decided that the roads around Brighton really weren't suitable for drunken driving.

Then, of course, there was (NAME ANOTHER SENIOR PERSON, PREFERABLY ONE WHO CAN TAKE A JOKE!). I found him wandering around on the roof of the hotel at two o'clock this morning. Somebody had told him that the drinks were on the house.

It really was some night. I overheard (YET ANOTHER SENIOR PERSON) talking to his secretary. He said, 'Drink makes you look really beautiful, (NAME—PLEASE MAKE SURE IT IS *NOT* HIS SECRETARY'S REAL NAME!).' She said, 'But I haven't been drinking!' 'No,' said (SENIOR PERSON). 'But I have.'

(AD-LIBBED SUMMARY OF COMMENTS ABOUT REORGANIZATION, TAKEN FROM PREVIOUS DAY'S PROCEEDINGS.)

So now, let's move on to the future. Yesterday, we heard from our two managing directors, (name) and (name), who showed us that there clearly is a determination on their parts and on the part of their teams, to provide real quality services which meet the needs of our customers. And they also pointed out to us that those customer needs are changing, and we can't go around with our heads in the sand selling products which frankly don't match up with what our customers are asking for. So I found it really very encouraging to see that kind of flexibility and determination coming through; that's just what every one of us here in this room would want. I'd like to thank (name) and (name) for that.

The next point, of course, is for the rest of us to match that. So, what is there to be done in our way ahead?

Well, we've got to continue to run a very high quality sales operation which is going to match that determination, and the quality products coming out of the businesses. We talked about that, yesterday. We patted ourselves on the back and we looked at how well we've done. But of course, we must never be satisfied with that. And we have to make sure that we *continue* to provide a high quality operation which will meet all the needs. That means constantly looking at ourselves, not allowing complacency to creep in, and always looking for new ways and new ideas to help us make sure we actually deliver the goods. If you'll forgive the pun.

Now, to do all this we have our way ahead; our reorganization.

But one thing I want to point out is that you mustn't be afraid of reorganization, as so many people are. When I was at (previous company), people got so paranoid about reorganization that I renamed it 'structural progression'. It was the same thing, but it didn't sound so ominous.

And just the other day, I heard of a very experienced businessman who was just as paranoid. He'd been quoted in some publication, as saying this . . .

We trained hard ... but it seemed that every time we were beginning to form up in teams we would be reorganized ... I was to learn later in life that we tend to meet any new situation by reorganization; and a wonderful method it can be for creating the illusion of progress while producing confusion, inefficiency, and demoralization.

SHOW SLIDE:
'GAIUS PERONIUS ARBITER, 10 B.C.'

Mind you, that *was* only a rough translation from the Latin. And as you can see, this particular businessman has been around even longer than I have.

So, cynicism about reorganization is nothing new. But we *have* got to lose that, if we don't want to finish up like the Romans did.

Yesterday, I showed you the current plan as to what the organization will be. But what about the timescale for this?

Well, there are no surprises in it. You know that we are committed to have everything in place by (date), 19XY. That's 19XY, not 19XX, so I'm not talking about next week; I mean in fifty-three weeks' time. But even so, to achieve that there are an awful lot of things to be done. That includes putting names to jobs, and getting all the training done to equip everyone to carry out their new roles. It means finding accommodation in the appropriate district offices, getting the (X) computers installed, getting the Telemarketing function up to speed, and getting the customer care function up and running well. And the timescale for achieving all these objectives looks like this ...

(TIMINGS GIVEN HERE.)

But let's get back to the year which starts *next* week ... our 19XX–19XY financial year. Well, I guess there are seven main objectives that form what we would formally call our business plan, and I'd like to look at them in turn.

(ETC.)

And now, we get to point number seven. What does all of this mean?

Well, finally, it means an overall increase in our *professionalism*. By now, you must be bored with (speaker's own name) standing on stage and talking about professionalism. What the bloody hell does it *mean*?

There's no great mystique to it. It means actually satisfying the needs of our customers ... as a sales force and individually. And we do that through training, through thinking about what we wish to achieve for the businesses and for ourselves, planning how to do it, getting out there and achieving those objectives ... and getting great satisfaction through doing so.

And, having got that satisfaction, we like it; it's like a drug. We go out and do it more, and more, and more. That's what I mean by professionalism; satisfying our customers. And who are our customers? It's the (name) business customers and the (name) business customers. But don't forget, it is the (name) business and the (name) business *themselves* who are our major customers too, and we have to satisfy *their* needs.

That's what professionalism is all about. That's what we are very good at. That's why we changed our culture so successfully. And that's why we have to actually spread the good word throughout both businesses.

(ETC.)

Finally, here is one (switched) gag which set the tone of an after-dinner speech, during which the speaker was to announce a number of prize-winners. The gag served to set the tone for the speech, which had some serious content, and was designed to congratulate the audience in an informal way.

(SPEAKER): Good evening, everyone, and let me welcome all of you to our 19XY Star Performance Road Show here tonight.

And star performance is an extremely appropriate title ... because 19XX, ladies and gentlemen, was our most successful year yet. It was the most successful year for us ... for you ... and to a great extent BECAUSE of you and the fantastic efforts you all put in.

Tonight we're gathered here to honour the MOST successful, among the successful. And that means our top earners ... people who have contributed most to our financial success, and indeed to their own.

Talking of financial success reminds me of one of our top earning salespeople some years back: Arthur Collins. To celebrate his high earnings, in addition to enjoying the conference venue that year—I can't remember where it was—anyway, Arthur took himself off for a spot of salmon fishing in Scotland.

As Arthur was getting into his waders one day a farm worker walked past him, hobbling in a somewhat strange way. Arthur was in a benevolent mood, and called the man over to where he was struggling with the waders. As the man approached he noticed that the sole on one of his boots had come unstuck and was flapping around, hence the funny walk.

Arthur said, 'I say, my man, haven't you got some decent boots to wear? That sole flapping about could be dangerous, you know. You might have an accident.'

The man looked up at Arthur and said, 'Well I know, sir, but I can't afford to have it repaired until I get my wages at the end of the week.'

So Arthur reached into his jacket pocket and pulled out an enormous wad of ten pound notes ... he'd had a pretty good year, as I told you ... and took off the elastic band that was holding them all together. Then he handed this to the farm worker.

'Here,' said Arthur, 'put it around your boot. That'll make it much safer.'

But of course Arthur was not typical of our breed of salespeople. He was a funny sort of chap. In fact after the (relevant) Act was announced we had to let him go.

Our salespeople today, are a breed of truly expert professionals ... like all of you here tonight. Nationwide, we currently have around 2750 people like you. And it is professionalism on this large scale, which is probably the greatest single contributing factor to our success.

I'd like to take the next couple of minutes to tell you just HOW successful we have all been, and where.

(ETC.)

Chapter 15

Themed events

In the main, large conferences and business meetings are more memorable, motivating and interesting if they are themed in some way. Often this can just be a verbal theme, perhaps backed up with a logo on screen, that is woven throughout and influences the ways in which speeches are written. Examples of this might be:

PROGRESS THROUGH PARTNERSHIP
THE WINNING TEAM
THE NEW TEAM FOR THE NINETIES
FORWARD INTO THE FUTURE

... and so on. These types of theme are fairly general, and normally do not require any special scriptwriting techniques other than ensuring that you structure each speech with the theme in mind, referring to it as appropriate here and there.

Many companies, though, like to have something rather more theatrical, and even involve their own staff in some acting. Often, conferences are intended to be amusing exercises where all participants—speakers and audience—should have a good time, as well as absorb information. The theory behind this is that people will be more uplifted and motivated if they remember the information they've absorbed in the context of having had fun and enjoyed themselves. Obviously, each case must be judged individually, but in certain circumstances the theory works very well.

What you must remember when you are writing for a show like this, is the same point you must remember when you're writing comedy for corporate TV purposes: don't let the tail wag the dog. You should always use the information and the underlying motivational messages to dictate the theme and the way it unfolds; never try to bend the information around a good stage play. If the theme is a recognizable one (e.g. James Bond or Startrek, as in the examples below) you must study the style and plot structures of the original, and then create your own plot based on that *style*, but developed around the products, activities and messages concerned.

If the performers are to be members of the company's staff, then no matter how keen they are, never write parts that are too difficult for them.

If they're expected to say a lot of lines in character, ensure that a teleprompter is available so that they do not have to learn the part by heart. Although some people in these circumstances can get very carried away with their acting roles, it's important to remember that their prime role is to impart information to the audience. Often you'll find it is up to you to make the circumstances as easy as possible for them to do so.

The complete story

One approach you can use for a themed event is to create a story which runs as a sub-plot throughout, continuing as links between presentations. Here, you should always involve as much that is of relevance to the company and the event as possible, including as many in-jokes as you can find.

The following example is an edited version of an event for a pharmaceutical company, who wanted to update their sales force on their product range and give them a good time as well. The theme (chosen by the client) was James Bond, and I developed a story for the show around the 'enemies' (in this case, bacteria and fungi) and the 'weapons' (the client's drugs) needed to wipe out the 'enemies'. To some it may seem a little childish, but the whole thing was a huge send-up which everyone thoroughly enjoyed. (The presentations were given as straight speeches, so as not to cast an amusing light on the pure business content.) The show continued over about three days, including a formal dinner after which there was a cabaret linked to the theme. In addition to the show, delegates were also involved in seminar sessions and competitive sporting events.

> (Please note that although (Client 3) plays Bond on stage, we will also use a narrator to link, who will act as Bond's 'thought bubble'. He speaks in the past tense, commentating on the events as if they had already happened, and obviously provides us with a very necessary link device between speakers. The voice-over artiste concerned will use the Roger Moore 'Bond' voice.)
>
> The set is in semi-darkness. We see (Client 1) in silhouette, quietly waiting at 'M''s desk. There are introductory slides on screen, and some music is playing. It is subtle, but suggests a build-up to something dramatic. Bond, in 'narrator' guise, tells us what's happening.

NARRATOR: My name is Bond ... James '(Company X)' Bond. And my job is ... well, you'll see what my job is, soon enough. But at this point, the story is just beginning ... and this was a very special occasion. After all, a personal visit from the Minister of Defence, fresh from the Cabinet Office, isn't something that happens every day. The Minister had already arrived. And he was *not* amused to find that 'M' still hadn't got back from lunch. Mind you, he did turn up early. But this was a *very* urgent mission. Finally, 'M' walked through the door ...

> (Client 2) walks in through the door. The lights come up, and (Client 1) greets him.

MINISTER: Ah, 'M'. Good lunch at the club, was it? Come and sit down. Don't mind me using your desk, do you? (NOT WAITING FOR A REPLY) Good.

> (Client 2) sits down obediently. (Client 1) then delivers his speech.
>
> INTRODUCTION TO (COMPANY X)
>
> At the end of the speech, (Client 1) returns to character.

MINISTER: Well, 'M', it's over to you now. You've got some work to do, and a team to assemble. And I would suggest that you get the best man to lead that team.

'M': Quite so, sir. Do you by any chance mean ...

MINISTER: (INTERRUPTING) Yes, I mean ...

'M': (INTERRUPTING) ... 007?

MINISTER: (EXITING) 007, 'M'. James Bond. He's the only man who can handle this little project. And he's the only man who can pick the best team in the country to help him. (HE GETS UP, ABOUT TO LEAVE.)

'M': Thank you, sir. Leave it to me.

> The 'Minister' says goodbye and exits. 'M' discreetly shifts back to his own chair, and then picks up a telephone on the desk.

'M': Miss Moneypenny? Find Bond for me, will you? (PAUSE) Yes, I know he's still on leave. I'm cancelling it. This is too important. PM's instructions. Minister asked for him personally. (PAUSE) Come, come, Miss Moneypenny. You should know where to look for him by now. (HE PUTS PHONE DOWN.)

> 'M' remains at his desk. The set goes dark, and we see a few slides of such places as an expensive restaurant, a casino, Cartier's, Gucci, etc. The introductory strains of the 'Bond' theme are playing, softly. Finally, we see a very

luxurious bedroom, followed by another shot of the doorway to the bathroom. The door is open, and we can see a marble sink. A man's tie is resting on its edge, and a pair of ladies' shoes are on the floor beneath. (Please note that these are just prop suggestions at this stage: in production it may be that suitable alternatives are used.) We hear sound effects of splashing water, and two voices ... one male, one female ... chatting and laughing in a particularly intimate way. Miss Moneypenny has finally found Bond ...

We hear the sound of a bleeper, and Bond's voice answers it tersely.

NARRATOR: Yes? Oh, not too bad. But I'm feeling a little, er, washed out right now. (PAUSE) The Minister? (PAUSE) I see. Very well. I'm on my way.

We hear a click as he switches off his radio.

NARRATOR: Sorry, darling. The boss wants to see me. You'll just have to finish that caviar by yourself.

Then, we cut to shots of Bond (a model, not (Client 3)!) getting dressed very quickly. The shots are close-ups, so we don't actually see a face, or any other indentifiable part! The music plays to a crescendo. After this, the lights come up in full, and (Client 3) walks on stage ... still doing up his tie, and with quite obviously wet hair ... (note to (Client 3): we can use gel rather than water, to avoid drips around your collar!)

(Client 3) greets (Client 2), and sits down. (Client 2) then briefs him on the mission.

THE MISSION, AND THE FIELD FORCE STRUCTURE

At the end of this section, (Client 3) gets up and says goodbye to 'M'. He walks over to the lectern, and 'M''s half of the set goes dark. (Client 2) then exits unobtrusively. (Client 3) then appears to be studying documents and the maps behind him, obviously working up a plan.

NARRATOR: Well, well. Assemble a NEW team, hmm? Had to be the best, of course. Only one thing for it. The other 00 agents ... licensed to kill. And that was the first dish on the menu: to kill the entire top table of BACTERIA. That's short for Bacterial Terrorist International

Assassination, in case you didn't know. Particularly good at germ warfare in respiratory tract infection, they are. Literally suffocate their enemies to death. Friendly bunch of chaps. And to think they were about to let loose with a campaign of terrorism here in Britain. We'd come up against them before, of course. But now, with a brand new, crack (Company X) team and our latest (product) missiles . . . well, it was high time we gave them a taste of, er, their own medicine. And that's precisely what we were about to do. I'd called all the 00 agents back from leave, poor devils. Special alert. Some of them didn't even have time to change.

> (Client 3), having completed his studying and 'silent' musing, now turns to the audience. He calls up each area manager in turn.

> Each area manager says a few words about his own area. Then, they go back to sit with their area teams. (Client 3) remains on stage for a moment, looking through his papers and studying the maps again.

(The presentations continue, with the themed links building up a tension towards the culmination of the battle . . .)

> The telephone on the desk rings. (Client 3) hesitates briefly, then picks it up. (Please note that (Client 3) will not speak these lines. He should turn his back to the audience and appear to be speaking on the phone, while the narrator actually does the talking. Hence, the dimmed set!)

NARRATOR: Bond here. (PAUSE) What? *Secret Agent* Angeline? Put her on through the scrambler. (PAUSE) Angeline, darling! How did you know where I work? (PAUSE) My God! Hold on a moment . . .

> (Client 3) flicks a switch on the phone, putting her on 'conference' so the audience can hear her.

ANGELINE: (OOV) James, I couldn't tell you. I'm so sorry, but I couldn't blow my cover. Not even for you. I'm working undercover with both organizations . . . with BACTERIA *and* with THRUSH.

NARRATOR: Terrorism, Hijack, and Revolution, Undercover, to Savage Humanity. THRUSH. Not them as well, surely!

ANGELINE: (OOV) Yes, both! But right now I'm on to BACTERIA, James! I'm sure they don't suspect me. I've been observing their operations. They're about to launch an offensive timed to coincide with the British winter. Oh, James, you've got to stop them! They've sent a special task force of mercenaries to try and *steal* a (product) from (location). So they can try to work up a resistance to it.

NARRATOR: They can't succeed, of course.

ANGELINE: (OOV) No. But they don't know that yet.

NARRATOR: Well, we'll just have to show them what (products) can do, won't we? In fact I think I'll get down there myself and put a (product) through its paces. In person.

ANGELINE: (OOV) What, fly one yourself? Oh, James. You're so clever! But please hurry, darling! Those BACTERIA mercenaries must be just outside (location of client's head office) by now!

NARRATOR: The chopper's standing by on the roof. I'm on my way.

> (Client 3) puts the phone down, and hurriedly exits.

> We hear the sound effects of a helicopter taking off, and the James Bond music.

> We then see the excerpt from Octopussy, from the moment just *after* the aircraft emerges from the phoney horse (we do not see the horse, as this would require too laborious an explanation within the (product)/bacteria plot).

> The excerpt ends with Bond in the craft at the gas station, telling the attendant to 'fill her up'.

NARRATOR: Well, the (product) certainly did its stuff. And just on two-star petrol, as well. Angeline had certainly done her stuff, too. But I couldn't help feeling that she was in danger. Now, she was on the track of THRUSH ... our next mission. I decided that from now on, I'd better keep an eye on our Secret Agent Angeline. For the moment, though, I had to send the field operatives off to plan their attacks. Our battle against BACTERIA wasn't over yet ... and by the next day, every one of our operatives had to be as familiar with the (product) weapons as I was. It was back to the training rooms, for the whole (Company X) team ...

> A slide comes up on screen stating that the audience should go to their syndicate rooms.

(At the dinner that followed this session, there was a themed cabaret, involving a foiled kidnap attempt on 'Agent Angeline'.)

(Final day: Another product range was discussed—Anti-fungal Preparations—themed around the 'T.H.R.U.S.H.' enemy gag. The character of Secret Agent Angeline was taken by the brand manager of the Anti-fungal Product range, whose name was Angela.)

(The presentations continued, up to and including a summary of the whole event.)

> After this, the two men re-establish themselves in 'M''s office. They looked more relaxed now.

'M': Fancy a snifter, old chap?

BOND: Thank you, sir. A vodka martini. Shaken, not stirred.

'M': This is the headquarters of MI5, 007. Not Harry's Bar. You'll have some of my excellent malt whisky and like it.

> (Client 2) goes over to the side of the set, where a decanter and two glasses are waiting on a tray. He goes about pouring the whisky (cold tea—or the real thing!) and taking the glasses over to the desk, as the narrator takes over for a while.

NARRATOR: It wasn't a bad little malt, actually. Birthday present to 'M' from (client)—that's agent 00 zero. Must have cost him most of his salary that week. Ah, well. It looked like we finally had the new threats from THRUSH and TINEA under control. The new team of (Company X) operatives was trained, and armed to the hilt. They're some of the finest field operatives in the world. Quite proud of them, really. The (product) weapons were safe in our hands ... and deadlier than ever if our terrorist friends *were* foolish enough to get in the way. We could relax. Except for one thing. I was worried about Angeline. She should have arrived by this time. Her plane was due to touch down at Brise Norton an hour earlier, and she was then taking the office helicopter to come and report to 'M'. It wasn't like her to be late.

> (Client 3) gets up, glass in hand, and stands downstage, peering out over the audience.

NARRATOR: I looked out over Whitehall, but there was no sign of her.

> (Client 3)'s gaze comes to rest on something at back of the hall. He looks intently at it.

NARRATOR: Two faces in the crowd. I'd seen them before. And I didn't like the look of them.

> (Client 3) calls (Client 2) over to look as well. He joins (Client 3) downstage.

NARRATOR: Then, I remembered where I had seen those faces. In the mugshot file on terrorist organizations. One was a BACTERIA agent; another was a senior operative from THRUSH ... and the third was one of the worst fanatics from the TINEA suicide squad. What were they doing, outside the office?

Suddenly, Angeline (alias client) appears, suitably spotlit, at the back of the hall. She is wearing a flying suit and boots, carrying a helmet. She walks slowly around the room, looking over her shoulder and all around her as she moves. When she gets about halfway along, three 'enemy agents' get up out of their seats and follow her at a discreet distance.

(Client 3) springs into action. (Please note that from here on, these are suggestions only. Further discussion will be necessary to plan the stunt appropriately.)

BOND: My God, sir! It's Angeline! And she's got a BACTERIA hit man, a THRUSH operative and a TINEA agent right behind her. May I use your telephone?

Without waiting for a reply, (Client 3) goes over to the desk telephone and calls Miss Moneypenny.

BOND: Moneypenny, darling. Get all the other 00 agents up here chop, chop, would you please? I think the dear old office is about to see some action. First time since the bombing in 1942. And see if you can rustle up any of our other agents in the building? We're going to need all the help we can get.

The area managers and as many of the other speakers who wish to participate come on stage. (Client 3) 'briefs' them, pointing out Angeline and the three enemy agents in the audience. (Client 3) then splits them into two groups, and despatches them off through the door. A few seconds later, we see the two groups prowling around the audience, looking at Angeline all the time.

Meanwhile, (Client 3) is on the phone again.

Bond: Weapon division? Get me one (product) and two (product) missiles and launchers. In 'M''s office. On the double.

He puts the phone down, and a couple of seconds later two very large tubes, labelled '(product)' and '(product)', plus another container labelled '(product)', are wheeled on stage. They are resting on small trolleys, so they look like miniature cannons. Three attendants accompany them.

Meanwhile, out in the audience, the pace is hotting up. Starting from the back of the hall, Angeline breaks into a brisk trot, and comes quickly towards the stage. The enemy agents catch up with her, and grab her arms, but she breaks free. She runs up on stage, puffing and distraught, into (Client 3)'s arms. The three agents also run up on stage after her, hotly pursued by three or four of the area managers/other speakers. After some carefully staged rugby tackles, the three enemy agents are brought down. But they get up and move off down the centre aisle of the audience. (Client 3) decides to play the trump card ...

BOND: Right! Stand clear. Fire (product) and (product) weapons!

The three 'weapons' are triggered with flashes of light and sound effects to suggest gunfire. The three enemy agents, now well and truly shot, fall down in an undignified heap in the centre aisle. All those on stage shout triumphantly, and congratulate each other. The Bond music begins, and plays us out.

The following is an excerpt from an event for a sister company to the one above. Their show was to run along very similar lines, with participation from the same top management team. This time, the theme (once again, chosen by the client) was *Startrek*, and I developed a similar story to that described above, linking the straight presentations and building up to a dramatic climax. The drugs to be discussed during the show were connected with the treatment of angina and hypertension (high blood pressure), so these became stylized enemy factions; the cardiovascular system became an innocent and undefended planet threatened by invasion of the enemy factions, and the client's products were the 'weapons' that would wipe out the invading enemy factions. Once again, the uninitiated could regard this as a little childish, although the *Startrek* series has become a cult with all age groups. However, the send-up aspect of the theme provided all concerned with the opportunity to let their hair down and enjoy themselves, while at the same time absorbing the necessary information.

After walk-in, we see the set in semi-darkness. Introductory music begins, and we see a starfield background on screen.

NARRATOR: Space ... the final frontier. These are the voyagers of the Starship (Company X) ...

We see, on screen, shots of key (Company X) figures in *Startrek* costumes. However, they are at work in their ordinary office environments. We also see, if possible, shots of the area managers—but not in costume.

NARRATOR: Our ten year mission . . . to explore the life-threatening activities of alien forces from Anginon and Hypertenzon . . .

We see product shots.

NARRATOR: . . . to promote new treatments through calcium antagonists . . . to boldly go, where no calcium antagonist has gone before.

Visuals continue as appropriate.

NARRATOR: Captain's log, stardate September 7, day sector one. We were picking up a faint distress signal from the Planet Cardiovascos . . .

We hear a woman's voice: that of Lt Uhura.

LT UHURA: (OOV) Captain! It's coming through now . . . the inhabitants of Cardiovascos are under siege from hostile aliens . . . wait. It's so faint, Captain! Ah! They request that we beam down medical supplies, urgently. It's a matter of life or death. Oh, Captain! Could they be under attack from Anginons? Or Hypertenzons? We must help them!

The narrator returns.

NARRATOR: This was serious . . . a major threat to the lives of these friendly beings on the Planet Cardiovascos. It was time to check that the Starship (Company X) was ready for anything the enemy Anginons and Hypertenzons could dream up. It looked like it was the Hypertenzons, this time . . .

We see flashing lights, and hear a selection of electronic bleeping noises, plus the voice of Scotty.

SCOTTY: (OOV) Aye, all systems at the ready, Captain. Photon phasers programmed and standing by. Full warp factor potential in force. Beam sensors live.

We return to the narrator, as the set now comes alive with sound and light; the arrival of a V.I.P. on the flight deck is imminent.

NARRATOR: Fortunately for the Starship (Company X), and for the Planet Cardiovascos, the governor of the Starfleet was with us on a special inspection. Earlier that day, he had beamed across from the Starship (Company Y), which had then departed on another mission. Now, he took command of this new threat to the civilizations of our galaxy, and prepared to brief the crew . . .

The doors of the flight deck open and (Client 1) walks on, in suitable costume. He takes his place at the lectern.

INTRODUCTION AND WELCOME BY (CLIENT 1)

(Client 1) exits.

NARRATOR: Captain's log, stardate September 7, day sector two. Obviously, the Governor was counting on us to destroy the threat of the Hypertenzons, to save the Planet Cardiovascos from certain annihilation. But this was no ordinary battle; it was probably the most demanding challenge the Starship (Company X) would face in a long time. Before we went into action, there was a lot of work to do ... I had to speak to my crew, right away: our mission was to go in peace, but if necessary, to shoot to kill.

The doors of the flight deck open, and (Client 2) walks on, in costume. He goes over to the lectern.

(COMPANY X): THE FUTURE, AND SELECTION OF THE TEAM LEADERS.

(Client 2) describes the 'new mission', then says he will now assemble the team leaders, and introduce them to the rest of the crew. He introduces them in turn, in character: it would be best if (Company X) were to allocate characters to the seven area managers, as they know which would be most appropriate for whom! Here is a selection of characters to choose from. All should be prefixed by the rank of Major.

Darth Vader
E.T.
R2D2
C3PO
Captain Kremmen
Mr Sulu
Mr Chekov
Doctor Who
Dalek
Alien
Trifid
Transformers

In some themed events, the dividing line between theme and serious business content need not be so obvious. This involves you in some careful writing to ensure that the business content is treated with respect, even though themed. In the following example, the theme was the FBI. Delegates (sales people from a company which manufactures and sells men's toiletries) were flown to New York, met at the airport by large men driving black limousines, driven to a Manhattan hotel where there was a gaggle of 'reporters' (actors) waiting with flashing cameras and mock TV crews, etc. Every moment of the event was themed, and needless to say the delegates enjoyed the whole thing immensely. Subliminally, too, they were flattered at the trouble and expense to which their company had gone to give them a good time, and the resulting uplift in motivation was reflected in the following year's sales figures. Many cynics would say that the cost of such an event is unjustifiable—but if it works, the money is well spent. First of all, this is the introduction delegates received from the actor who played the head of the FBI. This was the first time that the whole theme had actually been explained to them in full; until now very little had been said, to generate some suspense.

KURT: Good morning. You won't have heard my name before and naturally you won't be repeating it outside these four walls. But as a courtesy gesture, I will tell you that I'm Kurt Schlesinger, and I'm Head of the FBI here in New York. You may have guessed already, that FBI stands for Features and Benefits Investigation.

I'd like to welcome you here today, for the first New York briefing session of Features and Benefits Field Agent Investigators, in the (Company X) Sector. I'd also like to apologize for the secrecy surrounding your arrival in New York City, but as you know only too well we've got to take certain, er, precautions to make sure your cover isn't blown. And even with the strict security you'll have noticed that the news about your visit was leaked to the media.

> Kurt now notices that there is something happening on screen.

KURT: Yes, talking of the media. We have a newsflash coming through on our main screen right now.

> We now see the news reporter's opening piece to camera.

GAIL HAMILTON: (GESTURING TOWARDS HOTEL) The Marriott Hotel in downtown Manhattan ... this is the scene of some feverish activity here today, as the (Company X) Sector FBI agents all the way from Britain, meet in New York City for the first time. Crowds of reporters have been waiting since last night to get an exclusive on this important event on the Secret Service calendar. But as the limos pulled up outside the Marriott we could only wonder what important subjects these (Company X) specialists were going to be talking about in those top-security rooms inside.

Several delegates have been approached and asked to tell us the reasons for bringing this elite group of field agents together ... but no one's talking. There's obviously very important business going on in there, and we'll keep trying to find out just what that business is. So stay tuned for more news as soon as we get it. Until then, this is Gail Hamilton, NYBC News, outside the Marriott Hotel, Manhattan.

Kurt now concludes his introduction.

KURT: (DISAPPROVING, AS IF SPEAKING TO HIMSELF) This place's got more leaks than a Mexican toilet. (RESUMING AUTHORITATIVE MANNER) I know I can talk freely here, and I can tell you some of my colleagues were a little unnerved by these, er, indiscretions. They considered a move to silence the reporters. Some of the suggestions included ... (CASUALLY) impounding their cameras ... getting the Income Tax department to take a sudden interest in their freelance work ... arresting them for loitering ... rearranging the shape of their faces ... you know the kind of thing. But, my colleagues finally agreed with me to let it go this time, so we keep a low profile. However, if there are any further leaks the New York hospitals may have more than the normal number of broken legs to care for today.

So, let's get down to business. This morning we will remain here for a formal debriefing session, with a number of Special Agents who have been working under cover on our behalf for some time now. You must appreciate that these are some of the top Agents the FBI has ... put in as 'moles', as our colleagues in MI5 and MI6 would say back in England. The agents have infiltrated a number of organizations and operational areas which are of special interest to us here today.

The areas our Special Agents have been investigating are market research ... product quality ... product design ... advertising ... media planning ... Christmas strategy ... and, customer care.

All this input will help you achieve your vital goals out there in the field. That's because you'll be fully briefed on the features and benefits supporting you in the next operation, up to Christmas.

Later on you'll get the chance to interrogate these Special Agents yourselves, in small groups. The interrogation questions have been prepared by our Field Investigation operatives, and you'll find these have been concealed under your chairs for extra security. Needless to say they're under cover, in plain brown envelopes.

Right now, though, let's get the proceedings under way ...

Next, I've included part of one of the 'debriefings' conducted by Kurt with one of the 'Special Agents'. This part of the presentation was

intended to provide the sales force with useful background about the
behind-the-scenes activities undertaken by the company, including market
research, graphic design of packaging, media buying and advertising. The
section below is from the script I wrote for Kurt and a senior
representative of the company's advertising agency.

KURT: Now, Agent (name). Your brief was to report back on the creation
of advertising, I believe. I take it you've been working under cover in that
sector for a while now.

(ADVERTISING AGENCY PERSON): (Twenty years, or however long it
has been!)

KURT: Well, that's a good start. What is your cover title?

(ADVERTISING AGENCY PERSON): Creative Director, (name of
advertising agency), London.

KURT: I see from your haircut that you take the role pretty seriously.
(BEAT) Now. What does it take to put out good advertising?

(ADVERTISING AGENCY PERSON): Let's take an example. How about
the new (product) commercial?

KURT: Right. But before we do that, let's refresh our memories and take
a look at the (product) launch commercial. (Agency) developed that with
(Company X) back in 19XX. The title was (X).

We run the (X) launch commercial on V.T.

KURT: (X) was quite a success story, wasn't it?

(ADVERTISING AGENCY PERSON): Certainly was. It was a great film
that gave the product a unique positioning. The launch was highly
successful, and the sales results were as well.

KURT: So how do you go about producing a new commercial? How do
you follow that success?

(ADVERTISING AGENCY PERSON): I'll tell you. It started back in 19XY,
when creative development of (product) advertising was reviewed.

KURT: What areas were discussed?

(ADVERTISING AGENCY PERSON): Modernity—was the image right up
to the minute? Was the hero a bit old-fashioned, maybe? Surely our
consumers had moved on attitudinally. And their demands for creative
work had moved on as well.

KURT: So what was the conclusion?

(ADVERTISING AGENCY PERSON): That it was time for new copy. I mean, we knew this already, because we have the right experience, judgement and instincts to tell us the answers. But just to make sure and help us refine our thinking, we used creative development research. That was done by (name). And there was some qualitative research, too.

KURT: And what did that tell you?

(ADVERTISING AGENCY PERSON): Basically, that a lot of what the (X) commercial was saying, should stay. The impact, branding, range communication and showing ... it was all on target. It all showed that the products WORK, and that's what the consumer wanted to buy.

KURT: What opportunities for development came out of all that?

(ADVERTISING AGENCY PERSON): We learned even more about (product) users' inspirational values. These people are ahead of the game ... well organized types. So we had to make the props more relevant, and more motivating to the target audience in the late 19XXs.

KURT: Props?

(ADVERTISING AGENCY PERSON): Yes. The model, the music, all that.

KURT: So how did all this input come together?

(ADVERTISING AGENCY PERSON): In the form of a very detailed brief, which was put together, presented internally, fine-tuned, and then presented to (Company X). They added their input, it was developed further, and finally approved.

KURT: Painstaking process, eh?

(ADVERTISING AGENCY PERSON): It's the only way. A good brief is crucial.

The final excerpt in this chapter is from a very complicated, but very effective themed event for a major UK computer company. The theme was based on the 'back to the future' concept, and involved me plus a number of other scriptwriters in generating scripts for the company's various divisions across a number of tenses and time zones. The idea was that three company officials (played by actors) from the year 2010 had come back to the year of the event (early in 1989) via a time-warp device, to describe to the clients (they were in the present) what 'had' happened to the company in the future. The set was very simple, with the three actors sitting on a raised section and the clients concerned seated either side of them. All were reading from teleprompters. As no movement was involved, other than clients walking on and off set, the whole show was dependent on the dialogue to keep things interesting. Although there were a number of serious business messages involved (for example, through the actors describing what 'had' happened, warning delegates of what could happen if they were complacent about current success) there was to be a high satire content including plenty of in-jokes. To add depth, we characterized the three people from the future. Robert was a rather pompous, well-spoken Englishman with the very dead-pan humour of a style like that of 'Yes, Prime Minister'. Caleb was a Texan whose language, though colourful, reflected the fact that he was very shrewd. And Harriet was an English lady business executive who suffered from a bit of conflict between her professional expertise and flirtatious personality!

This particular script, for the company's marketing division, was the best of those I wrote. And although it drove me mad while I worked on it—trying to think and write in three tenses at once is not a job for beginners—it is one of the favourite scripts in my portfolio. I attended this particular show as well as sitting in on rehearsals, and was very gratified to see that the audience were chuckling, giggling and listening intently from one end to the other. Here are some excerpts from it! ...

(CLIENT TWO): So what are you going to tell us about the future, then? Nothing too dismal, I hope.

ROBERT: I may have to disappoint you there, Mr (name). What you're about to hear is the picture not just you, but the whole of (Company X) faced in the future. Assuming, that is, that you did not take heed of the impending changes in the marketplace, and carried on blithely with some of the company's present ideas.

CALEB: So y'all better listen up, and listen GOOD.

HARRIET: One of the most important issues to hit (Company X) was in 1992, when European standards became a reality rather than a looming sword of Damocles hanging over your heads. Of course you people in Europe had been banging on about this for some time, but it took quite a while for your colleagues across the pond to realize how important an issue it was and reflect European standards in their programmes. Meanwhile, (Company X) in Europe was lagging behind its competitors. Poor loves, I can't imagine YOU lagging behind anybody.

(CLIENT TWO): But what did we DO about our European standards?

HARRIET: When 1992 arrived, the technological scramble to get the standards right was so bad that (Company X) people were falling over each other in the rush. And it wasn't surprising to find that whereas one half of the personnel in Professional Services were sent for forced sabbaticals to health farms all over the UK, the other half staged a lightning walk-out and sit-down protest, totally blocking the North Circular Road outside the (location) site for several days.

ROBERT: This of course did not lead to any noticeable disruption in the normal traffic flow. (BRIEF BEAT) The European standards issue was not helped by the new US president, Oliver North, stating in his inaugural address in January 1993 that he intended to open negotiations with Europe, with a view to creating twelve new US states out of the EC countries. His remarks were well received by the various European leaders, who were all offered new jobs in the United States. Margaret Thatcher, who had been elected Prime Minister for the fourth consecutive time in 1991, was to be given the especially coveted title of Head of Catering at the Pentagon. Sir Austin Mitchell would give up his job in television and remain behind as Governor of the State of Britain, with Senator Norman Tebbitt as local head of the British CIA.

(CLIENT ONE): Bugger Norman Tebbitt. What was happening to (Company X)?

CALEB: The old die-hard attitude towards selling boxes, like you'd expect, became a thing of the past. The first reason was because hardware, far from being boxes, was gettin' so much smaller that most machines could fit into the palm of your hand. But more 'bout that later. The other problem was that relative costs were falling at an average rate of 35 per cent per year. So by the year 2001, a (Company X) (product) cost a bit less than £150 and it was cheaper to buy than a Sony Walkman. Basically, customers around the turn of the century didn't give a shit whether their hardware was a box or a plate of corned beef and hash browns.

HARRIET: What concerned them was systems, not bits of kit. They were interested in what their (Company X) system could do for them, rather than the metal it sat in. (Company X) was somewhat slow to see the light, but eventually did respond ... especially to the hard work put in by Professional Services, who had been telling them that for years.

(CLIENT TWO): And what about all the things we'd been saying for years?

ROBERT: You were in luck, my friend. Finally, the words of you long-suffering individuals in Central Marketing were heard, too. Although selling boxes had been easy money for (Company X) and its competitors way back in the seventies, times had changed. The new view was that if

(Company X) people didn't change, there wouldn't be a company to work for any longer. And they were right.

(CLIENT ONE): And then what?

HARRIET: (Product 1) as well as (Product 2) availability on UNIX was announced, but due to delays the marketplace became sceptical about your commitment to deliver them to the open market. As a result, (Product 2) sales declined, and both (Product 1) and (Product 2) were rejected by the CCTA as inappropriate. And your lead in fourth generation languages evaporated.

(Etc.)

(CLIENT ONE): Tell me about the new activity centres. I can't wait for this.

CALEB: Yep. They played an increasing role in (Company X) as the years went on. The three new office buildings in (City 1), (City 2) and (City 3) met with wide acclaim for their plush fittings and elegant decor. Your very own Prince Charles ... well, he just didn't think they was much to write home about.

(CLIENT TWO): Well, Prince Charles has always had a problem with architecture. Perhaps he should work for (Company X).

CALEB: Yeah. And in a major speech in 1994 the Prince talked about the buildings as (PUTS ON PSEUDO 'ENGLISH' ACCENT) 'carbuncles on the bum of the British computer industry'. He asked his audience (PSEUDO 'ENGLISH' ACCENT AGAIN) 'why on earth (Company X) couldn't create more wonderful buildings with character, like (location which was known to be very ugly)'. Well now, old (name) wanted to do the future King a favour. Don't forget he hadn't gotten his knighthood yet. So he promised to retain (location) and turn it into a charity hostel for homeless (Company X) fitters.

HARRIET: In 1995, (Company X) bought the world-famous art collection previously owned by Charles Saatchi, to adorn the activity centres. So popular was the collection with customers that (Company X) eventually decided to remove all products from the buildings as they just got in the way of the pictures.

(CLIENT ONE): I suppose computers would be getting pretty small by then. So they'd probably be dwarfed by the paintings anyway.

ROBERT: Quite so. Already in the mid to late 1980s, the number of components on a computer chip had increased from 20 000 to 400 000. A few years later, a computer chip could hold several billion components.

This meant that by 1993, a (Company X) UNIX product was the size of a dried pea and could be fitted inside the casing of a wristwatch. This naturally led to a clever move on the part of Central Marketing and Indirect Divison to sign up the Rolex organization of Switzerland as a major value-added reseller. High-level talks were also held around that time about a proposed merger between (Company X) and Matchbox Toys. However, the talks were unsuccessful as both (name) and (name) flatly refused to market (product name) products under the branding of Thomas the Tank Engine.

(CLIENT TWO): So what did our customers do with their computer rooms and computer centres? Turn them into warehouses?

CALEB: Yeah. And they're just dandy as shower cubicles for the (client) account team. And a special limited edition of the (Company X) (product) series was designed to be implanted directly into the human brain. This made it specially attractive to accountancy and finance users.

(CLIENT ONE): I'll bet. Our accountants need all the help they can get.

HARRIET: I'll bet you need some help sometimes too, darling. Of course the trend towards miniaturization saw a gradual redefinition of both mainframe architectures and (DELIBERATELY) 'PERPETUITY'. Back when (Company X) was formed in the mid 1980s, there were four mainframe architectures to be supported in 'PERPETUITY'. With the shrinking size of processors, by 1994 it was decided to settle finally on one architecture for all mainframes.

(CLIENT TWO): I wonder if they called it a PC ...

ROBERT: The shrinking size of machines also gave rise to some concern over the term 'PERPETUITY', and there were considerable fears that perpetuity, along with the products themselves, would eventually disappear up their own definitions. This being an unpalatable prospect, senior management decreed that perpetuity would, in fact, come to an end when either (a) the cows came home or (b) (name) took early retirement, whichever was the sooner.

CALEB: The (Company X) (despatch) function, previously troubled by products going missing on airplanes, now had the added problem of losing products which had been mistakenly transported by wasps, bees and other flyin' insects from (location where department was based.)

(CLIENT ONE): Oh, surely not. Now, what about working in partnership with other organizations? That's another important trend.

HARRIET: I'll be your partner any time you like, sweetie. And you're right about (Company X), too. That trend, which was set in the mid to late

1980s, where you would work in partnership with component manufacturers, third parties and customers, continued to develop at a cracking pace. (Company X) furthered its policy of buying many of these partner companies to expand its own operation. By 1993 it had purchased Marks and Spencer, Boots the Chemist and Tesco, in order to pursue its interests in the retail industry.

ROBERT: At the same time, (Company X) opened a large healthfoods hypermarket on the (name) site so that its three new partners could pursue their interests in computing. (Company X) did encounter something of a problem in the electric razor market, however, when Victor Kiam bought a (product) in 1994, used it for his own personal shaving, and liked it so much he decided to buy the company.

(CLIENT TWO): Well, I DON'T like his razors, so I hope he doesn't buy us.

HARRIET: Oh, darling. You look far too young to be SHAVING yet . . .

(Etc.)

(CLIENT ONE): So what was happening to the hardware side of the business?

HARRIET: Well, around about this time, the increasing compatibility and communications among (Company X) products led to the decision to streamline that, and produce only one machine that did everything. So by the end of the 1990s (Company X) announced its 'One machine, one company' strategy. That meant that the business consisted of one product the size of a human finger nail supplying the total computing needs for one major corporation made up of (Company X) and all its customers. However, the new single machine was still incapable of handling (Company X)'s own (product) system.

(CLIENT TWO): That must have made life easier for (despatch), at least.

ROBERT: Not really. It is to be regretted that (despatch) were still unable to trace the one remaining (Company X) product. They had confused the company's total production output in the year 1999 with a packet of flaked almonds. And, interestingly, reports in the tabloid press late that year spoke of a magical new almond-flavoured cake, that would provide total business solutions for senior executives at only 80 calories a slice.

(Etc.)

Chapter 16

Speaking on the broadcast media

This is an area in which little or no script should ever be written, because interviews should always sound unrehearsed. However, putting the words together for a broadcast media interview—whether you are the interviewee, or you're helping to prepare an interview for a colleague—involves much of the same *thinking* that goes into scriptwriting, even though you don't write words down in a formal manner.

In Chapter 12 of this book, I covered corporate TV and AV interview techniques, largely from the point of view of how to conduct such interviews—although if you're to be a corporate interviewee, you should be able to learn quite a lot from that chapter as well. In this chapter, however, we're talking about broadcast, or, in other words, journalistic interviews. And although on the surface the two types of interview may seem similar, there are some very significant differences. Probably the most important difference is that whereas in a corporate interview everyone, interviewer included, is playing on the same team—i.e. putting the interviewee and the whole interview in the most favourable possible light—in a broadcast interview, the whole point is to create interest and even entertainment for the viewer or listener. And if that means doing it at the expense of the interviewee, even putting that person on the spot and making him or her look silly, it makes 'good TV' (or radio)—and that's what the interviewer gets paid to do.

Not surprisingly, therefore, broadcast media interviews—i.e. going on radio or television to talk about your business or other activity—have become an art in themselves. Radio and TV interviewers are trained and very experienced at asking questions, often awkward ones, and practised interviewees are just as good at responding in a way that makes them or their companies look good no matter how much pressure the interviewer puts on them to do otherwise. For the inexperienced interviewee, a good interviewer with a plastic smile and sharp verbal teeth can be terrifying. But with a little knowledge on how to handle interviews, you can come through the harshest experience unscathed.

In nearly every major city in the Western Hemisphere, you can take a course on media interviews. This training facility has become big business, often run by ex or current media interviewers who put you through a 'mock' interview, record it on videotape, take your performance apart and then show you how to put it back together properly. For most executives whose companies play a significant part in a community, one of these courses is a good idea. Even local radio and TV will sometimes want to interview a representative of Bloggs Bearings Ltd if the factory is facing potential closure, they plan to build a new plant, their chimneys are puffing out what the district conservation society thinks is toxic smoke, the local frog population is threatened with reduced breeding grounds in the factory's car park, or any other activity which is likely to affect the neighbourhood. Company representatives will be called upon for an interview, to put their side of the story. To refuse can be seen as an admission of culpability. To do the interview, and get it wrong, can make the company look bad even if it doesn't deserve to. Knowing how to put your case becomes essential.

Another, rather more positive reason why two or three people in a company should know how to be interviewed, is for promotional purposes. Press releases, suitably worded and sent to a broadcast station stating some piece of genuine news about a company, can interest the editorial people there and result in a request for someone to go on air and elaborate.

Finally, going on air in a non-specific capacity—the managing director of Bloggs Bearings Ltd answering questions about how to grow orchids on a radio phone-in show, and casually mentioning the company's name—can help to gain recognition for Bloggs Bearings. That's all part of the PR process. But all the MD needs to understand about the PR relevance of the exercise is that more than one or two discreet plugs for Bloggs would be a no-no. Wall-to-wall plugs would have two consequences: (1) the MD would never be asked to discuss orchids again, and (2), he or she would put Bloggs Bearings in a bad light. Discretion is vital; but the spin-off PR, with press releases about the MD's radio stardom going to local newspapers and internal PR with an article about the radio show in the company newsletter, could be useful.

Where the knowledge of how to put words together really counts, is in the first two categories: defending your position, and promoting a new product or service. Let's take a look at a few tips on how to get your words right; however, bear in mind that a full training course for the likely interview candidates in a company will teach them much more than is possible in this book.

The first thing to consider is that radio and TV stations are uncharted waters for the average business person, and the sheer unfamiliarity of the place can make you nervous to start with. It's important to remember that these stations are ordinary places of business, just like yours. The fact that there are people in headphones lurking behind double thicknesses of glass, and that strange machines are whirring around you, is purely a matter of course in the running of the station's business. If you took one of the station's technicians down to your place of work, he or she would probably feel just as out of place and uncomfortable watching your production line or computer activity as you do in the sound-proofed recording studio. It sounds incredible and it can be, the first few times, but the red glow of the 'on air' or 'recording' light in the radio or TV studio does not signal Armageddon; it merely tells everyone that it's time to go to work. Keep the whole thing in perspective, and keep reminding yourself that broadcasting, just like your own industry, is not entirely staffed by man-eating tigers.

It helps a lot to do a little preparatory research before you are interviewed. Sometimes, of course, this isn't possible—especially when there has been a sudden piece of news and you need to comment on it immediately. However, in normal circumstances you will have a little time to learn something of the broadcast station, and the programme, on which you will appear. Listen to, watch, or tape the programme concerned beforehand, so that you know its style and approach.

Make sure you and the broadcast station know what to expect of each other. If you have a PR consultant, he or she will normally do this for you; if you don't, do it yourself. Before the programme, and preferably well before the programme, find out just what aspect of the topic the interviewer wants to highlight. This will give you some time to prepare your material. You should also make sure that the broadcast station knows who you are and what you and your company do; a short, tightly written briefing document should be sent to them as early as possible.

Get to the broadcast station as promptly as you can. Don't arrive three hours in advance, as you'll build up excessive nerves and probably wire yourself up on their coffee which will make things even worse. Just allow enough time to park your car, go to the bathroom, smoke a cigarette (unhealthy, but soothing for some!), settle in comfortably, and *relax*. Then, try to have a chat with the interviewer before you go on. This isn't always feasible, especially if you're to make an appearance on a three-hour drive-in time radio show, where you're likely to be ushered into the studio during a commercial break or weather report and start a few seconds later. But with TV, you're likely to have time to talk to the person who will interview you, or at least a researcher who will then brief the interviewer. The purpose of this conversation is to run through the questions the interviewer may ask, and generally get to know the person a little. Not many interviewers will tell you the actual questions you should expect and—as is the case with corporate interviews—this isn't intended to catch you off your guard. From the interviewer's point of view, he or she will want your replies to sound spontaneous, and so will want to keep one or two small surprises up the professional sleeve. That makes good radio or television, and as long as you know your subject matter you'll handle any surprises easily. But most interviewers will give you a good general idea of what will be asked, so you can call those issues up on your brain's computer and have them handy.

How to approach the interview

One very basic tip is to listen carefully to the questions. This sounds ridiculous, but when you're a bit nervous in your unfamiliar surroundings, staring at a dangling microphone in a radio studio or at a cold, hard camera lens on TV, you can be sufficiently distracted to let questions go in one ear and come out of the other. Remember that any kind of studio microphone, radio or TV, is very sensitive and can pick up a fly buzzing ten feet away. Don't shuffle your feet or tap the furniture with your fingers, as the sound may well come through. Sit still, breathe deeply, and concentrate on the interviewer.

Even with radio, you should always look at the interviewer when you're replying to questions. That will help you to concentrate, as a human face responding to what you say is reassuring. Don't be put off by the fact that the interviewer doesn't *say* anything while you're talking; he or she may well smile or nod to encourage you, but grunts, 'Yes's, 'No's, 'Oh really's, and so on that are common in normal conversation are out of the question because more than one voice at a time will confuse the soundtrack. It's purely a technicality, so don't worry about it. (See Chapter 12.)

With radio, remember that the audience does not have the benefit of seeing you. All you've got to put across your message is your voice. So try to speak in a lively tone, avoid clichés and jargon, and avoid plugging your product or service *unless it's relevant* to the subject matter. Be natural; to quote John Yates (one of Britain's leading direct mail writers) entirely out of context, address the listeners 'as if you were standing next to them in a pub or cocktail bar'. Don't be pompous or opinionated, and remember that all but a few of the listeners will know nothing whatsoever about your business—so speak in simple, understandable language.

With television, you do have the benefit of being seen, but that's a double-edged sword. Remember, one of the biggest shocks many people get is seeing themselves on television or video; you never look as you expect to. One of the great advantages of doing a media interview training course is that you're likely to get the chance to watch yourself on videotape. And you'll be surprised how what your Mother always called an endearingly crooked smile looks like an evil, twitching leer. The camera doesn't lie, really; it just magnifies all your acne scars, open pores, nervous tics, and uncomfortable posture. A gesture with your hand, eyebrow, etc., that would hardly be noticed in real life makes you look like a demented windmill through the cruel eye of the camera. Many stage actors have had to learn to reduce their exaggerated theatre 'body language' when they've turned to acting on TV or film, for exactly the same reason. Seat yourself as comfortably as possible, look at the interviewer, and no matter how hostile you feel towards him or her, be pleasant. Keep your hands still, as far as possible, without looking as if the interviewer has tied them behind your back, and keep your head still no matter how animated your discourse. Even slight movements of the head can look as though you're bobbing for apples. If all the above guidelines make you feel nervous just to think about them, do a training course; or failing that, practise with a good friend who can play the interviewer's part and observe your behaviour.

Your clothes should be carefully chosen, too. Don't forget, your clothes speak volumes, or wardrobes, about you and the organization you represent. Loud, jazzy numbers reflect precisely that on your image. Dress according to how you want viewers to perceive you and your company. And there are also a few technical points to observe. TV stations can be hot, especially under the powerful studio lights, so use an antiperspirant and avoid thin clothes through which any perspiration could show. Also avoid vivid patterns, stripes, etc., plus the colours red and white, as these can create fuzzy reactions with the camera. If the studio uses chromakey (colour separation overlay, a technique whereby you project background pictures apparently behind the subject) you should also avoid the colour blue, but this is something you can check out before you go to the TV station for your interview. In either radio or TV interviews, it's a good idea to avoid wearing heavy metal watches or bracelets because if you should put your wrist down on a table or desk top, the resulting clunking noise might be picked up by the microphones. Even the rustle of crisp, freshly ironed cotton or linen can be picked up by a sensitive lapel microphone, but don't worry too much about that one—the technicians at the broadcast station can usually sort it out.

One final word on the approach to the interview: watch the booze. Those of us in the business who advise speakers on anything, be they conference presenters or potential broadcast media interviewees, sympathize with the speaker's view that one drink will help to relax the nerves and smooth the conversation—however, we don't support it. The police say that even one small alcoholic drink can impair your judgement in the driving seat of a car; the same is true of your ability in the hot seat of the interview studio. If you must, just have *one*; but you're better to stick to juice, tea or coffee.

The interview itself

Once again, a good training course will put you through detailed studies of how to go about answering questions and handling the interviewer. However, there are a few basic tips that will help you if you get caught on the hop, before you've had a chance to enrol on a course.

Let's look first at the straightforward type of interview which has been set up for PR purposes, i.e. by you or your PR consultancy, in order to gain recognition for your company and its products and services. You may be required to participate in an interview as a 'generic' industry spokesperson, or your company may have announced a new product, service or activity which is of local or national interest. However, you can bet your bottom dollar that the interviewer is not going to sit there and cue you to perform as a walking, talking, breathing, advertising commercial. The interviewer will be looking for an angle that is likely to be of interest to the listeners or viewers, and what most interests them is not necessarily what most interests you or your sales director. If you even attempt to do a sales pitch the interviewer is likely to become hostile and stop you, and to an extent this is understandable because a sales pitch is likely to make the listeners or viewers feel hostile towards the broadcast station. And that's bad for the interviewer's business.

The interviewer is likely to be interested in issues that are relevant to as large a sector of the audience as possible. This is likely to centre around human matters, or commercial matters that are pertinent to the good of the community or a significant group within it.

It's important that you accept this, and answer the questions accordingly. When answering, try to put yourself in the listeners' or viewers' shoes, and structure your statements with them in mind. However, do remember that, provided you have something important to say, it is not a crime against society to use radio or TV as 'free advertising'. And to be fair, if the broadcast station has done its homework it will have ascertained beforehand just what you do have to say, and will naturally assume that you will work in a mention of your company, products or services. So unless you overdo the plugs, no professional interviewer should get hostile with you for a fair and reasonable mention of what you have to sell.

Probably the best and most acceptable way to work in your own messages, benefits, achievements, etc., is through *examples* that you can give to illustrate your direct answer to the interviewer's questions. Examples are wonderful things in PR terms, because they can be set up as a genuine part of the overall non-commercial response you're giving, and can subtly bring in a number of facts about you and your company at the same time.

Let's say that Bloggs Bearings has just won a huge, long-term contract from a customer, and the extra work involved is going to generate fifty new jobs in the area. You, as the spokesperson for Bloggs, are being interviewed on local radio about it. The interviewer is keen to find out if this is just a temporary boost to local economy, so asks you ...

INTERVIEWER: Fifty new jobs—that's good news. But we hear a lot these days about growing competition from foreign manufacturers in engineering, making goods of high quality and selling them here for lower prices. How do you see British manufacturers competing against that sort of threat? What have you got that the foreign competitors haven't?

YOU: Well first of all there's British companies' loyalty to and moral preference for British-made goods. That counts for something. Okay, our prices are higher in some cases, but then we pay higher wages to our workforce to keep up with the higher standards of living we have here. Most of our British customers appreciate that. More important in a competitive field, though, is that our service is reliable, with the sort of long-term experience we have, and because of the fact that we are on the spot rather than hundreds or even thousands of miles away. That's worth paying a little more for, in itself. Then, there's quality; we pride ourselves on quality in the British engineering industries, and it's something we work very hard to keep at the forefront of. So with first-class service and top quality, we're genuinely giving our customers added value. Let me give you an example. Last month one of our biggest customers telephoned me at Bloggs Bearings, and said they needed five thousand titanium bearings for a very special new machine, by Monday morning. This was Friday afternoon. So, our workforce dropped all their plans for the weekend and designed the bearing using our new computer-aided design technology, got tooled up and manufactured the whole order of five thousand, carried on working through the nights as well, and we got that order delivered to the customer's door at nine o'clock Monday morning. We didn't charge any more for the bearings than the usual market price; the rush order and special design are all part of our service. I daresay many of our colleagues in British engineering might have done the same. But how many of our foreign competitors could have managed that?

Congratulations. You've answered the broad question—why customers should pay more for British-made goods—and you've also managed to bring in the facts that your workforce is good, you've got the latest technology for design, your dedication to quality is absolute, and your service is excellent. You then managed to bring the conversation back to general terms, by generously suggesting that some of your British competitors might be almost as good. And you haven't got the interviewer's back up, because you've worked your own message into a genuine overall statement that genuinely answered the question. The sell came into the example, not the reply itself, and didn't sound out of place.

Some interviewers like to ask 'awkward' questions in the belief that putting interviewees on the spot makes for more entertaining radio or TV. If you should experience this, don't be intimidated, and whatever you do don't try to fluff your way through it. That will make you seem shifty and uncertain of your ground. If you believe the question is awkward and/or difficult, say so; honesty is very important in any type of interview. Say that this is a difficult question to answer, and then say why it is. Finally, outline whatever main points you can, in response to it.

The last, and most important point to remember about even the most straightforward of broadcast interviews is to *know* your subject. Even the unsighted world of radio can expose your innermost weaknesses to the public ear, and television doubles the risk. Trying to bluff your way out of a question to which you don't know the answer will drop your credibility rating right down. If the worst comes to the worst, *say* you don't know, but will find out and let the viewers know the answer. But that is a measure which should be reserved only for emergencies. No matter how busy you are, a broadcast media interview is very important to your company in PR terms, so make sure you find the time to prepare for it properly. Not only will you save your company from the embarrassment of looking bad through its representative—you—but you will also save yourself from being any more apprehensive than is strictly necessary. There's nothing like ignorance and lack of preparation to make any interviewee climb the walls with stagefright.

The defensive interview

This is the type of interview that no PR consultant in his or her right mind would ever seek for you. There has been a problem with your company—real or manufactured—and the press are after you to comment and/or to defend yourselves. To a large extent the following few paragraphs apply to press interviews as well, but at least with reporters from newspapers you don't have to worry about *how* you sound or how you look. You just have to choose your words carefully.

With the broadcast variety, it is vital that you stay calm and don't panic. If you handle the problem properly, not only will you be seen to defend your company well, but you can even turn the whole issue around so that it does your company some good, on the PR side.

Radio and TV reporters love to 'doorstep' unsuspecting victims when there has been a sudden newsworthy occurrence. In fairness to them, as news reporters it is their job to find out what's going on, get the various parties involved to comment, and report the details to their audience as soon as possible; that's why they turn up on your doorstep very quickly—not because they deliberately want to catch you and your colleagues unawares. However, the effect on you can be much the same. It's essential not to over-react to doorstepping, because there's nothing worse for the image than a company representative humming and ha-ing, trying to make something up. If you do not yet know what's going on, say so; and then quickly point out that an immediate enquiry has been launched into the accident/incident/whatever, and that you'll have more information for them in so many hours' time. Once you have the information, give it to the reporters; you must be seen to keep your word.

Whatever you do, don't dehumanize any problem. All reporters, unless they write for the specialized business press, are interested in the 'people' issues of any crisis or incident involving companies. Don't preface a rebuff by saying 'it's not our company policy to . . .' no matter how tempted you may be to use it. Even if it isn't company policy to talk to the press, the alternative if you're doorstepped is to make your company look hard and uncaring, which is bad news from every imaginable point of view. So it's better to say that you don't know the answer to that question yet and that, rather than speculate, you're going to find out the facts and let the public know just as soon as the investigation is complete.

Another common instance of doorstepping is when there is a dispute between the management of your company and the trade unions, or between the company generally and an external group. Reporters, in the correct belief that a public argument is entertaining for viewers or listeners, will attempt to get both sides airing their views. Don't be drawn into this one, even if you're told that the other side has given an interview saying you're about as amenable as Attila the Hun. Let's say there has been a lightning strike at Bloggs Bearings, and you're told that the union negotiator has just given an interview saying that although you'd been ensconced in a meeting for eight hours no progress had been made. The interviewer asks for your comments:

> *YOU:* It's still early days yet, although it was a long meeting today. With an issue as important as this, we can't expect any quick, easy answers. As it happens, I thought we *did* make some progress (IF THIS IS TRUE), and we'll be back in there first thing tomorrow to continue. We've all got much more work to do, and if you'll forgive me, I must get on with mine now.

This way, even though you privately may think the union negotiator would earn his or her living more effectively as an organ-grinder's monkey, you kill the public argument stone dead and deflect any further controversy. If the union person is watching, he or she can't argue with the fact that there's more work to be done, or with the fact that you're intending to do your share.

If you're lucky, you may have a little more time to prepare yourself for a defensive interview. In this case, you might well turn a negative into a definite positive. Let's take an example: Bloggs Bearings is selling some land to a property developer who intends to build executive homes on the site. Local people are worried that this might mean Bloggs is in financial trouble and is cutting back, with the possible loss of jobs. The interviewer leads up with all this, then asks you why the land was sold instead of using it to expand your business and create more jobs:

> *YOU:* Well, like a lot of companies these days we are under a certain amount of financial pressure, yes. Competition is growing, especially from overseas manufacturers who have much lower overheads and can undercut our prices. And, as you know, expansion costs money. To do that, we have to borrow money, which gets expensive in interest rates. But by selling this land, we have released quite a lot of money which we can now invest in the company. That means all the existing jobs are secure. It also means there's some money to invest in new machinery, which we badly need to stay competitive. The way things were looking before we sold the land, we might have had to stop making some of our components here and imported them from Japan. This way, with our new machines, we keep all our products one hundred percent British, and may even need to increase our workforce once the new machines are installed.

> *INTERVIEWER:* But surely you need that land to expand into?

> *YOU:* No. The new ways of manufacturing our products, with new machines, take up less space. And, in any case, we still own fourteen

acres of land around the factory, which we can use in the future should we need it. But expansion these days means smaller, more efficient machinery, with more room for the people who work with it to move around and do their jobs better. Take our XYZ bearing, for example; the machine we're currently using to make that takes up eighty-five square metres. The new one we can now afford to buy takes up just forty square metres, although the number of people working it remains the same. In fact, we're planning to buy a second one to make XYZ's next year, which will double our output, create ten new jobs, and all in virtually the same factory space.

INTERVIEWER: So do you foresee any job redundancies at Bloggs Bearings?

YOU: No. As I just said, we plan to double the output of the XYZ bearing next year, with ten new jobs. And that's just one of our range of two hundred products.

You have not only deflected the bad news aspect of the interviewer's questions, you have also caught him or her on the hop. Often an interviewer will keep trying to cast a negative or aggressive light on the interview even after he or she should have stopped; if you're quick to spot this, you can turn it to your advantage. In the last few lines, you have pointed out that the XYZ expansion will result in ten new jobs, and that your other products may experience similar growth. You have managed to cover a number of sales points, and reassured the viewers and listeners of the fact that Bloggs Bearings is on the up and up. You have also given a very fair and honest answer to the interviewer's question before you got into the sales points, which satisfies the media's need for truth, and your need to make your company look deservedly good.

Chapter 17

Your part in the production process

Before we get into the part you actually play within the production process, it's worth taking a look at the various production routes that are possible within the corporate field. If you know this already, then I apologize for boring you; if you don't, or you're not sure about the precise roles involved, reading the following sections will clarify things for you.

Who makes your programme?

Production can be broken down into three main groups of responsibility. Productions are, in the main, made by any one or any combination of these three:

- an in-house production studio or department
- an outside production company
- an outside facilities company.

Before we go any further I should define the difference between production and facilities, as even within the business itself there is often a grey area on that topic. Production consists of making an entire programme, film, or business theatre presentation, from start to finish. This involves everything from the initial concepts and treatments, through to scripts and storyboards where applicable, all the way down the line to the finished product. Facilities organizations, whether they consist of one person and a dog or a cast of thousands, provide only a part of that process; and the part they provide is always a function that occurs after the treatment and script have been done. Therefore, facilities can mean: (1) a company that produces computer graphics; or (2) a company that does cartoon work; or (3) a company that provides videotape or film editing; or (4) a company that makes hundreds of copies of a film, videotape or slide-tape master. Many of these facilities outfits will describe themselves as production companies, but unless they offer clients a concept service from scratch—i.e. they will take the project from an initial brief through to completion—they do not offer true, *total* production services.

There is one exception to this principle. That is in the area of television and radio commercials, where organizations advertising themselves as production companies seldom if ever get themselves involved in the writing of scripts and the drawing of storyboards. These latter functions are normally performed by an advertising agency or consultancy; although in the case of a client going directly to a production company (i.e. who chooses not to use an advertising agency or consultancy) the production company will normally find people to script and storyboard the client's commercial. However, the story of advertising is one that has been very thoroughly dealt with in other books and is not examined here.

So, we get back to the realms of the production department, the production company, and the facilities house. Let's take a look at each one in a bit more detail.

Production companies

The definition of a production company is as near to the riddle of 'how long is a piece of string?' as it is to anything else. In the same way as the in-house production department, the production company can be anything from one person, a desk and a telephone, to a large audio-visual factory employing dozens of staff.

You're more likely to find a common denominator in what the production company does: creating total productions. The variation comes in on the subject of workers to carry out the different functions of such a process; the one person, one desk variety will hire freelance individuals and facilities for everything, whereas the large organization will provide all but a few functions under its own roof.

Not surprisingly, there are two very clear schools of thought on this difference of approach. There are those who favour the small, tightly knit production company which hires freelance people to do all the key jobs like directing, camera operation, graphics, etc. The argument in favour of this approach is that the production company is free to hand-pick the best and most suitable people for the job, with a far wider choice of personnel than would be the case with a virtual Hobson's choice of in-house staff. Freelance specialists tend to be very good at their jobs, too—that's why they go freelance in the first place. And because you're only ever 'as good as your last job' in the freelance world, they tend to be good every time if they want to continue to pay their mortgages and feed their families.

The argument against compiling teams out of freelance people and small facilities set-ups is that these people get around, know what every production company and client is up to, and could present some sort of security risk. And, to be fair, there are clients who become nervous over the fact that some of the people working on their production are not on the production company's payroll, and therefore may not be sufficiently loyal. However, any successful freelance operator, or any successful facilities outfit, will tell you that the most valuable asset anyone can have in this business is a tightly buttoned lip. Anyone indulging in even the merest trifle of industrial espionage or disloyalty will only ever get the chance to do it once. Word of such undesirable activity spreads like an epidemic, with disastrous results for the perpetrator. And with competition among freelance individuals and operations increasing just as fast as it is for larger companies, the last thing any of them is likely to do is jeopardize future work by leaking sensitive information.

Another, less serious argument against the small-is-beautiful production company arises out of the question of professional pride. A small production company's one or two directors may not like to admit to clients that they haven't exactly got a personnel register the length of Metro Goldwyn Mayer's. And it is true to say that some clients may feel more reassured by a production company with several employees on the payroll; but at the end of the day it is quality, not quantity, that produces the best work. Most clients or organizations commissioning productions recognize the validity of this point only too well—especially if they find it out through experience of indifferent work having been produced by a large production company. It's what the production company does that counts, not how many people it employs to do it.

At the other end of the spectrum, you have the large production company that provides almost every facility it's ever going to need under its own roof. Companies answering to this description are found mainly in business theatre production, where there are very good reasons for having such facilities in-house, quite apart from those of the economic variety. Speed, for example, is one of those other reasons; the speed at which some conferences are designed, written, prepared and despatched is often quite alarming. It frequently involves teams of people toiling night and day to get all the work done on time. Also, by cutting back on travelling time as well as avoiding the delays caused by the complications of work going on in several places, precious time can be saved.

Another benefit of the large production company is in quality control. It is obvious that supervision is a great deal more efficient with all work being processed in one place; many producers find it a lot easier to coordinate and control a production when they can physically lay hands on everybody concerned at the same time. And because business theatre production is particularly labour-intensive, quality control is as important as it is difficult to maintain.

Film, videotape and slide-tape production companies of a medium size—and it is in this category that you'll find the vast majority of production companies—tend to work to a compromise. Key personnel such as producers, visualizers, production managers, along with more junior staff like slide mounters and general maintenance technicians, will be employed on a full-time basis. More specialized and, therefore, less frequently needed people like scriptwriters, directors, graphics artists, animators, camera operators and stills photographers are usually freelance in this business, although there are of course some exceptions. Medium-sized production companies will hire such people in on a time or total fee basis, or will sometimes have some kind of retainer arrangement with their favourites in each category. That way the freelancer is free to work for other organizations and keep his or her earnings up, and the production company doesn't have to bear the strain of the high salaries these people would require.

However, with key personnel of a more general nature on staff, there is a flow and continuity which is suitable for clients' requirements. Indeed, many clients who are more experienced in the audio-visual area prefer the approach adopted by the medium-sized production company; they can have the best of both worlds, with continuity on the production/ management side and the pick of the best in the country for specialized creative work.

Whether the production company hires specialists and facilities or employs them all in-house, it must never lose sight of its primary job—to devise, create and produce productions on behalf of its clients. The production company's role within industry, institutions and education is to listen to the client's requirements, learn about the client's operation or business, and then create the solution to the client's audio-visual problem with a production that meets as many of the criteria as is humanly possible. That may sound like an inhumanly impossible task; but there are many, many production companies out there achieving these goals every day of the week.

A word about specialization

A large number of production companies will offer production in any of the main media, i.e. videotape, film, slide-tape, multi-image and business theatre. The chances are, though, that they will in fact specialize in one area like conference work or videotape, but be able to offer any of the others through subcontracting to other production companies or facilities outfits.

Some clients are a little afraid to put the work of one medium through a production company whom they believe specializes in another. It is impossible to give clear guidelines about this dichotomy, because each case has to be assessed on its own merits. Some production companies, of course, specialize quite unashamedly in one medium only, and will simply turn away requests for work in other media. But with the production companies that offer a total audio-visual service, the picture is not so clear. On the one hand, from a technical point of view it is easy to see the merits of choosing horses for courses and having videotape productions made by videotape specialists, slide-tape programmes made by slide-tape specialists, etc. But when a client company has established a very good rapport with a production company—for example, when the production company's staff have come to know the client's business or other activities very well through, say, producing several conferences and meetings for it—what then? If that same client suddenly finds a need for a videotape programme, should the project be taken to another production company which specializes in videotape but doesn't know the client's needs from Adam's? Or should the client go to the original business theatre production company who may have to hire a videotape expert or two to handle the nuts and bolts of the job, but will have a better, and quicker, understanding of the real, deep needs of the client's videotape project? A question to ponder, and one to which there are no easy answers.

For the sake of argument, however, it is right that I should list the main areas of production company specialization. Here they are:

- *Videotape*   Commercials, documentary, corporate, industrial.
- *Film*   Advertising commercials.
- *Film/videotape*   Advertising commercials, rock music promotional productions, documentary, corporate, industrial.
- *Television (independent)*   Videotape or film, mostly for broadcast, although some will do non-broadcast productions.
- *Television (broadcast)*   A number of ITV broadcast companies in the UK now have corporate departments, competing directly with corporate video production companies.
- *Feature film*   Precisely this, although some will make documentaries.
- *Audio-visual*   Slide-tape, multi-image up to medium-sized productions, and slide-tape programmes to be transferred to videotape. Some also make videotape programmes, but care must be exercised to avoid those production companies whose people don't understand the difference in

creative approach. Some can also produce small to medium-sized conferences.

● *Conference*   Business theatre, plus multi-image and film or videotape which is often bought in or subcontracted. These specialists are experts in staging and theatrical work, and will act as impressarios hiring dancers, choreographers, set-builders, actors, presenters, in fact everything down to the performing seals. Because they are normally trained to think big, they are not always the best people to go to for small shows and productions, but there are exceptions—particularly if the client concerned is a regular and also uses them for bigger projects.

● *Sound or radio*   Produce radio commercials and other audio productions, including audio-visual soundtracks.

In-house units

Many large organizations which have a regular and extensive need for audio-visual communications have set up their own studios and production departments to handle varying levels of production involvement. If your organization already has such a department and you're not yet familiar with what it can do, you should spend a little time finding out before tackling a script project which they are to produce.

In-house units can involve anything from two people sitting either side of a desk, organizing and coordinating the activities of a variety of outside production and facilities companies, to large departments with broadcast standard videostudios, fully equipped, that produce regular in-company video magazine programmes as well as a range of video training programmes, sometimes interactive, plus one-off videotape programmes, slide-tape programmes, and speaker support material.

Obviously, a large international organization which has truly recognized the advent of the video age will spend a great deal of money each year on audio-visual communications of many different kinds. Once the annual expenditure on such activities exceeds a certain level, the idea of starting an in-house department becomes increasingly attractive and cost-saving. Some companies still prefer to retain their independence where buying in services is concerned, and will employ a small production team that acts as an overall coordination point for a variety of specialist production or facilities companies. Others who may have a more singular requirement— e.g. only videotape—will contemplate the establishment of their own studio not only to produce programmes but also to shoot them, edit them and even make copies to be distributed throughout their own network.

Such organizations—no matter how thorough their own set-up—may still buy in specialized facilities like computer graphics, special videotape effects, and so on. They may also buy in the production services of scriptwriters, directors and producers. This is because no matter how widespread the audio-visual activities of the company concerned, it is very seldom that it makes economic sense to install such specialized—and expensive—equipment or personnel. It is also rare to find an in-company studio or department that employs full camera crews or slide production staff as, apart from very rare circumstances, this would not be cost-effective.

Obviously, for a company to set up its own audio-visual production department, and justify the expense, there has to be quite a regular through-put of work. Some companies with a trickle rather than a flow of such work may merely tack on a small extra capacity to their advertising or public relations departments. However, the majority of companies that use audio-visual communications in a small-to-medium capacity—which does not justify more than a token acknowledgement in terms of in-house staff—will engage the services of a production company.

Facilities companies

In general terms, 'facilities' is taken to mean the machinery, services and relevant operators you need to make films and programmes. The most obvious areas here are companies that hire out camera equipment and crews, and editing set-ups. Then comes the sound studio which, when sound is an integral part of a production (as it normally is), counts as a facility rather than a stand-alone production element. After that comes the sound stage or television studio, which provides a suitable indoor area for filming or videotape recording, with plugs in all the right places, areas for cameras and lighting to be manoeuvred in, seats and control panels for the production staff, people to make tea and coffee and fresh sandwiches, etc.

In most major centres of the industrialized world there are facilities companies that offer, in one centre, almost everything the film or VTR maker needs. Even huge organizations like the Burbank Studios in California and Pinewood Studios in the UK are, at the end of the day, facilities operations—albeit famous, glamorous and very large. For the purposes of this business, however, Burbank and Pinewood are perhaps a little too ambitious, and are so expensive that they would give the average production manager his or her first coronary. But smaller, more modest and very efficient centres do exist in most major cities and provide the programme or film maker with everything required.

Depending on the project concerned and its cost-efficiency implications, production companies and in-house units will also buy their facilities from several different sources. For example, they might use a superb sound engineer at one studio to mix a soundtrack for a film; edit the film at another address where there is an editor who specializes in that kind of subject matter; they'll get their opticals (special graphics and effects) done by a further expert around the corner; and they'll have the final dubbing and editing done by yet another expert supplier three streets away.

So how do you fit in?

As suggested elsewhere in this book, whoever writes the script for a programme or presentation of any kind is normally the person who starts the production ball rolling, perhaps in tandem with the producer. If you are an in-house manager or executive in charge of a project and choose to write the script yourself, then the decision to make a programme or presentation may be yours in the first place. However, whatever your level of management decision-making, your role is always crucial because it is normally your concept and approach which will shape the entire production. The earlier chapters in this book describe how to go about the actual briefing, research, approach and scripting activities. But however much the project in hand is your 'baby', you will normally have to work closely with a number of other people and processes in order to generate the finished product.

Rather than isolate your role, therefore, you'll probably find it far more useful if I include the part you play in the context of examples of entire productions. In this way you not only see how your work should be approached, but you also see how it interacts with the other jobs that have to be done. The sections which apply directly to you, as the scriptwriter, are shown in italics.

The simple VTR (or film)
Let's assume that this typical simple production will include one or two live action interviews, perhaps a top-and-tail approach with a studio presenter (introducing and summarizing the programme) and narration over tape or footage, interspersed with some 'lip sync' sections of natural, unscripted dialogue among workers in a factory, forming the remainder. This would be quite a representative example of a modest-budget corporate or training production.

- The in-house team or chosen production company is briefed by the commissioners of the programme. *This should happen as early as possible, preferably before you begin writing your script and even before you begin research. Much as the final production may be your responsibility, the other members of the production team may well have some useful input at this stage. If you have already established a budget figure, for example, the producer will be able to guide you at this stage as to what shooting/editing it will be possible to achieve for that money.*

Pre-production

- *Working as closely as possible with the producer (to ensure that budget levels are not exceeded, and that all your ideas can be produced within the agreed timescale) you develop the treatment for the programme.*

- A full costing is prepared on the basis of the treatment, and a production schedule is also drawn up.

- The treatment, costing and production schedule are shown to the client (or to your superiors/colleagues—referred to from here on just as 'the client'); any necessary alterations are made, and the client gives approval. *If you want to save yourself some time later on, it's a very good idea to ensure that the treatment you write is as comprehensive and detailed as possible. If you recall, in Chapter 2 I suggested that a treatment should be like a short story, whereas the script is the screenplay of the same story. For people who are not used to reading scripts (and very few business people are) it is far easier for them to grasp the concept and content of a programme if they can read it as if it were a magazine article. If your treatment is short and cryptic, though, readers won't get the full picture until they see the script or, worse still, they won't realize what you meant until they see the off-line edit. Should any changes become necessary this late in the day, you will be involved in extra expense as well as extra time. Ensure that all changes and alterations to content are made at this stage, as well, and if necessary re-present the altered treatment before anyone goes any further.*

- A director is hired, if there isn't already one on staff. This may also happen at the very start, rather than at this stage. In other circumstances the producer will also be the director; and sometimes the writer and director are one and the same. For a very small production it is even possible for one person to do all three jobs; and provided the production schedule is quite straightforward that person won't suffer too many sleepless nights. Anything other than a very simple programme or film, though, requires at least two or preferably three pairs of hands. *Assuming there are three pairs of hands and yours is one of them, you will need to work with the director now. He/she may suggest changes and/or additions to the treatment and ways of fleshing out and improving some of your ideas, especially on the visual side. Don't feel that these suggestions are impertinent, no matter how possessive you're beginning to feel about your treatment! Remember you're all playing on the same team and you all have the same objective—to create the best possible programme with the available resources. If the director suggests content changes and you feel they are inappropriate, you can always fall back on 'the client' who has already approved your version in detail (or so you can say). Of course it is always better to involve the director right at the beginning of the project, so you, the director and the producer can pool resources before anything gets carved in tablets of stone. But do remember that directors are not just in charge of the pictures, just as you're not only responsible for the words. Directors have even been known to come up with good narration and dialogue ideas, so keep an open mind.*

- All relevant locations, and a studio if the client or production company doesn't have one, are booked and confirmed.

- *The script is written* and a storyboard is prepared.

- *The client is presented with the script and storyboard; any necessary alterations are made, and approval is given. If all you're doing within a production is to write the script, this is where you bow out.*

- The camera crew is hired, if such people are not already on the production company's staff. All equipment required for shooting is made available—in this case, it's only likely to consist of a single camera and either video recorder or audio recorder (depending on whether you're shooting VTR or film), lights, and power accessories. Some production companies which also have their own facilities will have all the necessary equipment; if not it will have to be hired. In either case it will then have to be checked, and any necessary maintenance carried out.

- Dates for location and studio shooting are confirmed, and all relevant performers taking part in the production should be confirmed as available on those dates.

- If the production company does not have its own editing facilities, these should be booked at this stage of the production—if not earlier. Off-line videotape editing can often be done at the production company's premises, by transferring the master tape on to VHS or

U-matic and working it through on simple, inexpensive editing equipment. On-lining, though, must be done on as high-quality a format as possible and although some production companies own this expensive gear, there aren't too many of them.

- Consequently it is likely that a good videotape edit suite will have to be booked for the on-line at least. With film, a rough cut can often be produced on the production company's premises, although unlike the videotape variety film editing—even the earliest stages—is best done by an expert editor on the highest quality equipment. Large production companies are likely to have their own editing arrangements or 'cutting rooms', but the smaller ones are likely to go to a specialist film-editing operation. There are normally several good film-editing facilities outfits in major cities.

Production

- Live action shooting is done (both on location and in a studio.) *If you go along to watch the shoot, even in an advisory capacity, do remember that when a project is in production the director is the boss—even if you're 'the client' and you're paying him or her. If you notice something that doesn't seem right, never approach a performer, interviewee or crew member directly. Always wait until an appropriate moment and make your comment to the director. It's then up to him or her to act on your recommendation if you agree it together.*

- Graphics are prepared for inclusion at editing stage, and any other relevant material like library stills or footage is prepared.

- Rostrum filming/recording is done.

Post-production

- An off-line edit—or rough cut, if it is a film—is prepared by the director. This will follow the approved script and storyboard. *Sometimes the writer attends the off-line edit to ensure that the script intentions are followed and that interview content is appropriate to the requirements of the project.*

- *The narration script is re-adjusted if necessary— depending on the way in which the off-line or rough cut has been prepared. In some cases the narration script will only be written at this stage, to form accurate links between freshly edited sections of live action.*

- The client is shown the off-line programme, or a rough cut of the film with the soundtrack played back in sync, but on another system; this is sometimes called a 'double head' as both film and audio tape go through the same machine. Once any necessary changes have been agreed, the client then gives full approval. *He or she is also shown any alterations to the narration script, or the original narration script if it has been done at this stage, and gives approval.*

- The narration is recorded/dubbed on to the master.

- The final master videotape (on-line edit) or show print of a film is made. Any special video effects or film 'opticals' are incorporated.

- Copies are made from the master.

- Copies are given to the client or distributed on his or her behalf.

Needless to say, of course, production schedules are not always as disciplined as this, and often the order in which things happen changes according to circumstances. Flexibility within a schedule is very necessary, as you'll frequently find that its stages are shifted around for reasons beyond anyone's control. And if completion of a programme or a film by a certain deadline is essential, then a flexible schedule gives you a fighting chance of getting the show on the road on time.

The simple presentation

With a small meeting of, say, a couple of hours' duration with around three or four speakers presenting to an audience of up to, say, one hundred, and once again a small budget, there will be very little in the way of staging required of the production company. In the following example we're assuming that there is no set to be built; we'll just use a presentation room as it stands, with the venue's own lighting, lecterns, seating, etc. There will just be slides, without another medium to project, and the slide input will consist of one multi-image module plus some speaker support slides. There will be no teleprompter; speakers will cue their slides by pressing the cue light button on the lectern. This all represents a fairly typical example of the small shows many companies produce by the dozen every year, and form the mainstay of the 'audio-visual' industry's bread and butter. With business theatre—if you want to get the terminology right—a show goes 'into production' when it is being prepared, and goes 'out' when it is actually at the venue in rehearsal or performance. If it is going to travel to more than one venue it will be called a 'roadshow', and the crew and performers will be 'touring' the show; but this example assumes that there is only one show in one venue. Once again, the sections which are directly relevant to you, as the writer, are shown in italics.

- The in-house team or production company is called in by originators or client company. An overall brief, production schedule and budget are agreed, and preferred venues decided upon. *If you are an in-company person, you are likely to be involved at this stage whether as 'the client' or as part of the client team. Sometimes external scriptwriters are involved this early, too, but not always. In my view, though, the earlier the writer gets involved the better, as he or she can provide a useful contribution to the overall shape and theme of an event, as well as creating the speeches and modules.*

- Venues are 'recce'd'; the most preferable booked. Any necessary equipment is hired and/or checked.

- *The scriptwriter is called in, and together with the producer takes a fuller brief from the client. Or, if you are the client, you now develop the creative content of the show in outline form. Remember that in business theatre you do not normally have a director—this role is performed by the producer, or by 'visualizers'.*

- *The writer and producer create a treatment for the module, and probably a draft script as well. The way you go about doing this is much the same as you would with a videotape programme. With AV, though, as there is less to include in the way of camera and editing jargon, scripts are easier for the lay person to read and therefore it isn't so crucial to prepare a detailed treatment first. However, it helps to present a treatment to accompany the script, simply describing the overall feel and shape of the module. This gives readers a general overview as well as the details. Once these are presented and considered, any necessary changes are made and approval is given to proceed.*

- The module goes into production.

- *The client presents the production company either with their own thoughts on speeches, detailed notes from which the scriptwriter can work, or tape recordings of conversations between speaker and writer outlining the needs of each presentation. (See appropriate chapters on the speechwriting process.)*

- *The scriptwriter prepares a draft of each speech and presents it back to the clients. They make any necessary changes, and give approval.*

- The speech scripts are visualized for speaker support slide material, and the visualizations shown to the client. The client makes any necessary alterations, and gives approval.

- Speaker support slides go into production.

- Once most of the slides are ready and the soundtrack for the module has been done, the client is invited to the production company's premises for a preview. This takes the form of a stagger-through rehearsal (although not at the venue) of the speeches. Some production companies will provide a trained actor or stage director to coach the speakers at this point, helping them to get their messages over more effectively. The client will also preview the programmed module, although there may still be some late slides temporarily replaced by 'write-ons'. *This is the last opportunity speakers will have to make changes to their scripts and speaker support slides. If you attend this meeting—and normally scriptwriters do, whether they're of the in-company variety or not—you must bear in mind that even the slightest change to a script may have serious consequences to the slide content. By this time speaker support slide content of speeches will be fairly far advanced. So, although script changes are in order should the speaker want them, if you're there assisting the speakers you must be careful to take note of every change no matter how minor, and inform the producer of every one. If you are a speaker yourself, do bear this point in mind and restrict all changes to those which are strictly necessary. Capricious or whimsical word changes can alter slide cues and complete programming sequences, which can cost you (the client) substantial sums of money.*

- Finalization of the module and speaker support slides takes place.

- All equipment is packed. Speaker support slides and the module, all programmed in show order, are packed, too.

- All hardware and software are transferred to the venue. The crew (probably only a few people) do the 'get-in' and rig the equipment.

- The crew performs a technical rehearsal to ensure that all cues are on time and that everything is running smoothly.

- The speakers join in and a full rehearsal takes place, with speakers running through their presentations several times if time permits. *There is still time to make the odd word change to speeches if they are strictly needed. Naturally all such changes must now take place within the existing slide cues, with no changes involving visual alterations being possible at this late stage without incurring a great deal of expense and potentially damaging delays.*

- The show takes place.

- The crew performs the 'get-out', loads all the hardware and software, and returns to base.

Perhaps it may sound repetitive, but once again: not all productions will run to this exact pattern, especially if the lead time between briefing and show day is short. In an ideal world, however, the above would probably allow a comfortable production period with plenty of time for everyone's performance to be polished and perfected.

Index